GREAT IDEAS IN RETAILING

D0993245

RETAIL MANAGEMENT
A STRATEGIC APPROACH
EIGHTH EDITION

GREAT IDEAS IN RETAILING

RETAIL MANAGEMENT
A STRATEGIC APPROACH
EIGHTH EDITION

Barry Berman • Joel R. Evans

Both of Hofstra University

Prentice
Hall

Upper Saddle River, New Jersey 07458

Acquisitions editor: Bruce Kaplan
Associate editor: Anthony Palmiotto
Production editor: Leah Crescenzo
Manufacturer: Integrated Book Technology, Inc.

ISBN 0-13-027967-6

10 9 8 7 6 5 4 3

PREFACE

Great Ideas in Teaching Retailing: A Case and Exercises Book is specifically designed to accompany *Retail Management: A Strategic Approach,* 8th Edition.

Great Ideas in Teaching Retailing : A Case and Exercises Book is divided into four parts:

- Long cases—This section consists of 7 cases ranging in length from 2-18 pages. All of these cases, including the shorter ones, are suitable as major class assignments. You may wish to assign them for presentation by teams.

- Short cases—This section is comprised of 46 shorter cases that range in length from 2-3 pages. These are suitable for shorter assignments or for in-class discussion.

- Chapter-Based Exercises—There is one exercise per chapter. These are suitable for smaller assignments and for in-class discussion.

- Problems in Retail Mathematics—There are a total of 80 problems on the following topics: store location (Chapter 9), operations management (Chapter 12), financial merchandise management (Chapter 16) pricing (Chapter 17), and key business ratios (Chapter 20).

Our goals in developing *Retail Management* and in editing *Great Ideas in Retailing: A Case and Exercises Book* have been to focus on the exciting and dynamic aspects of retailing (and a course in retailing) and to provide instructors with a large amount of flexibility and background material. We hope that you will comment on this approach..

Barry Berman (mktbxb@hofstra.edu)
Joel R. Evans (mktjre@hofstra.edu)

CASE CONTRIBUTORS

We thank these individuals for contributing cases to this book:

Patricia M. Anderson, Quinnipiac College
Joe K. Ballenger, Stephen F. Austin State University
Mary Bartling, Mount Mary College
Anne Heineman Batory, Wilkes University
Stephen S. Batory, Bloomsburg University
Marianne C. Bickle, Colorado State University
Doreen Burdalski, Philadelphia University
John Callahan, Eastern Financial Federal Credit Union
James W. Camerius, Northern Michigan University
Kenny K. Chan, California State University, Chico
James W. Clinton, University of Northern Colorado
Dean Cohen, Quantum Storage Systems
Howard W. Combs, San Jose State University
Andrew Cullen, The Pennmor Group
William P. Darrow, Towson University
B. John D'Auria, Metro-Dade County
Roger Dickinson, University of Texas at Arlington
Molly Eckman, Colorado State University
Jack Eure, Southwest Texas State University
Larry Goldstein, Iona College
Jonathan N. Goodrich, Florida International University
Michele M. Granger, Southwest Missouri State University
Edward Heler, Heler^2 Consultancy, LLC
Lisa A. Henderson, Drexel University
Terence L. Holmes, Murray State University
David C. Houghton, Northwest Nazarene University
Brian R. Hoyt, Ohio University
Gail Hudson, Arkansas State University
Michelle Smoot Hyde, Brigham Young University
Karen Hyllegard, Colorado State University
Gale A. Jaeger, Marywood University
Carol Felker Kaufman, Rutgers University, Camden
William W. Keep, Quinnipiac College
Patrick Kemp, Medic Aid Communications
Doris H. Kincade, Virginia Tech University
Algin B. King, Towson University
Gail H. Kirby, Santa Clara University
Antigone Kotsiopulos, Colorado State University
Mark R. Leipnik, Sam Houston State University
Richard C. Leventhal, Metropolitan State College
Michael R. Luthy, Bellarmine College
Kathryn L. Malec, Manchester College
Raymond A. Marquardt, Arizona State University-East
Suzanne G. Marshall, California State University, Long Beach
Sanjay S. Mehta, Sam Houston State University

Allan R. Miller, Towson State University
Deborah M. Moscardelli, Central Michigan University
Jennifer Paff Ogle, Colorado State University
Sharon S. Pate, Illinois State University
Melodie Philhours, Arkansas State University
Carolyn Predmore, Manhattan College
Stan Rapp, Cross Rapp Consulting Group
Lynn Samsel, University of Nebraska-Lincoln
Sangeeta M. Sarma, University of Kentucky
Bridgette Shields, Crucial Technology
Leslie Stoel, University of Kentucky
Susan C. Strickler, South Dakota State University
Rodney L. Stump, Morgan State University
William R. Swinyard, Brigham Young University
K. Denise Threlfall, Old Dominion University
Connie Ulasewicz, San Francisco State University
Ginger Woodard, East Carolina University

Barry Berman
Joel R. Evans

HOFSTRA UNIVERSITY

Matrix Linking Long and Short Cases
with *Retail Management: A Strategic Approach*, 8E Text Part Numbers

	Part I	Part II	Part III	Part IV	Part V	Part VI	Part VII	Part VIII
LONG CASES:								
1.: Artistic Impressions	X	X			X			X
2.: Geo. Inf. Systems				X				
3.: Kmart	X					X		X
4.: Quincy, John CPA	X		X					X
5.: Richland Dodge			X				X	
6.: Selling 'Hood'	X			X				X
7.: Wal-Mart	X	X			X			
SHORT CASES:								
1.: Ace Hardware	X	X		X	X			
2.: Amazon.com		X	X					X
3.: Assess. So. America	X							X
4.: Assortment Planning						X		
5.: Avon's Search	X	X						
6.: Bagels, More		X				X		X
7.: Basically Bagels							X	
8.: Beverages and More!	X	X						X
9.: Buying Lesson Activity						X		
10.. Crucial Technology		X						
11.: Custom Ski Pants					X	X		
12.: Deep Water Diving						X		
13.: Dolphin Bookstore	X	X						
14.: Duds for Dudes	X	X	X					
15.: Eastern Fin. Financial	X							X
16.: Flushing Fine Furniture		X					X	
17.: Focus Group Strategy			X					
18.: Food Zone			X					
19.: Golden Fleece						X		
20.: Green and Growing			X					
21.: Haddonfield				X				
22.: Hiring Dilemma					X			
23.: J. Peterman Company		X	X					
24.: J.C. Penney.Com		X						
25.: J.T.'s General Store		X						
26.: Joburg Health & Fitness	X		X				X	
27.: L&T Enterprises						X		
28.: Large Retail. Demands	X	X				X		
29.: Larry's Barber Shop	X		X					
30.: Licensing						X		

Matrix Linking Long and Short Cases
with *Retail Management: A Strategic Approach*, 8E Text Part Numbers

	Part I	Part II	Part III	Part IV	Part V	Part VI	Part VII	Part VIII
31.: Lines-R-Too Long					X		X	
32.: Mall Anchors Away		X						
33.: Negotiation Ratio						X		
34.: Old Navy		X	X					
35.: Patagonia	X	X						
36.: Pool & Wellness			X			X		
37.: Prince of Cruises				X				
38.: Racquet Club	X		X		X			
39.: Sanchez Property Mgt.				X				
40.: Service Orientation	X				X			
41.: Spacejams		X						
42.: Thomson's Computer					X			X
43.: Trawick Hotels	X		X		X			
44.: Venice Island				X			X	
45.: Walgreen's				X				
46.: Williamson-Dickie	X	X						

TABLE OF CONTENTS

CHAPTER-BASED EXERCISES

RETAIL MATHEMATICS PROBLEMS

LONG CASES

CASE 1

Artistic Impressions, Inc.: Developing An Entrepreneurial Growth Strategy

This case was prepared and written by Professor James W. Camerius of Northern Michigan University and Professor James W. Clinton of the University of Northern Colorado and is intended to be used as a basis for class discussion rather than to illustrate either effective or ineffective handling of an administrative situation. All rights reserved to the authors. Copyright © 1998 by James W. Camerius and James W. Clinton. Reprinted by permission.

COMPANY AND INDUSTRY BACKGROUND

Artistic Impressions is a rapidly-growing direct seller of affordable art works for the home and office. Most of Artistic Impressions' art was sold to African-Americans via home-based party presentation formats. The firm sold paintings and other art works through a network of over 2,700 sales people in over 40 states. Artistic Impressions' planned to achieve sales of $25 million in 1998. Twice ranked in the top 500 fastest growing private companies in the United States, according to *Inc.* magazine, the company's sales had increased more than 962% in the past five years.

Bart Breighner, founder, president and chief executive officer of Artistic Impressions, Inc. Breighner called a meeting of his staff to discuss repositioning the firm for the future. He asked the staff to respond to the following issues: "What do we need to do to get us where we want to go, to reach the kind of customer we want to reach, and to recruit and maintain the kind of sales force that will grow the business?" According to Breighner,

> I think that there's plenty of opportunity out there and I don't think that we're scratching the surface in the African-American market. But the reality is that African-Americans make up only 10% of this country's population of close to 300 million. I want the whole shot, so we're going to do things to grow the Caucasian market.

Bart Breighner's Background

Bart Breighner had a 30-year track record in the direct-selling field, primarily with World Book Encyclopedia. In his 21-year career with World Book, he built the firm's field sales organizations. In his last seven years with World Book, Breighner held the position of Executive Vice President and Director of North American Sales. Reflecting on those years he noted:

> They sent me through the Harvard University Advanced Management Program. As part of my job responsibility I traveled around the world. ...that was an exciting career. But the company was sold twice, and I wasn't politically adept at dealing with the

1

paternalistic environment. I wasn't comfortable and I did move on. I decided to become an entrepreneur.

After two brief positions in consulting and other positions, Breighner decided to return to direct selling. "I missed direct sales and the psychic rewards the business offers," he noted, "I looked into possibilities and capital requirements." He decided to study the field to identify an unsatisfied market need. He felt that he wanted to "control his own destiny" at that mid-career point in his life. A number of fields in direct sales are relatively crowded, such as nutrition and cosmetic and facial products, but there are very few successful home enhancement companies. He founded Artistic Impressions, Inc., in 1985 with the intention of being the dominant company in its industry.

The Direct Sales Environment

The direct selling industry consisted of a few well-established companies and many smaller firms that sold a broad range of products: toys, animal food, plant-care products, clothing, computer software, and financial services, etc. Among the dominant companies are: Avon (cosmetics), Amway Corporation (home cleaning products), Shaklee Corporation (vitamins and health foods), World Book, Encyclopedia Britannica, Tupperware (plastic dishes and food containers), Kirby (Vacuum Cleaners), and Mary Kay (cosmetics). By the 1980s, many retail analysts believed that the industry was in a mature stage of development, including a high concentration of firms selling nutritional products (vitamins) and facial products (cosmetics).

The spectacular sales growth of the 1960s and 1970s, had given way to a pattern in which many firms had stagnant revenues and profits. Industry problems were typically blamed on the increasing number of full-time working men and women, which reduced number of recruits as well as the ability to reach potential customers during daytime hours. Problems were also blamed on an improved economy, which encouraged some potential customers to avoid purchasing items from part-time sales persons, and the increased sophistication of consumers.

Breighner felt that Artistic Impressions offered a career in direct sales that appealed to individuals who wanted to be independent; particularly those who feared being displaced through corporate "downsizing. Breighner also believed that individuals who had successful careers, but were frustrated in their present positions, would find satisfaction through sale of the company's products.

A review of the direct selling field in 1984, led Bart to conclude that there were very few successful "home enhancement companies." One firm, Home Interiors, had annual sales of about $500 million. Several smaller companies also existed. While Brieghner respected their product lines and their retail strategies, he felt that the market could support a more upscale art product for the home.

The Sales Organization

Artistic Impressions was a privately held, multi-level direct sales organization. A multi-level organization is one in which a hierarchical network of distributors is created to sell and distribute a product line. In this format, each distributor is not only seeking to sell goods and services to the final consumer, but also is seeking distributors to join his or her distribution network. By recruiting and training new distributors, the recruiter becomes a master distributor that earns commissions and bonuses on the retail sales of all distributors within the network.

Artistic Impressions' primary business was selling framed art via the party plan. The party plan method of at-home retailing requires a salesperson to make sales presentations in the home of a host or hostess, who has invited friends and relatives to a "party." Usually, the party plan includes various games and other entertainment activities in which participants receive small inexpensive gifts. A salesperson takes orders from the guests attending the party. Advantages of the party plan are the referrals from the host, and the ability of guests to see actual art works and prices. Some executives at Artistic Impressions felt that many of its customers were either intimidated by traditional galleries and/or felt they could not afford gallery art.

Although Breighner was Caucasian, 90 percent of the company's sales force of Artistic Impressions was African American as were 90 percent of its customers. According to Deborah Thompson-Widmer, Artistic Impressions' director of promotions and communications for Artistic Impressions. "It's very hard to find African American art out there. We hit a gold mine out there (in this area), and (our products) really met a need." Thompson-Widmer oversaw three departments: field service, promotion, and marketing. Field service processed new applications for sales representatives, monitored the productivity of sales representatives and generated reports for team managers. Promotions developed contests to motivate the sales force, such as special incentives, contests, customer specials, and hostess specials. The third department, marketing, developed promotional materials and videos.

THE RETAIL MIX

Identifying A Market Need

In the 1980s, market research conducted by World Book Encyclopaedia revealed that the field of home beautification was going to grow in the future. "I made a mental note at that time that the field was hot and was going to continue to be hot," suggested Bart Breigner. "I made lists of what business I could be in. Later that factor plus my more than 20 years of experience of recruiting, training, and developing direct sales people combined to show me a way to capitalize on my assets."

In his trips to Europe, Breighner appreciated and accumulated a collection of moderately-priced art works. While searching for a new home, he observed that the art in people's homes was often not very attractive. Often, ordinary posters served as the centerpiece of home decoration.

Breighner felt that he could provide products to the American public that would enhance their quality of life.

Although sales for the first year of his business were $500,000, the company lost $120,000. In its second year, sales tripled to $1.5 million, then doubled to $3 million in its third year. Sales increased to $6.5 million in the firm's fifth year of business. The company currently recorded 91 months of consecutive increases over the previous month. Breighner anticipated doubling sales over the next three years.

Product

Artistic Impressions featured art created by artists that the company contracted on an independent basis. The appeal of religious art was very strong in the African-American community. Many of its most popular items were replicas of such famous art works as "The Last Supper," or "Praying Hands," but done in darker flesh tones. Other art works depicted African-Americans in various life experience situations. The product line also included landscapes, florals, still life, and abstracts that put less emphasis upon ethnicity. Another emerging market niche that the company was just beginning to explore was Hispanic Art. The firm has a very strong group of sellers in Puerto Rico who were constantly asking for more Hispanic art.

Artistic Impressions product development executive, attended art shows around the country and regularly contacted artists about their work. A product committee reviewed the art works to evaluate their market potential. The committee also worked with regional managers to identify regional tastes. Committee members followed regional trends in decorating, color schemes, and styles, noting that what was popular in California might not be in New York.

The product line featured over 375 hand-painted originals, serigraphs, lithographs and prints with over 150 specialized framing options. The company also sold limited edition figurines and collector plates. These items were illustrated in its 100 page catalog. Artistic Impressions' management also published new catalog supplements periodically to introduce new products.

Promotion

The marketing system of Artistic Impressions was made up of approximately 2,700 sales people who operated in more than 40 states. In 1997, representatives of the company conducted over 40,000 art shows. They arranged with hosts to invite friends, relatives and acquaintances into living rooms to view 60 or more paintings, many of which were the original artwork. Guests were prescreened before each show to identify their personal art interests. This means that each home party was customized to the guests. For example, if a hostess prefers burgandies and greens, he or she is sent 20-30 paintings with these color schemes.

The consultant arrives at the host's home and displays up to 40 framed samples in a one-hour presentation to 5 to 10 guests.. Following the show, the guests have an opportunity to purchase the paintings. Hosts were eligible to purchase paintings from the company's product line at substantial discounts. Future hosts were often selected from guests at the show.

A consultant can earn up to $40 to $50 per hour. The hostess gets 10 percent of the show's sales, which average $1000 as well as $100 off a piece of art work. If two of his/her guests ask to do a host in the future, the current host will be entitled to get another $100 off another piece of artwork for each new hostess. The typical art consultant who worked one night a week earned more than $10,000 a year. Special incentives to motivate associates included discounts on art, prizes, and trips to London, Switzerland, Hawaii, and Acapulco. Commissions for consultants start at 22 percent and increase based on sales volume.

Sales consultants were encouraged to qualify for management opportunities by recruiting others to become consultants. In this multi-level organization, consultants were eligible to initially become sales directors (the first level of management) after recruiting three people as consultants. As sales directors, they earned commissions and bonuses on sales made by their new recruits. The next level was the regional manager, who supervised two sales directors. Some of the senior regional managers supervise up to several hundred independent contractors. The next level, zone manager, included two regions with 12 people (in additional to 6 people under them). The top level is the executive manager level that supervised four zones in the hierarchy: consultants, sales directors, regional managers, and zone managers. Commission and bonuses increased as one moved up the hierarchy.

To motivate sales associates, the company held an annual convention at a hotel in the Chicago area. The three-day event was designed as a business and networking environment. It featured a series of meetings of consultants, team competition, new product introduction previews, entertainment, motivational sessions, and sales performance recognition. The artists who created the artwork sold by the company displayed their latest work and met with the company's representatives. Each year, Artistic Impressions recognized top achievers at all levels in personal sales, number of shows given, recruiting of new consultants, etc. Attendees paid their own expenses to attend the convention. The company did no national or regional advertising. Publicity was limited to feature stories on the company and its activities in magazines like *Black Enterprise*.

Distribution

Sales associates were not required to purchase inventory or deliver merchandise. The company shipped all products by United Parcel Service (UPS) from a distribution center adjacent to corporate headquarters in Lombard, Illinois, to the show host, who delivered them to customers. Approximately 7,000 framed paintings per week were shipped to show hosts.

Pricing

Listed prices of art works included the choice of frame from a line of 30 basic frames. The company was concerned that the price of its product be kept within an affordable range for its customers. The price range for the majority of artwork sold was $69 to $149. Additional charges were made if the customer chose the artwork of an upscale designer, frame liners ($10 to $30 additional) or higher cost frames (between $10 to $80 additional). Limited editions of figurines and plates sold exclusively by Artistic Impressions start at $29.95.

Corporate Responsibility

Bart Breighner served as chairman of National Foundation for Teaching Entrepreneurship (NFTE) where he raised over $500,000 in donations in a five-year period. NFTE provided entrepreneurial and motivational training for inner-city youth. Artistic Impressions was honored with the "Vision for Tomorrow" award from the Direct Selling Association in recognition of its "contribution to support and launch the careers of disadvantaged youth."

The Challenge

Bart Breighner was certain that his firm was ready to appeal to a much broader market. Some members of his executive team were not so sure. They felt that the firm already was struggling in 1998, just to get 7,000 paintings per week shipped to its current customers. Others thought that any attempt to enter new markets would distract from the highly successful niche strategy that the company had developed since its inception.

Breighner concluded:

> The business we're in is selling art, framed art, and we do it primarily with a party plan, the home show method. But we're going to redo the mission because frankly, we're an opportunity-driven company.

Questions:

1. Define and identify some common characteristics of entrepreneurs. How can this definition and these characteristics be applied to Bart Breighner, the founder of Artistic Impressions?

2. Review the marketing concept and show how it is used in the strategy of Artistic Impressions.

3. Discuss Artistic Impressions as a multilevel marketing organization. How does this type of organization differ from more traditional retail organizations?

4. Identify and discuss the nature of the strategic marketing planning process. Describe the extent to which Artistic Impressions management has successfully carried out these steps.

CASE 2

Geographic Information Systems

This case was prepared and written by Professors Sanjay S. Mehta and Mark R. Leipnik, Sam Houston State University. Reprinted by permission.

BACKGROUND

Geographic Information Systems (GIS) are a powerful tool for marketers to analyze locational and demographic issues. Some applications of GIS include store location, understanding the distribution of existing and potential customers, and so on. In order to use GIS, an analyst would need to have: (1) GIS software such as Mapinfo or ArcView, (2) a specially structured set of digital map and tabular data, and (3) specific data about the location of an actual or potential unit and/or its customers. Customer and/or unit data could take the form of street addresses or telephone numbers and/or zip codes, but it must be *geocoded* by placing it into the GIS at the appropriate location.

Getting GIS Data:

The most popular source of GIS data for marketing is the Topologically Integrated Geographic Encoding and Referencing system (TIGER). TIGER is a uniform nationwide set of streets with address ranges for each block, along with boundaries of census block groups, tracts, cities, divisions, counties, and states. TIGER data can be obtained from the U.S. Census Bureau and from vendors such as Wessex/GDT in an *enhanced* version with streets updated within the last two years (rather than being up to ten or more years out of date). The street data provide a framework for determining addresses and geocoding. The boundary information provides a wealth of demographic data about communities. TIGER allows users to understand who and where their current and potential customers are. Nonproprietary GIS data will not include vital information on business unit or competitor location, nor will it include the addresses of actual customers. This data must be placed into GIS from an existing customer data base or from a survey. Likewise, unit locations must be geocoded.

Using GIS

The view, query, measurement, and spatial analysis capabilities of GIS allow analysts to quickly answer questions such as what is the median income, age composition, racial, and gender make-up of persons living in proximity to a current or potential unit. Characteristics of the people in the enclosing block group, census tract, or larger community can be determined based on a variety of distance measures: a circle of a specified radius, a specified distance along the street network radiating from a unit, or for the area within a given travel time from a unit.

Considerations

Growth of the use of GIS in marketing has paralleled the availability of TIGER data. Analogous data sets are becoming available in other countries (e.g., the United Kingdom and Switzerland). However, TIGER data has a number of important limitations. Since it is generated by a census that may be ten years or more out of date, market potential of areas experiencing rapid growth will be underestimated using TIGER unless care is taken to incorporate population projections. Use of only a few key variables such as median income of the hundreds of demographic parameters derivable from TIGER data is common but can also be misleading. In many cases, more accurate and up-to-date GIS data can be obtained for specific communities from sources such as municipal governments and appraisal districts.

Questions:

1. Why might a 1990 population count provide a misleading impression of market potential in the year 2000? Would data from the 2000 census (available starting in 2001) solve these problems? Explain your answer.

2. What types of mistakes in retail site location planning can be made as a result of using a ten-year-old set of street data?

3. Why do major retailers such as Radio Shack and Toys "R" Us geocode their store locations using addresses and their customer locations using zip code and/or telephone number information?

4. How could the issue of cannibalization be studied using GIS?

5. Are there any other types (layers) of information besides streets, census demographics, and customer and business unit locations that might be relevant to a retailer? Explain your answer.

6. Use Mapinfo or ArcView to generate the following maps:
   a. Your state and county.
   b. Your county with census tracts delineations.
   c. Your city with major streams and streets.
   d. A new business (e.g., Stake and Ale). Plot its primary and secondary trade areas.
   e. The census block groups in and around your city.
   f. The median family income by block groups of your city.
   g. The percentage of African-Americans in each block group.
   h. The median family income by block groups of a neighboring city.
   i. Go to the local GIS manager and obtain the current population information and compare it to the information provided in the TIGER data.

CASE 3

Kmart Corporation: A Corporate Strategy Dilemma

This case was prepared and written by Professor James W. Camerius, Northern Michigan University. It is intended to be used as a basis for class discussion rather than to illustrate either effective or ineffective handling of an administrative situation. All rights reserved to the author. Copyright © 1998 by James W. Camerius. Reprinted by permission.

INTRODUCTION

Floyd Hall, chairman, president, and chief executive officer of Kmart Corporation since June 1995, was pleased. Net income for the quarter ended April 29, 1995 rose to $47 million as compared with 14 million for the same period one year before. This financial information convinced Mr. Hall that the new corporate strategy that he recently introduced would revitalize Kmart's core business, its 2,136 discount stores, and put the company on the road to recovery. Industry analysts had noted that Kmart, once a industry leader, had posted 11 straight quarters of disappointing earnings and had been dogged by persistent bankruptcy rumors. Analysts cautioned that much of Kmart's growth reflected the overall economy's strength and that uncertainty continued to exist about the company's future in a time period of slower economic growth.

Based upon its sales revenues, Kmart was the third largest retailer and the second largest discount department store chain in the United States. After several years of restructuring, it was composed largely of general merchandise businesses in the form of traditional Kmart discount department stores, Big Kmart (consumables and convenience) stores, and Super Kmart Centers (food and general merchandise). It also had equity interests in Meldisco subsidiaries of Melville Corporation that operated leased departments in Kmart's footwear departments. Kmart's units operated in all 50 of the United States, as well as in Puerto Rico, Guam, and the U.S. Virgin Islands.

The discount department store industry was perceived by many retail analysts to have reached maturity. Kmart's overall retail management strategy was developed in the late 1950s and revised in the early 1990s. It now needed to develop a new overall retail strategy that would reposition Kmart in a fiercely competitive environment.

THE EARLY YEARS

The adoption of the "nickel and dime" or "variety store" concept, pioneered by F.W. Woolworth Company in 1879, led to rapid and profitable development of what was then the S.S. Kresge Company. Kmart was the outgrowth of an organization founded in 1899 in Detroit by Sebastian S. Kresge. The first S.S. Kresge store represented a new type of retail institution that featured low-priced merchandise for cash in low-budget, relatively small (4,000 to 6,000 square foot) buildings with sparse furnishings.

Kresge believed it could substantially increase its retail business through centralized buying and control, standardized operating procedures, and the addition of new stores located in heavy traffic areas. In 1912, when the retailer was incorporated, it had 85 stores with sales of $10.3 million. At that time, it was the largest variety chain in the world, next to Woolworth. Over the next 40 years, the retailer experimented with mail-order catalogs, full-line department stores, self-service merchandising, a number of different price lines, and the opening of stores in shopping centers. However, throughout this time period, Kmart's continued emphasis was on variety store formats.

By 1957, Kmart's corporate management became aware that the development of supermarkets and the expansion of drug store chains into general merchandise lines had made inroads into market categories that were previously dominated by variety stores. It also became clear that a new form discount, the full-line discount house, was emerging.

The Cunningham Connection

In 1957, in an effort to regain its competitiveness, Frank Williams, then president of Kresge, nominated Harry B. Cunningham as general vice-president. Mr. Cunningham, who had worked his way up the ranks of the Kmart, was being groomed for its presidency. Harry Cunningham was ask to study existing retailing businesses and make specific retail strategy recommendations to Kmart's board of directors.

In his visits to Kresge stores, and those of the competitors, Cunningham became interested in discounting, particularly a new operation, E.J. Korvette. Korvette stores had a mass-merchandising emphasis that featured low prices and profit margins, high inventory turnover, and departmentalized units. Many of its locations had ample parking and were located in the suburbs. Cunningham was impressed with the discount concept, but he knew he had to first convince the Kresge's board.

He studied the retail industry for two years and presented Kresge's board with the following recommendation:

> We can't beat the discounters operating under the physical constraints and the self-imposed merchandise limitations of variety stores. We can join them -- and not only join them, but with our people, procedures, and organization, we can become a leader in the discount industry. In a speech delivered at the University of Michigan, Cunningham made his management approach clear by concluding with an admonition from the British author, Sir Hugh Walpole: "Don't play for safety, it's the most dangerous game in the world."

The Board of Directors accepted Harry Cunningham's recommendations. When Frank Williams retired, Harry Cunningham became the new president and chief executive officer and was

The Birth of Kmart

Management conceived the original Kmart as a conveniently located, one-stop shopping facility where customers could buy a wide variety of quality merchandise at discount prices. The typical Kmart had 75,000 square feet, all on one floor. Kmart stores generally were located as self-standing units in high-traffic, suburban areas, with plenty of parking space. The store layout in all stores were very similar.

Before the first Kmart opened in 1962, in Garden City, Michigan, the retailer made an $80 million commitment in leases and merchandise for 33 stores. As part of its overall retail strategy, Kmart's management decided to rely on the strengths and abilities of its management team rather than employing external consultants.

The main difference in Kmart's strategy, as compared with Kresge's, is that the Kmart stores had a much wider merchandise mix. Kmart management had the knowledge and ability to merchandise roughly half of the departments in Kmart's merchandise mix, and contracted for operation of the remaining departments, mostly to licensees. In the following years, Kmart eventually took over most of these leased departments, except shoes.

By 1987, the 25th anniversary year of the opening of the Kmart's first store, sales and earnings of Kmart Corporation were at all-time highs. The company was the world's largest discount retailer with sales of $25.6 billion and with 3,934 general merchandise and specialty stores. On April 6, 1987, Kmart Corporation announced that it agreed to sell most of its remaining Kresge variety stores in the United States to McCrory Corporation.

THE NATURE OF THE COMPETITIVE ENVIRONMENT

A Changed Marketplace

The retail sector of the United States went through a number of dramatic and turbulent changes during the 1980s and early 1990s. Many retailers were negatively affected by increased competition, reduced consumer spending, slower than anticipated economic growth in North America, and recessions abroad. As one retail consultant noted:

> This changing environment particularly affected the discount department store industry. Nearly a dozen retailers such as E.J. Korvette, W.T. Grant, Arlans, Atlantic Mills, and Ames were forced into bankruptcy or reorganization. Other retailers like Woolworth's Woolco division had withdrawn from the field entirely after years of disappointing sales and earnings. May Department Stores sold its Caldor and Venture discount divisions, and Venture announced liquidation in early 1998. Most of these retailers were successful five to ten years ago. Kmart's management felt that retailers who were successful had a very difficult time in adapting to change, especially at the peak of success. Since the retailers' management would wait too long to adapt, they typically had to react too quickly to regain their competiveness.

Wal-Mart was an exception. It was especially growth-orientated and had emerged in 1991 as the nation's largest retailer, and largest discount department store chain in terms of sales volume. Wal-Mart operated under several formats, both nationally and internationally, including Wal-Mart stores, Wal-Mart Supercenters, and Sam's membership warehouse clubs. Wal-Mart's retail strategy consisted of cultivating rural markets, everyday low pricing, and the control of operations and inventory restocking through sophisticated technology linking cash registers to corporate headquarters.

Sears, Roebuck, & Co., in a state of stagnated growth for several years, completed a return to its retailing roots by spinning off to shareholders its $9 billion controlling stake in its Allstate Corporation insurance unit and the divestment of financial services. After unsuccessfully experimenting with an everyday low-price strategy, Sears' management chose to refine its merchandising program to meet the needs of middle-market customers, by focusing on apparel, home, and automotive products. Other retailers such as Target (Dayton Hudson), which also adopted the discount concept, attempted to go generally after an upscale customer. Other "pockets" of population were served by retailers like Zayre, which had served consumers in the inner city before being acquired by Ames Department Stores.

Kmart executives found that discount department stores were being challenged by several retail formats. Some retailers were category killers, such as Toys "R" Us and Home Depot. Other retailers, such as Zayre and Marshall's, were experimenting with the "off price" apparel concept where national brands were sold at 20 percent to 70 percent discounts. Still others opened drug supermarkets that offered a wide variety of high turnover merchandise in a convenient location, such as Jewel-Osco and Rite Aid. Kmart's management viewed each of these retail formats as competitive threats since they each competed in important merchandise categories with Kmart. An industry competitive analysis is shown in Table 1.

Expansion and Contraction

When Joseph E. Antonini was appointed chairman of Kmart Corporation in 1987, he was charged with the responsibility of maintaining and eventually accelerating the chain's record of growth, despite a mature retail marketplace.

As he noted, "Our vision calls for the constant and never-ceasing exploration of new modes of retailing, so that our core business of U.S. Kmart stores can be constantly renewed and reinvigorated by what we learn from our other businesses."

In the mid-1970s and throughout the 1980s, Kmart acquired or developed several new operations. Kmart Insurance Services, Inc., acquired as Planned Marketing Associates in 1974, offered a full line of life, health, and accident insurance centers in 27 Kmart stores. In 1982, Kmart initiated its own off-price specialty apparel concept, Designer Depot A variation of this concept, called Garment Rack, was also opened. Neither venture was successful.

Table 1
An Industry Competitive Analysis
1997

	Kmart	Wal-Mart	Sears	Dayton Hudson
Sales (millions)	$32,183	$117,958	$41,296	$27,757
Net Income (mil.)	2.4%	12%	8%	9%
Profit margin	.8%	2.9%	2.9%	2.7%
Sales/sq.ft	211	N/A	318	226
Return/equity	5.0%	19.8%	20.0%	16.8%

Number of Stores:

Kmart Corporation
 Kmart Traditional Discount Stores – 2,037
 Super Kmart Centers – 99

Wal-Mart Stores, Inc. (includes international)
 Wal-Mart Discount Stores – 2,421
 Supercenters – 502
 Sam's – 483

Sears, Roebuck & Co.
 Full-Line Stores – 833
 Hardware Stores – 255
 HomeLife Furniture Stores – 129
 Sears Dealer Stores – 576
 Sears Tire Group:
  Sears Auto Centers – 780
  National Tire & Battery Stores – 326
 Sears Parts Group:
  Parts America Stores – 576
  Western Auto Stores – 39
  Western Auto (locally-owned) – 800

Dayton Hudson Corporation
 Target – 796
 Mervyn's – 269
 Department Store Division – 65

Source: Company annual reports.

In 1984, Kmart acquired Home Centers of America which operated warehouse-style home centers. The new division, renamed Builders Square, had grown to 167 units by 1996. This division capitalized on Kmart's real estate, construction, and management expertise and Home Centers of America's merchandising expertise. Builders Square was sold in 1997.

Waldenbooks, a chain of 877 book stores, was acquired from Carter Hawley Hale, Inc. in 1984. Borders Books and Music, an operator of 50 large format superstores, became part of Kmart in 1992 to form the "Borders Group," a division which would include Waldenbooks. The Borders Group, Inc. was sold during 1995.

In 1987, Kmart formed a joint venture with Bruno's Inc. to develop large combination grocery and general merchandise stores or "hypermarkets" called American Fare. The giant, one-stop-shopping facilities of 225,000 square feet traded on the grocery expertise of Bruno's and the general merchandise of Kmart to offer a wide selection of products and services at discount prices. A similar venture, called Super Kmart Center, represented smaller format combination stores. In 1998, Kmart operated 99 Super Kmart Centers, all in the United States.

In 1988, the company acquired a controlling interest in Makro Inc., a Cincinnati-based operator of membership club stores. PACE Membership Warehouse, Inc., a similar operation, was acquired in 1989. The club stores were sold in 1994.

PayLess Drug Stores, which operated super drug stores in a number of western states, was sold in 1994 to Thrifty PayLess Holdings, Inc., a entity in which Kmart maintained a significant investment. Interests in The Sport Authority, an operator of large-format sporting goods stores, which Kmart acquired in 1990, were disposed of during 1995.

On the international level, an interest in Coles Myer, Ltd, Australia's largest retailer, was sold in November 1994. Interests in thirteen Kmart general merchandise stores in the Czech and Slovak Republics were sold to Tesco PLC at the beginning of 1996, one of the United Kingdom's largest retailers. In 1998, Kmart stores in Canada were sold to Hudson's Bay Co., a Canadian chain of historic full-service department stores. The interest in Kmart Mexico, S.A. de C.V., was disposed of in fiscal year 1997.

Founded in 1988, OfficeMax, with 328 stores, was one of the largest operators of high-volume, deep discount office products superstores in the United States. It became a greater than 90 percent owned Kmart unit in 1991. Kmart's interest in OfficeMax was sold during 1995.

In 1998, Kmart maintained an equity interest in Meldisco subsidiaries of Melville Corporation, operators of Kmart footwear departments.

Consumer Research at Kmart

Kmart's corporate research revealed that on the basis of convenience, Kmart served 80 percent of the population. One study concluded that one out of every two adults in the United States shopped at a Kmart at least once a month. Despite this popular appeal, strategies that had allowed the firm to have something for everybody, were no longer felt to be appropriate for the 1990s for several reasons.

One, Kmart was often perceived as aiming at the low-income consumer. The financial community believed the Kmart customer was blue collar, low income, and working class. Two, although Kmart had made a major commitment in more recent years to secondary or rural markets, these were areas that had previously not been cultivated. Furthermore, in reassessing these markets, Kmart discovered that its assortments in rural areas were too limited and that it did not fully understand these consumers. For example, Kmart overestimated the importance of merchandise lines such as overalls and shovels and underestimated demand for such appliances as microwave ovens.

Kmart's goal was not only to attract more customers but also to get the customer spending more on each shopping trip. Once in the store, the customer was thought to demonstrate more divergent tastes. In the process of trying to capture a larger share of the market and get people to spend more, the firm began to attract a more upscale shopper. Based on Kmart's trading area research, the retailer found that the demographics of its stores' trading area and Kmart's customer profile to be very similar. Thus, Kmart was effectively serving its suburban consumers with its existing locations. In 1997, Kmart's primary target customers were women between the ages of 25 and 45 years old, with children at home and with household incomes between $20,000 and $50,000 per year. The core Kmart shopper averaged 4.3 visits to a Kmart store per month. The purchase amount per visit was $40. And 95 percent of consumers who visited a Kmart, actually purchased at least one item. Kmart estimated that 180 million people shopped there in an average year.

In studying the family makeup and working status of its shoppers, Kmart found that its shoppers were more likely to be from two-income families and had fewer than average number of children. Kmart customers also tended to be homeowners. Lastly, Kmart's customers wanted better quality merchandise products at competitive prices. According to a Kmart annual report, "Consumers today are well educated and informed. They want good value and they know it when they see it. Price remains a key consideration, but the consumer's new definition of value includes quality, as well as price."

The Renewal Program

Kmart's management considered the discount department store as a mature retail institution. This presented an opportunity to increase sales through upgrading Kmart's image. Elements of this strategy included an accelerated store expansion and refurbishing program, strengthening important life-style departments, centralizing merchandising, investing in retail automation, developing and implementing a focused advertising program, and development of new specialty retail formats. This five-year, $2.3 billion program would involve virtually all Kmart discount stores. There would be approximately 250 new full-size Kmart stores, 620 enlargements, 280 relocations, and 30 closings. In addition, 1,260 stores would be refurbished to bring their layout and fixtures up to new store standards.

One area receiving initial attention was improvement in the way products were displayed. While the traditional Kmart store was organized by product category, newer stores utilized the shop concept. For example, while Kmart's management recognized that it had a sizable "do-it-yourself" store, nobody was aware of the opportunity since the hardware, paint, and electrical departments were located in different areas of each store "All we had to do," management contended, "was put them all in one spot and everyone could see that we had a very respectable 'do-it-yourself' department." The shop concept resulted in a variety of new departments such as "Soft Goods for the Home," "Kitchen Korners," and "Home Electronic Centers." The goal behind each department was to sell an entire life-style-orientated concept to consumers, making goods complementary so shoppers would want to buy several interrelated products rather than just one item.

The program also involved remodeling and updating virtually all existing U.S. Kmart discount stores. The new look featured a broad "poppy red" and gold band around interior walls as a horizon; new round, square, and honeycombed racks that displayed garments; relocation of jewelry and women's apparel to areas closer to the entrance; and redesigning of counters to make them look more upscale, as well as to enable them to hold more merchandise.

National brands were added in soft and hard goods lines as management recognized that the customer transferred the product quality of branded goods to perceptions of Kmart's private label goods. Kmart increased its emphasis on such major national brands as Rubbermaid, Procter & Gamble, and Kodak. In addition, it began to develop such private label brands as Kathy Ireland, Jaclyn Smith, and Sesame Street in apparel; K Gro in home gardening; American Fare in groceries; and Penske Auto Centers in automotive services.

Kmart retained such celebrities as golfer Fuzzy Zoeller, auto racer Mario Andretti, and cook and garden expert Martha Stewart. The "Martha Stewart Everyday" home fashion product line was introduced successfully in 1995 and expanded again in 1996 and 1997. A separate division was established to manage the retail strategy for Martha Stewart-label goods and programs. Merchandise was featured in the redesigned once-a-week Kmart freestanding insert that always carried the advertising theme: "The quality you need, the price you want."

Several thousand prices were reduced to maintain "price leadership across America." As Kmart's management noted, "It is absolutely essential that we provide our customers with good value -- quality products at low prices." Although lowering of prices hurt margins and contributed importantly to an earnings decline, management felt that high inventory turnover of items with lowered prices would be an effective strategy in the long run.

A "centralized merchandising system" was introduced to improve communication. A computerized, highly-automated replenishment system tracked how quickly merchandise sold and was effective in getting fast-selling items back on the shelves. Satellite capability and a point-of-sale (POS) scanning system were introduced as part of the program. Regular, live satellite communication from Kmart headquarters to the stores enabled senior management to communicate with store managers and allow for questions and answers. The POS scanning system allowed a record of every sale and transmission of the data to headquarters. This enabled Kmart to respond quickly to determine which new merchandise is in demand, and what existing merchandise is selling poorly at the individual store level.

A new corporate logo was introduced as part of the new program. The logo featured a big red "K" with the word "mart" written in smaller white script inside the "K." It was designed to signify the changes taking place inside the store.

The company opened its first Super Kmart Center in 1992. The format combined general merchandise and food with emphasis upon customer service and convenience and ranged in size from 135,000 feet to 190,000 square feet. The typical Super Kmart operated 7 days a week, 24 hours a day and generated high traffic and sales volume. The centers also featured wider shopping aisles, appealing displays, and pleasant lighting to enrich the shopping experience. Super Kmarts featured in-house bakeries, meats, fresh seafood, delicatessens, cookie kiosks, cappuccino bars, in-store eateries, and salad bars. Many locations also provided video rental, dry cleaning, shoe repair, beauty salons, optical shops, and express shipping services. Emphasis was placed on cross merchandising. Toasters, for example, were featured next to fresh baked breads, kitchen gadgets were positioned across the aisle from produce, and baby centers featured everything from baby food to toys. At the beginning of 1998, the company operated 99 Super Kmart Centers in 21 states.

THE PLANNING FUNCTION

Part of the role of senior management at Kmart was to recognize the need for change. Good planning, if done on a regular and timely basis, was assumed to result in improved performance. Kmart's Michael Wellman, then Director of Planning and Research, contended:

> Planning, as we like to stress, is making decisions now to improve performance tomorrow. Everyone looks at what may happen tomorrow, but the planners are the ones who make decisions today. That's where I think too many firms go wrong. They think they are planning because they are writing reports and are aware of changes. They don't say, "Because of this, we must decide today to spend this money to do this to accomplish this goal in the future."

Kmart management believed that it had been very successful in its use of strategic planning.

> "When it became necessary to make significant changes in the way we were doing business," Michael Wellman suggested, "that was accomplished on a fairly timely basis." When the organization made the change in the 1960s, it recognized there was a very powerful investment opportunity and capitalized on it -- far beyond what anyone else would have done. "We just opened stores," he continued, "at a great, great pace. Management, when confronted with a crisis, would state, 'It's the economy, or it's this, or that, but it's not the essential way we are doing business.' " He noted, "Suddenly,

management would recognize that the economy may stay like this forever. We need to improve the situation and then do it." Strategic planning was thought to arise out of some difficult times for the organization.

Kmart had a reasonably formal planning process that involved a constant evaluation of what was happening in the marketplace, what competition was doing, and what kinds of opportunities were available. The planning group at Kmart represented a number of functional areas of the organization. Management described it as an "in-house consulting group" with some independence. It was made up of three groups: financial planning, economic and consumer analysis, and operations research. The chief executive officer was identified as the primary planner of the organization.

Reorganization and Restructuring

Kmart's financial performance for 1993 was clearly disappointing. The company announced a loss of $974 million on sales of $34,156,000 for the fiscal year ended January 26, 1994. Chairman Antonini, noting the deficit, felt it occurred primarily because of lower margins in the U.S. Kmart stores division. "Margin erosion," he said, "stemmed in part from intense industrywide pricing pressure throughout 1993." He was confident, however, that Kmart was on track with its renewal program to make the more than 2,350 U.S. Kmart stores more "competitive, on-trend, and cutting merchandisers."

Tactical Retail Solutions, Inc., a retail consulting company, estimated that during Mr. Antonini's seven-year tenure with the company, Kmart's market share in the discount arena fell to 23 percent from 35 percent. Other retail experts suggested that because the company had struggled for so long to have the right merchandise in the stores at the right time, it had permanently lost customers to its competitors. Kmart's aging customer base was also cited as a reason for its loss in market share.

In early 1995, following the posting of its eighth consecutive quarter of disappointing earnings, Kmart's Board of Directors announced that Joseph Antonini would be replaced as chairman. Antonini relinquished his position as President and Chief Executive Officer in March. After a nationwide search, Floyd Hall, 57, and former Chairman and CEO of the Target discount store division of Dayton Hudson Corporation, was appointed Chairman, President, and Chief Executive Officer of Kmart as of June 1995.

In 1996, Kmart announced a restructuring of its merchandising organization that was aimed at restoring sales and profitability through improving product assortments, implementing category management, and achieving a better focus on customers. The company sold many of its noncore assets, including the Borders group, OfficeMax, the Sports Authority, and Coles Myer. In addition, Kmart closed 214 underperforming stores in the United States, and cleared out $700 million in aged and discontinued inventory in the remaining Kmart stores.

Kmart's revised corporate mission was "to become the discount store of choice for middle-income families with children by satisfying their routine and seasonal shopping needs as well as or better than the competition." Management believed that the actions taken by the new president would have a dramatic impact on how customers perceived Kmart, how frequently they shopped in the stores, and how much they would buy on each visit. Increasing customers' frequency of visits and the amount they purchased each visit were seen as having a large impact on the company's efforts to increase both profitability and sales.

In 1996, Kmart renovated and renamed as "Big Kmart" 152 of its traditional stores. These stores emphasized those departments that were viewed as most important to its core customers and offered an increased mix of grocery and related items at the front of each store. These items were typically priced at lower levels than the major competitors in each market. In an addition to the pantry area, Big Kmart stores featured improved lighting, new signs that were easier to read, and store layouts that generated a smoother traffic flow

Floyd Hall felt Kmart's financial results for 1997 and early 1998 reflected the major financial restructuring that was underway at the company. Since joining the company, his top priority has been to build a management team with "a 'can-do' attitude that would permeate all of our interaction with customers, vendors, shareholders, and one another." Major changes were made to the management team. In total, 23 of the company's 37 corporate officers were new to the company's team since 1995. The most dramatic restructuring had taken place in the merchandising organization where all four of the general merchandise managers responsible for buying organizations joined Kmart since 1995. In addition, 15 new divisional vice-presidents joined Kmart during 1997. Significant changes also were made to the Board of Directors with nine of 15 directors new to the company since 1995. Hall argued that the company had turned a corner and that it was "finally and firmly on the road to recovery." Appendixes A and B detail important financial performance data for both Kmart and Wal-Mart.

Questions:

1.   Evaluate the strategies that Kmart has introduced as part of its marketing program of the return on investment in existing stores.

2.   How much importance is placed on the planning function at Kmart? What are some constraints that are likely to decrease its effect on the development of the organization?

3.   Why do you think planning is important to a retailer like Kmart?

4.   How does retail planning fit into the management process at Kmart?

5.   Discuss the importance of changes in the external environment. How much impact do they have on strategic plans in retailers like Kmart?

6.   What conclusions can be drawn from a review of Kmart's financial performance in the

period 1988 to 1995?

7.   What new directions are needed to "position" Kmart to meet the challenges of the next 20 years?

8.   Review alternative strategies that Kmart might implement as part of its new marketing programs.

Appendix A
Kmart Corporation
Financial Performance 1988-1997

Year	Sales (000)	Assets (000)	Net Income (000)	Net Worth (000)
1988	$27,301,000	$12,126,000	$803,000	$5,009,000
1989	29,533,000	13,145,000	323,000	4,972,000
1990	32,070,000	13,899,000	756,000	5,384,000
1991	34,580,000	15,999,000	859,000	6,891,000
1992	37,724,000	18,931,000	941,000	7,536,000
1993	34,156,000	17,504,000	(974,000)	6,093,000
1994	34,025,000	17,029,000	296,000	6,032,000
1995	31,713,000	15,033,000	(571,000)	5,280,000
1996	31,437,000	14,286,000	(220,000)	6,146,000
1997	32,183,000	13,558,000	249,000	6,445,000

Net income is after taxes and extraordinary credit or charges.

Data from 1995, 1996, and 1997 reflects disposition of subsidiaries

Source: Fortune, Kmart Annual Reports, and *Fortune* financial analysis.

Appendix B
Financial Performance
Wal-Mart Stores, Inc.: 1988-1997

Year	Sales (000)	Assets (000)	Net Income (000)	Net Worth (000)
1988	$20,649,001	$6,359,668	$ 837,221	$3,007,909
1989	25,810,656	8,198,484	1,075,900	3,965,561
1990	32,601,594	11,388,915	1,291,024	5,365,524
1991	43,886,900	15,443,400	1,608,500	6,989,700
1992	55,484,000	20,565,000	1,995,000	8,759,000
1993	67,344,000	26,441,000	2,333,000	10,753,000
1994	82,494,000	32,819,000	2,681,000	12,726,000
1995	93,627,000	37,541,000	2,740,000	14,756,000
1996	104,859,000	39,604,000	3,056,000	17,143,000
1997	117,958,000	45,384,000	3,526,000	18,503,000

Source: Wal-Mart Annual Reports and *Fortune* financial analysis.

CASE 4

John Quincy, CPA

This case was prepared and written by Professor Jonathan N. Goodrich, Florida International University. Reprinted by permission.

INTRODUCTION

John Quincy was born to a poor family in Kingston, Jamaica, in 1940. As a young man, Quincy attended high school in Kingston and completed some courses in accounting. In Jamaica, he held a series of high-ranking accounting positions in well-known Jamaican companies, such as Corporate Secretary, Financial Controller, Manager of Budgets, Management Accountant, and Auditor. Even though Quincy did well financially in Jamaica, in 1977, he and his family migrated from Jamaica to Houston, Texas.

Quincy got a job as an accountant in the Bank of Houston, but left after two years for a similar but better-paying position in a rival bank. During the evenings, Quincy pursued his B.S. degree in business and commerce at the University of Houston. He completed his degree in 1980, with a specialization in accounting. Two years later, he passed the CPA exam.

Quincy had a difficult time living in Houston. He was fired from his bank job due to insubordination after he wrote a caustic memo about his boss's mismanagement of the bank's accounting department. Quincy still wonders if he did the right thing in writing that memo, but claims that he had discussed his misgivings with his boss to no avail. Quincy remained unemployed in Houston for two years and decided to move his family to Atlanta during the summer of 1986.

Since moving to Atlanta, Quincy dreamed of opening his own CPA firm. This dream had been fueled by his bitter work experiences in Houston, as well as his desire to be his own boss.

OVERALL RETAIL STRATEGY

Location

In January 1991, Quincy opened his accounting firm in a strip shopping center in Stone Mountain, Georgia. The shopping center, located in a middle-income area, contained 20 or so small businesses. Other tenants included an auto parts store, a beauty salon, a shoe maker, a women's clothing store, and a Caribbean restaurant. While the strip center was located at the intersection of two roads, it had poor visibility since it was in the middle of the shopping center and not visible from either of the intersecting roads.

Quincy's overall office space was long and narrow, about 20 feet wide by 60 feet long. The overall office space was divided into two smaller offices by a partition. A small waiting area, with several couches and chairs, was located in front of both offices.

While Quincy preferred to meet clients at his office (due to ready access to his computer files, books, and computer software), about 20 percent of the time, he performed his accounting work at the client's office. Some work, such as auditing and setting up an accounting control system, had to be performed onsite.

Target Market

From January 1991, when he first opened his CPA firm, to around June 1995, Quincy primarily targeted small retail business clients. These included hair dressing parlors, barber shops, and restaurants. Typically, each of these retail firms had between four to eight full-time employees, as well as several part-time personnel. Each of these retailers had gross sales of between $100,000 and $200,000 per year.

Around June 1995, Quincy decided to target companies with annual sales of between $5 million and $10 million per year. There were several problems with Quincy's initial target market customers. One, many of the clients were underfunded and had difficulty paying Quincy. They, therefore, wanted Quincy to perform his accounting services at a very low price. Two, since many of the clients knew Quincy on a social basis, they expected him to provide his accounting and consulting services free. Lastly, many of these clients were unsophisticated retailers who had difficulty implementing Quincy's financial plans and controls.

Services Rendered

Tables 1 and 2 list the major accounting services offered by John Quincy, CPA.

Table 1
Services Performed By John Quincy, CPA

- Payroll
- Monthly Income
- Business Problem Solving
- Income and Cash Forecasting
- Income Tax Returns -- Individuals, Partnerships, Corporations
- Financial Planning
- Management Advisory Services (e.g., taxation, accounting systems, implementation of accounting controls)
- Audit, Review, and Compilation
- Business Planning
- Estate Planning

Table 2
Sample of Federal Tax Forms Prepared by John Quincy, CPA

Form 1040	Federal Income Tax Return for an Individual
Schedules A and B	Itemized Deductions and Interest and Dividend Income
Schedule C	Profit or Loss from Business (Sole Proprietorship)
Schedule D	Capital Gains and Losses
Schedule E	Supplemental Income and Loss
Schedule EIC	Earned Income Credit
Schedule F	Profit or Loss from Farming
Form 2106	Employee Business Expenses
Form 2119	Sale of Your Home
Form 2441	Child and Dependent Care Expenses
Form 3093	Moving Expenses
Form 4684	Casualties and Thefts
Form 8283	Noncash Charitable Contributions
Form 8586	Low-Income Housing Credit
Form 8809	Request for Extension of Time to File Information Returns

Quincy was the only full-time member of his firm. His youngest son and wife each worked several hours per week inputting data, filing important papers and documents, and answering correspondence.

Pricing

The prices for Quincy's accounting services were generally below the going rate. For example, Quincy's flat rate for preparing and filing a federal income tax return was $100. Other accountants charged between $150 and $175 for a similar service. The flat fee for preparing other forms that were more detailed, could vary from $200 to $350, depending on the number of forms and work required. In addition to the flat-rate pricing, Quincy charged a billing rate of $100 per hour for work done for firms and nonprofit organizations. Such work included audit, review, and compilations; income tax returns for partnerships and corporations; and management consulting. Quincy also performed pro bono work (free of charge) for a few poor individuals and some very small sole proprietorships.

Advertising and Promotion

John Quincy promoted his accounting business through networking through membership in various organizations (such as the American Institute of CPAs, the Georgia Society of CPAs, and Toastmasters International); mailing out flyers that listed Quincy's accounting services to clients and friends; and through pro bono work. See Table 3.

Table 3
Methods of Advertising and Promotion Used by John Quincy, CPA

- Use of Stationery and Business Cards -- Quincy's letterhead highlighted his membership in the American Institute of CPA's, Georgia's Society of CPAs, and the Texas Society of CPA's.
- Business Cards -- The back of each business card listed Quincy's services.
- Networking -- Quincy attended accounting-related events in the Atlanta, Georgia, area, as well as selected events outside of Georgia.
- Active Membership in a Number of Organizations -- Quincy is an active member of Toastmaster International, his church, and other local organizations. Quincy networked among members of all these organizations.
- Use of Flyers -- Quincy mailed out flyers to 100 selected small businesses located in Atlanta and Stone Mountain. The flyers provided information about Quincy's qualifications and services.
- Public Speaking -- Quincy accepted speaking invitations. During such speaking engagements, Quincy was often asked about his background. His response included his educational and business background, as well as his ownership of John Quincy, CPA.
- Pro Bono Work -- Quincy did pro bono work for a few individuals, as well as the church he attended.

Other Businesses

Quincy and his wife also managed a real estate brokerage firm, Clayton Realty, primarily out of Quincy's accounting office (some clients would come to his home). Many of these clients were recommended by Clayton's friends and relatives. These are some of the specific real estate services that Clayton's Realty engaged in:

- Residential home sales.
- Rentals of residential property.
- Property appraisals.
- Real estate investment advice.

Clayton had commission revenues of about $1,000 per month.

Clayton's third business, Technical Temp Pool, Inc. (TTP) was a temporary staffing agency that specialized in providing temporary clerical staff that was trained to perform basic word processing and bookkeeping services. TTP would charge its clients an hourly fee for each staff member sent to a company. A flat weekly rate was negotiated if the client needed a temporary staffing member for more than one week. Most of TTP's clients were banking institutions.

Problems

None of Quincy's three businesses were successsful. Quincy's income from his accounting services was less than he could earn as a salary from an local accounting firm. Clayton Realty also suffered from low revenues. Technical Temp Pool was plagued by a few inept and/or tardy workers, about whom clients complained. This was a paltry sum for Quincy, who worked tirelessly, and who thought that owning his own business was going to be his way to financial independence.

The poor performance of all the three businesses also put a strain on Quincy's marriage. While Quincy was working hard to keep his three businesses afloat, he fell further and further into debt. He is wondering what to do to get out of his dismal situation.

Questions:

1.   What are the main problems faced by Quincy, CPA? What solutions do you suggest?

2.   Comment on the target market Quincy selected for his accounting business.

3.   Should Mr. Quincy concentrate on one business rather than on three? If so, which one? Why?

CASE 5

Research, Advertising, and Sales Promotion at Richland Dodge, Inc.

This case was prepared and written by Professors Melodie Philhours, and Gail Hudson, Arkansas State University. Reprinted by permission.

INTRODUCTION

Mr. Ben Brooks, chief financial officer of Richland Dodge (located in Jonesboro, Arkansas), sat down with his copy of the research report delivered to him by Dr. Logan Nonis, a marketing research professor at Arkansas State University. Concerned primarily with the car dealership's low advertising budget, Mr. Brooks requested that Dr. Nonis' class study the buying behavior and media usage of recent vehicle buyers in Northeast Arkansas as its semester-long class project. With the results in hand, Mr. Brooks now has to determine if the research was properly conducted and analyzed, as well as the impact of its findings on Richland's overall retail strategy, and on its promotional strategy.

Mr. Brooks had talked with Dr. Nonis' class of 25 students at the beginning of the semester about Richland's current situation. Richland Dodge was a relatively small and new dealer in the Jonesboro new car and truck market. Established in 1986, pickup trucks and sports utility vehicles (SUVs) comprised about 90 percent of Richland's sales, which was typical of rural areas. Mr. Brooks mentioned having had "some service problems in the past. We've got a new service manager now and we're working on that. What I really want to deal with right now is advertising." He had set the advertising budget at $150 per vehicle sold, which is about $6,000 per month. According to the National Auto Dealers Association (NADA), the average dealer spent $217 per new vehicle retailed (PNVR). Mr. Brooks estimates that his largest local competitors, Blackwell-Baldwin Ford, Central Chevrolet, and Aycock Pontiac/Nissan, spend in the range of $18,000 to $35,000 per month, or about $200 per vehicle sold." Mr. Brooks' sales estimates of new and used vehicles and advertising expenditures by these dealerships are summarized in Exhibit 1.

Exhibit 1
Vehicles Sold and Advertising Expenditure Per Month

DEALER	VEHICLES SOLD PER MONTH	ADV. EXPENDITURES PER MONTH
Blackwell-Baldwin Ford	175	$35,000
Central Chevrolet	125	$25,000
Aycock Pontiac/Nissan	90	$18,000
Richland Dodge	40	$ 6,000

In addition to being outspent by his competitors, Mr. Brooks is also concerned about how to best allocate his limited advertising budget among the various media. The media sales reps called on him often.

According to Mr. Brooks:

> They all have great presentations and numbers, but will contradict much of the industry figures based on their particular slant. I also talk with Little Rock dealers who'll report how well their radio spots perform, but I'm not sure the Jonesboro market works this way plus they spend even more in the larger areas like Little Rock and Memphis, maybe $300 per car there. We spend about 75 percent of our budget on newspaper, the *Jonesboro Sun*, and the remainder on local TV and radio. Our current focus as far as advertising content goes is price.

Richland Dodge participates in a "zone ad group" controlled by Dodge. This group is allowed about $200 per car purchased in advertising dollars. "We can get $50 to $75 per car of that back if it's not spent by the zone ad group, but it almost always is," according to Mr. Brooks.

Given this background information, the students prepared the following report:

MARKET RESEARCH REPORT

Prepared for Mr. Ben Brooks, CFO, Richland Dodge, Inc.

The Trading Area and Competitive Environment

Because of its shopping centers, shops, restaurants, and other attractions, Jonesboro, Arkansas, was the major trade, cultural, and medical center for 500,000 people in about 7,000 square miles of northeast Arkansas. Jonesboro is home to Arkansas State University, the second largest institution of higher learning in the state, with approximately 10,000 students.

In Jonesboro, three automobile dealerships, Aycock Pontiac/Nissan, Central Chevrolet, and Richland Dodge, are all located very close to one another south of the Highway 63 Bypass. Richland Dodge was the first dealership to locate to this area, with Aycock and Central following within a year. The other dealerships are located north of the bypass at various locations throughout Jonesboro. Blackwell-Baldwin Ford, the largest dealership in Jonesboro, is located near Indian Mall, Jonesboro's regional shopping center. Blackwell-Baldwin's advertising consistently included mention of its location as "the money-saving side of the bypass." Other local dealerships include University Motors (Honda, Mazda), McCarty Motors (Isuzu, Lincoln, Mercury), Williamson Buick-Toyota, and Jonesboro Motors (Chrysler, Plymouth).

Demographic data are summarized for Jonesboro and the competing trade areas of Little Rock and Memphis in Exhibits 2, 3, and 4. Among Little Rock's zip codes, the predominant consumer life-style type is "newly formed households." This is a moderate income market that are physically active in various sporting activities. In comparison, Memphis' predominant type was "upper-income empty nesters." In general, this group consists of business owners and managers that tend to join various organizations such as country clubs, religious organizations, and veteran's organizations. The predominant consumer life-style in Jonesboro was "semirural life-style" (27.6 percent) and "small-town working families" (16.5 percent). Semirural life-styles are interested in home projects, home furnishings and electronics. Small-town working families enjoy such activities as entertaining, barbeques, bowling, hunting, and fishing.

Exhibit 2
Population and Age Distribution: Jonesboro, Little Rock and Memphis

	Population	0-17	18-34	35-44	45-64	65+
Jonesboro	68,956	19,525	22,128	11,834	17,033	9,306
Little Rock	13,117	150,065	145,139	92,969	119,406	62,465
Memphis	1,007,306	313,906	283,004	186,008	229,815	112,509

Exhibit 3
Household Income Per-Capita Income, and Auto Sales:
Jonesboro, Little Rock and Memphis

	Household Income	Per-Capita Income	Auto Sales ($000)	Passenger Autos
Jonesboro	$41,698	$15,895	$ 208,803	33,150
Little Rock-North LR	$52,379	$19,837	$1,924,769	191,152
Memphis	$58,775	$21,279	$3,353,370	629,104

Exhibit 4
Number of Licensed Drivers: Jonesboro and Little Rock (1996)

Jonesboro, Craighead County, Arkansas	Little Rock, Pulaski County, Arkansas
54,980	272,102

THE MARKETING RESEARCH PROCESS

The marketing research process is conceptualized as a six-step process, consisting of problem definition, development of an approach to the problem, research design formulation, field work, data preparation and analysis, and report preparation and presentation.

Problem Definition

As a group, the class defined the management decision problem as follows: How can Richland Dodge best allocate its limited advertising budget to reach potential car purchasers? As a group, the students defined these specific research problems, which were reviewed and agreed upon by Mr. Brooks.

- Identify all advertising media consulted by Jonesboro/Craighead County consumers who have purchased vehicles in the past four weeks.

- What was the relative influence of each medium?

- What information was sought from these various sources?

- What were the demographic and psychographic characteristics of these consumers?

- What brand of vehicle was purchased?

Development of an Approach to the Problem

Several secondary sources were consulted to gain a better understanding of the problem and to better guide the research design. Most noteworthy were two findings. One, that in addition to advertising media, other sources of influence for automobile buyers included dealer visits, talking to friends, test drives, and consumer magazines. A second major factor in this project's research design is the "forgetting factor." According to several articles, the amount of time elapsed since the car purchase and the interview should be less than four weeks. However, the reported information may still be useful if gathered within one year of purchase.

Research Design Formulation

Based on the defined research problems and their readings, the students determined that the appropriate population for study should include very recent buyers (within the past four weeks, if possible) of any make of vehicle. While Mr. Brooks offered to buy such a list from The Polk Company's Registration Information System (REGIS^R), this information was unavailable in Arkansas due to state privacy laws.

While Mr. Brooks provided a list of buyers of new vehicles from Richland Dodge from the past four weeks, the population size was so small that the students decided to extend the time frame to include the past three months. Mr. Brooks also spoke with the managers of Aycock Pontiac/Nissan and Central Chevrolet who agreed to provide the names and phone numbers of their buyers in exchange for a copy of the final research report. After eliminating business buyers and buyers residing outside Craighead County, the resulting population consisted of 49 buyers from Richland Dodge, 142 from Central Chevrolet, and 141 from Aycock Pontiac/Nissan. See Exhibit 5.

A telephone questionnaire was developed by the class. This survey instrument was primarily quantitative and included a number of different types of scales: Likert scales, ordinal scales, nominal scales, and open-ended questions. See Appendix A.

Exhibit 5
Sample Responses

Dealer	Initial Population		Resulting Sample	
Aycock Pontiac/Nissan	141	42%	59	43%
Central Chevrolet	142	43%	52	38%
Richland Dodge	49	15%	21	15%
Other			6	4%
Total	332	100%	138	100%

Field Work

The students received instruction in class as to how to administer the survey. They carefully reviewed and practiced using the survey prior to conducting the telephone interviews. Each student contacted approximately 14 respondents. In total, 138 completed questionnaires were received, which represented a response rate of 41.5 percent. Telephone logs were kept by each interviewer so that verification of any gathered information would be possible.

Data Preparation and Analysis

The first research problem addressed was the identification of advertising media consulted by recent vehicle buyers. Summary statistics were calculated in which the mean, standard deviation and frequency distributions were identified for Section I of the questionnaire. The sources were then ranked in order of importance based on their mean response. These were reported in Table 1.

To determine the importance of these media sources to the respondents, cross-tabulations were calculated between the sources of information noted in the first section as "somewhat important" and "very important," and the reported frequency of consulting these sources in the third set of questions. These were reported in Table 2.

The type of information sought by the respondents from each media was identified using frequency distributions. Those information sources identified in Section I as "somewhat important" and "very important" were then cross-tabulated with the type of information sought as reported in Section III of the questionnaire. See Table 3. The words and symbols that communicated the sought information to respondents were also reported and summarized in Table 4.

Summary statistics were calculated to determine the demographic, psychographic, and media choice characteristics of the respondents, as well as the brand of vehicle purchased (Questions 27-29). These were reported in Charts 1 through 4.

The students evaluated the four customer groups (Richland, Aycock, Central, and Other) for differences across age, education, and media usage. No statistically significant differences were found. The means for importance of information sources and frequency of using information sources are reported in Tables 5 and 6 for the four customer groups.

Summary statistics were calculated for the likelihood of the respondent to make a repeat purchase from each dealer. These are reported in Table 7. Various analyses were performed to determine any significant differences in responses from consumers who purchased from the various dealerships. No significant differences were found.

Report Preparation and Presentation

The class has summarized the research process and its findings in Tables 1 to 7 and Charts 1 to 4. Dr. Nonis delivered the report to Mr. Brooks. Dr. Nonis offered to be available to Richland Dodge management to clarify any questions it may have regarding the survey's methodology or findings.

Questions:

1. Assess the marketing research process used for Richland Dodge. What is the significance of each step and were they used appropriately? Was the process adequate/appropriate for the needs of the client?

2. Based on the research findings and without regard for cost, list in order of effectiveness media choices for Richland Dodge.

3. Based on the research findings, what advertising content is appropriate for Richland Dodge? Create an ad for newspaper, tv, radio, and billboard using the research findings.

4. Describe in detail the specific newspaper, radio and tv/cable media vehicles available to Richland Dodge for the Jonesboro market.

5. Given that Richland Dodge has a very limited advertising budget, what is the most important overall promotional tool for attracting and keeping customers? Identify various "non-advertising" promotional activities for Richland Dodge.

6. Given the importance of word of mouth communication to the automobile purchaser, what is the significance of Table 7 to Richland Dodge and Mr. Brooks?

Table 1
Results of Importance of Advertising Mediums Consulted By Consumers Who Have Recently Purchased Automobiles and Live in the Jonesboro/Craighead County Area

Type of Source	Rank by Importance	Mean	Standard Deviation	% Frequency of those said the source to be somewhat important or very important
Talking With Family and Friends	1	3.39	1.53	64.50%
Car/Consumer Magazines	2	2.37	1.52	30.40%
Newspaper Ads	3	2.23	1.48	26.80%
TV Ads	4	1.87	1.21	14.50%
Radio Ads	5	1.74	1.15	13.00%
Web Sites/Internet	6	1.64	1.27	14.40%
Billboards	7	1.47	0.97	7.90%

Mean definitions: 1 = not important at all   2 = fairly important   3 = neutral
4 = somewhat important   5 = very important

Table 2
Percentage of Time Spent on Each Source by Consumers
Who Said the Source was Important In Their Information Search
Time Spent Searching

Information Source	Never	Rarely	Once a Week	2-3 Times a Week	Daily	Total
Car/Consumer Magazines	19.0%	28.7%	31.0%	11.9%	9.5%	100%
Newspaper Ads	2.70%	10.8%	18.9%	29.7%	37.8%	100%
TV Ads	10.0%	20.0%	15.0%	30.%	25.0%	100%
Radio Ads	5.60%	16.7%	5.6%	22.2%	50.0%	100%
Billboards	0.0%	27.3%	27.3%	27.3%	18.2%	100%

There may be slight rounding errors in this table.

Table 3

Ranking of Information Sought from Specific Sources by Consumers

(Consumers Who Felt the Source Was Somewhat or Very Important)

Rank of Information Sought in Order of Importance and Frequency of Responses

Source	1	2	3	4	5	6	7	8
Newspaper Ads	Price	Vehicle Quality	Service Quality, Vehicle Selection	Available Options	Brand Name	Dealer Location		
TV Ads	Vehicle Quality	Price	Service Quality	Vehicle Selection Dealer Reputation	Available Options	Brand Name	Dealer Location	
Radio Ads	Service Quality, Vehicle Quality	Price	Vehicle Selection, Dealer Reputation	Available Options	Brand Name	Dealer Location		
Car or Consumer Magazines	Vehicle Quality	Price	Service Quality	Dealer Reputation	Vehicle Selection	Available Options	Brand Name	Dealer Location
Web Sites on the Internet	Vehicle Quality	Price	Dealer Reputation	Vehicle Selection, Available Options	Service Quality, Brand Name	Dealer Location		
Billboards	Vehicle Quality, Price	Service Quality, Selection Available Options	Dealer Location	Brand Name				
Talking to Family/ Friends	Vehicle Quality	Price	Vehicle Selection, Service Quality	Dealer Reputation, Available Options	Brand Name			

Table 4
Words or Symbols Used to Communicate the Types of Information Sought

"Other" responses given to question #9:
What words or symbols communicated information relating to price to you?

* Low price
* Bought car there before—pleased with service
* Mid-range or high
* Newspaper ads
* Physical price
* Chevy
* Safety
* JD Power & Associates
* Crash test results
* Structural steel
* Safety features
* Paid no attention to ads
* $2,000 rebate written on car
* Sales tax paid
* In right price range
* The Make/Model indicated price range
* Willing to work with you

Question #10:
What words or symbols communicated information relating vehicle quality to you?

* Prior knowledge
* Reliability
* Brand
* Dealer
* Owned this type of vehicle before
* American made
* Brand name indicated quality

Question #11:
What words or symbols communicated information relating service quality to you?

* Reputation
* Main reason
* Warranty
* Brand
* Dealer service department
* Dealer
* Aycock had bad service, but good price

Question #12:
What words or symbols communicated information relating to brand name to you?

* Chevy
* Reputation of brand
* American made

Question #13:
What words of symbols communicated information relating available vehicle options to you?

* Tilt
* Most options
* Price
* Cruise
* Add on option—on Internet
* Power windows
* Didn't want to order

Question #14:
What words or symbols communicated information relating dealer location to you?

* Convenient
* Here in town
* Trade at home—Jonesboro area

Question #15:
What words or symbols communicated information relating vehicle selection to you?

* Size of lot
* Mind was made up
* Wife
* Only drives Chevrolet
* Passenger available

Table 5
Importance of Information Sources to Customers of Each Dealership

Car Dealership		Newspaper Ads	TV Ads	Radio Ads	Car or Consumer Magazines	Web Sites On the Internet	Billboards	Talking to Family/Friends
Central Chevrolet	Mean	2.29	1.77	1.71	2.19	1.54	1.23	3.83
	N	52	52	52	52	52	52	52
	Std. Deviation	1.53	1.20	1.14	1.43	1.09	.58	1.40
Aycock Pontiac/Nissan	Mean	2.34	1.90	1.78	2.54	1.71	1.54	3.19
	N	59	59	59	59	59	59	59
	Std. Deviation	1.49	1.14	1.19	1.60	1.39	1.04	1.54
Richland Dodge	Mean	1.90	2.05	1.86	2.14	1.90	2.00	3.00
	N	21	21	21	21	21	21	21
	Std. Deviation	1.41	1.43	1.24	1.49	1.48	1.38	1.64
Any Others	Mean	1.83	1.83	1.17	3.00	1.00	1.00	3.00
	N	6	6	6	6	6	6	6
	Std. Deviation	1.33	1.33	.41	1.67	.00	.00	1.55
Total	Mean	2.23	1.87	1.74	2.37	1.64	1.47	3.39
	N	138	138	138	138	138	138	138
	Std. Deviation	1.48	1.21	1.15	1.52	1.27	.97	1.53

Table 6
Frequency of Using Information Sources by Customers of Each Dealership

Car Dealership		TV Ads	Newspaper Ads	Radio Ads	Billboards	Magazine Ads
Central Chevrolet	Mean	2.46	2.62	2.27	1.77	1.81
	N	52	52	52	52	52
	Std. Deviation	1.34	1.33	1.44	1.10	1.05
Aycock Pontiac/Nissan	Mean	2.61	3.07	2.37	1.85	2.05
	N	59	59	59	59	59
	Std. Deviation	1.40	1.46	1.48	1.14	1.21
Richland Dodge	Mean	2.71	2.86	2.43	2.24	1.95
	N	21	21	21	21	21
	Std. Deviation	1.42	1.59	1.57	1.48	1.24
Any Others	Mean	3.5	3.00	3.33	3.50	2.83
	N	6	6	6	6	6
	Std. Deviation	1.64	1.90	1.63	1.76	.75
Total	Mean	2.61	2.86	2.38	1.95	1.98
	N	138	138	138	138	138
	Std. Deviation	1.39	1.45	1.49	1.25	1.15

Table 7
When asked, "How likely is it that you will purchase from this dealer again?"

Car Dealership			Frequency	Percent
Central Chevrolet	Valid	Might or might not buy again	9	17.3
		Probably would buy again	23	44.2
Mean = 4.21		Definitely would buy again	20	38.5
S.D. = .72		Total	52	100.0
Aycock Pontiac/Nissan	Valid	Probably would not buy again	1	1.7
		Might or might not buy again	5	8.5
		Probably would buy again	34	57.6
Mean = 4.20		Definitely would buy again	19	32.2
S.D. = .66		Total	59	100.0
Richland Dodge	Valid	Definitely would not buy again	2	9.5
		Probably would not buy again	1	4.8
		Might or might not buy again	5	23.8
		Probably would buy again	7	33.3
Mean = 3.67		Definitely would buy again	6	28.6
S.D. = 1.24		Total	21	100.0

Chart #1
Most Read Newspaper

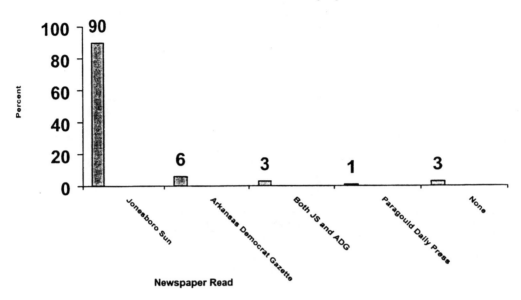

Newspaper Read

Chart #2
Most Read Newspaper Section

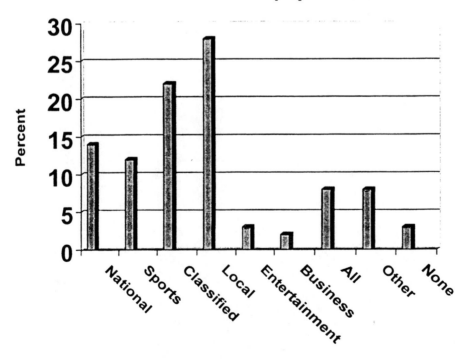

Section of the Newspaper

Chart #3
Most Watched TV Station

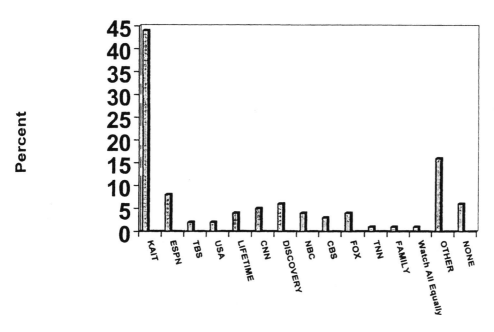

Television Station

Chart #4
Most Recent Brand Purchased

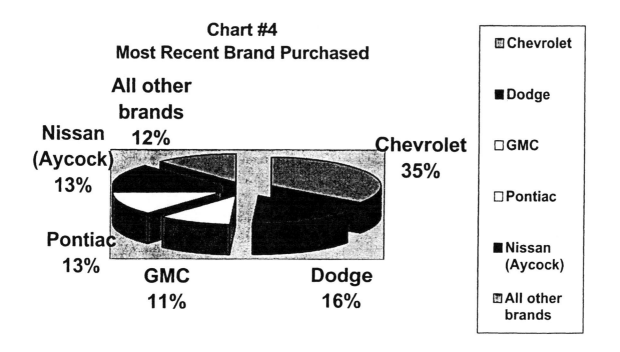

- Chevrolet
- Dodge
- GMC
- Pontiac
- Nissan (Aycock)
- All other brands

All other brands 12%

Nissan (Aycock) 13%

Chevrolet 35%

Pontiac 13%

GMC 11%

Dodge 16%

Appendix A
Richland Dodge Questionnaire

_____ I.D.   Phone Number_____

Introduction:
Hello, my name is _____. I am a marketing student at ASU and my research class is conducting a survey about a consumer's decision to purchase an automobile. Has anyone in your household recently made an automobile purchase? If no, thank them. If yes, ask, **May I please speak to them?** (If not the person to whom you are speaking, reintroduce yourself and proceed.) **I need about 10 minutes of your time to answer a few short questions. Would you be willing to help me complete my class project?**

        Yes, go to question #1   No, read the following:

Because your help is extremely important to my project, is there another more convenient time that I might call back? _____(recall date and time). If no, thank them for their time.

Please answer the following questions with regard to your most recent vehicle purchase. Many times when someone decided to purchase a vehicle, they begin to look for information. The following is a list of information sources that you might have used before you made your most recent vehicle purchase. 1 = Not important at all, 2 = Fairly unimportant, 3 = Neutral, 4 = Somewhat important, 5 = Very important.

	1	2	3	4	5
1. Newspaper Ads	1	2	3	4	5
2. TV Ads	1	2	3	4	5
3. Radio Ads	1	2	3	4	5
4. Car or consumer magazines	1	2	3	4	5
5. Web sites on the Internet	1	2	3	4	5
6. Billboards	1	2	3	4	5
7. Talking to Family/Friends	1	2	3	4	5
8. Other, specify_____	1	2	3	4	5

When you searched these information sources, what kind of information were you looking for? I will read a list of vehicle information, indicate a yes or no as to whether or not you were looking for this information in the sources you consulted. For info. answered yes, ask, **what words or symbols communicated this information to you?**

9. Price	Yes	No _____
10. Vehicle quality	Yes	No _____
11. Service quality	Yes	No _____
12. Brand name	Yes	No _____
13. Available vehicle options	Yes	No _____
14. Dealer location	Yes	No _____
15. Vehicle selection	Yes	No _____
16. Dealer reputation	Yes	No _____
17. Other, specify_____	Yes	No _____

During the time when you were considering your most recent vehicle purchase, how frequently did you read, listen to or notice any of the following automobile/dealer advertisements? 1 = Never, 2 = Rarely, 3 = Once a week, 4 = 2-3 times a week, 5 = Daily.

	Never	Rarely	Once a week	2-3 x a week	Daily
18. TV Ads	1	2	3	4	5
19. Newspaper Ads	1	2	3	4	5
20. Radio Ads	1	2	3	4	5
21. Billboards	1	2	3	4	5
22. Magazine Ads	1	2	3	4	5

23. Which radio station do you listen to the most? (Check one) – Don't read list.

_____KBTM-News Talk 1230   _____KISS FM 101.9
_____KFIN Super Country 107. 9FM _____KDEZ FM Z-100
_____KTBX FM mix 106.7   _____KDXY Fox 104.9 FM
_____Other, or none, specify_____

24. Which newspaper do you read the most? (Check one) – Don't read list.

_____Jonesboro Sun   _____Arkansas Democrat-Gazette
_____Commercial Appeal   _____Other, or none, specify_____

25. In which section of the newspaper do you spend the most time reading? (Check one) Read if necessary.

_____National news   _____Local news
_____Sports   _____Entertainment
_____Classifieds   _____Other, or none, specify_____

26. Which TV station do you watch the most? (Check one) – Don't read list.

_____KAIT-TV Channel 8   _____Lifetime Cable
_____ESPN Cable   _____CNN Cable
_____TBS Cable   _____TNT Cable
_____USA Cable   _____Other, or none, specify_____

27. In which of the following categories does your age fall?

_____18-25   _____46-55
_____26-35   _____56-65
_____36-45   _____over 65

28. In which of the following categories does your education fall?

_____Some high school   _____College graduate
_____High school graduate   _____Some graduate school
_____Some college   _____Masters degree or beyond

29. From which dealer did you make your most recent vehicle purchase? (Don't read list)

_____Central Chevrolet _____Aycock Pontiac   _____Richland Dodge

30. Including your most recent purchase, how many times have you purchased a vehicle from this dealer?

_____

31. How likely is it that you will purchase from this dealer again?
_____Definitely would not purchase
_____Probably would not purchase
_____Might or might not purchase
_____Probably would purchase
_____Definitely would purchase

32. What is the make and model of your most recent vehicle purchase?

Thank you for your help!

CASE 6

Selling in the 'Hood': A Case Study of an Inner City Retailer

This case was prepared and written by Professor Rodney L. Stump, Morgan State University. Reprinted by permission.

This case is to be used in conjunction with an EXCEL worksheet (HOOD-REGIONALSTATISTICS) which needs to be downloaded from the student site—http://www.prenhall.com/bermanevans.

INTRODUCTION

Whether you call it "urban wear" or merely casual wear, selling clothing and footwear like jeans, sweats, T-shirts, sneakers, and boots to teens and young adults is a tough, dynamic business – and is perhaps more challenging when your target is African-American males. Downtown Locker Room (DTLR), a small regional chain of men's clothing stores in the Baltimore-Washington, D.C., metropolitan area, must be doing something right to have grown to 17 stores since 1984. The success of DTLR and its parent company, LevTran Enterprises, is also chronicled by its appearance on the inaugural "Inner City 100" list established by *Inc.* magazine and the Initiative for a Competitive Inner City (ICIC), a national nonprofit organization devoted to revitalizing U.S. inner city neighborhoods. ICIC was established by Michael Porter, the noted Harvard economist.

Company Background

DTLR is the flagship line of stores operated by LevTran Enterprises, a privately owned corporation headquartered in Baltimore, Maryland. At the outset, the founders, Rick Levin and Tony Trantas, both had extensive experience in urban business -- but neither had any direct experience in apparel retailing. Each operated family-owned businesses, a liquor store, and dry cleaning service, respectively, that happened to be situated near one another in downtown Baltimore. Over the years, the two men came to know each other and a friendship blossomed, which ultimately led to the decision to partner together to acquire and operate an Athletic Attic athletic shoe and clothing store franchise.

This franchised store was situated in a mall located in a northern suburb of Baltimore. Initially, merchandise was shipped from manufacturers to Levin's downtown liquor store, where it was readied for the sales floor. After a while, Levin and Trantas began hearing comments from the liquor store customers, where African-Americans historically had accounted for a significant proportion, indicating how much they wished that this type of merchandise was more available in the city. Their experiences with their franchise store also led them to realize that much of the clothing and footwear purchases being made at their store were motivated by fashion moreso than athletics. This led to friction with the franchiser, who failed to concur with their view of locating a store downtown that specifically targeted African-Americans. Nor did the franchiser support the merchandising changes Levin and Trantas sought. Frustrated with this, the two men decided to open their own store -- one that would reflect their own retailing strategy.

Levin and Trantas settled on the name Downtown Locker Room, in part because of its similarity to a national chain of stores devoted to athletic footwear. The first DTLR store was opened in 1984 to the west of Baltimore's central business district near the Lexington Market. Rather than systematically performing a site analysis, the store location was selected primarily because this Lexington Street location was near to the two family businesses, which would enable the two owners to "keep an eye on the store." Within four years, the Lexington store was followed by several others in Baltimore and its western suburbs. There now exist seven DTLR stores in the Baltimore metropolitan area. In 1989, DTLR trained it sights to the south and opened its first store in Washington, D.C. Through 1999, an additional six stores were added in the district and the adjoining Prince George's County in Maryland.

General Information on African-American, Inner City Consumers, and Hip-Hop Culture

In general, there is growing evidence of the wisdom of retailers targeting African-Americans and inner city residents. A recent study by the Selig Center for Economic Growth at the University of Georgia documents that African-American households spend far more on apparel than is the national average (7.3 percent of after-tax money income versus 5 percent). While the average after-tax money income of African-Americans lags the national average by 28 percent, this still translates into average apparel expenditures of $1,774 for African-Americans versus $1,693 for all households, a 5 percent difference. Overall, the Selig Center estimates that the nation's African-American buying power totaled $533 billion in 1999, and has been growing at a 6.3 percent compounded rate during the 1990s. To put things into perspective, this growth rate has far outstripped the increase in total U.S. buying power, the U.S. gross domestic product, and projected increase in the African-American population during the same time period.

Recent efforts by Porter's ICIC organization and several national consulting firms has begun to document the attractiveness of U.S. inner city neighborhoods and the paucity of retailing outlets found there. The ICIC defines inner city neighborhoods as "distressed urban areas (zip codes) that have significantly lower income, and higher poverty and unemployment than the Metropolitan Statistical area average." It estimates that inner city neighborhoods account for $85 billion in annual retail buying power nationally. Comparing the inner-city buying power with retail sales in the same zip code areas indicates that unmet demand tops 25 percent in many urban markets, which translates into an estimated $21 billion in unmet demand nationally. It argues that winning strategies for penetrating inner city markets require a high level of operating flexibility and tailored products and services.

However, little systematic research has been focused on inner city consumers and their shopping habits. A pioneering study by PricewaterhouseCoopers and the ICIC has documented that inner city consumers are a very heterogeneous and racially diverse population. They report that inner city consumers are more interested in fashion and apparel shopping than U.S. shoppers as a whole. This trait is even more pronounced when these residents are minorities. Not only are inner city shoppers fashion and style conscious, but they are more oriented to brands and service. These shoppers are also more likely to patronize specialty stores than discount department stores when shopping for apparel. What is even more striking is the expenditure patterns for apparel, where African-Americans account for the largest share of purchases in this product category. African-American households reported spending an average of $663 on women's apparel (20 percent higher than the overall average for inner city households), $745 on men's apparel (75 percent higher than the overall average), and $1,032 on children's apparel (50 percent higher than the average).

Another factor that has boded well for DTLR is the rise of the Hip-Hop culture, an urban, "street"-oriented lifestyle that has heavily influenced both fashion and music trends. Originating from African-American inner city neighborhoods during the 1980s, Hip-Hop has become mainstream and is now embraced not only by other minorities, but also by Caucasian suburban youths throughout the United States. Hip-Hop is also increasingly popular around the globe in industrialized countries like Germany and Japan.

Demographic and Retailing Profile of the Baltimore-Washington, D.C., Metropolitan Region

On a more local basis, both Maryland and the District of Columbia are found on the top-ten list of total buying power that is attributable to African-Americans. Overall, nonwhites account for 32.8 percent of Maryland's 5,275,000 residents (2000 estimate). In Washington, D.C., this proportion is 64.8 percent of the estimated 523,000 residents. The Maryland aggregate figures are somewhat misleading, since the state's minority population is heavily concentrated in the city of Baltimore and the Baltimore-Washington suburban counties. In Baltimore, 68.2 percent of the city's 625,000 residents are nonwhites. In the surrounding five counties that along with the city comprise the Baltimore metropolitan region, the population totals 1,842,000, with 17.6 percent being nonwhites that are concentrated in Baltimore, Howard, and Anne Arundel Counties. In the Washington, D.C., Maryland suburban counties, the population totals 1,844,000, with nonwhites representing 41.2 percent of this total. Like the Baltimore suburbs, nonwhites are heavily concentrated, in this case predominantly in Prince George's County, one of the nation's most affluent counties with a predominantly African-American population. Other demographic trends for the area are displayed in Table 1.

While as a whole, the trends for the two cities and their Maryland suburbs are positive, both Baltimore and the District of Columbia are experiencing ongoing population declines. In Baltimore, this reduction is accounted for by decreases in the population of both African-Americans and Caucasians. In contrast, in the District of Columbia, the population of Caucasians has increased while the population of African-Americans has decreased.

Overall, the retail trade in the Baltimore and Washington regions of Maryland and the District of Columbia appears to be vigorous, growing 17 percent to total $41.3 billion in 1997. However, the growth in retail trade performance for the focal area lagged the 23 percent rate experienced by the entire state of Maryland and the 35 percent rate for the entire United States. More importantly, this overall trend masks very different trends within the two core cities and the related Maryland suburban regions. In the District of Columbia, both the number of establishments and total retail

Table 1-- Regional Population Trends 1995-2005 (All figures shown in thousands)					Page 1 of 2
Geographic Locale	**Race**	**1995**	**2000**	**2005**	**% Change (since 1995)**
MARYLAND	Total	5,042	5,275	5,467	8%
	Whites	3,496	3,546	3,580	2%
	Blacks	1,347	1,489	1,609	19%
	Other Minorities	199	240	278	40%
BALTIMORE REGION	Total	2,433	2,467	2,542	4%
	Whites	1,714	1,716	1,738	1%
	Non-Whites	720	751	804	12%
Anne Arundel County	Total	460	486	507	10%
	Whites	389	405	416	7%
	Other Minorities	72	81	90	25%
Baltimore City	Total	693	625	615	-11%
	Whites	247	199	185	-25%
	Non-Whites	446	426	430	-4%
Baltimore County	Total	714	727	737	3%
	Whites	580	568	553	-5%
	Non-Whites	134	160	183	37%
Caroll County	Total	139	155	167	20%
	Whites	135	149	160	19%
	Non-Whites	5	6	6	20%
Harford County	Total	209	225	238	14%
	Whites	186	198	207	11%
	Non-Whites	23	27	30	30%
Howard County	Total	218	249	279	28%
	Whites	178	198	217	22%
	Non-Whites	40	51	63	58%

Table 1 -- Regional Population Trends 1995-2005 (All figures shown in thousands)					Page 2 of 2
Geographic Locale	**Race**	**1995**	**2000**	**2005**	**% Change (since 1995)**
WASHINGTON REGION	Total	1,747	1,844	1,951	12%
	Whites	1,077	1,085	1,106	3%
	Non-Whites	670	759	845	26%
Frederick County	Total	175	194	217	24%
	Whites	163	179	200	23%
	Non-Whites	12	14	17	42%
Montgomery County	Total	806	860	910	13%
	Whites	605	616	622	3%
	Non-Whites	201	244	288	43%
Prince George's County	Total	765	790	825	8%
	Whites	309	290	284	-8%
	Non-Whites	456	500	541	19%
Washington, DC	Total	554	523	529	-5%
	Whites	183	184	194	6%
	Blacks	352	321	316	-10%
	Other Minorities	19	18	19	0%
Data Sources:	Maryland Office of Planning (http://www.op.state.md.us/MSDC/map.htm) U.S. Department of Commerce, Census Bureau (http://www.census.gov/population/projections)				

trade dropped precipitously during the 5 years ending in 1997 (-46 percent and -22 percent, respectively). Retail sales in the District of Columbia totaled $3.6 billion in 1997. For the city of Baltimore, the number of establishments dropped by 42 percent, yet retail sales increased 8 percent during this timeframe to total $3.2 billion. For the overall Baltimore region, the number of establishments declined 32 percent, while sales climbed 24 percent to total $17.3 billion. For the Washington region in Maryland, a 29 percent reduction in stores occurred while sales increased 19 percent to total $17.2 billion.

During the mid-1990s, several notable retailing trends occurred in the Baltimore-Washington, D.C., area. One was the rapid introduction of new discount department stores (Wal-Mart and Target) and conventional department stores (Nordstrom and Kohl's) and the proliferation of "big box" shopping centers in the suburbs that are filled with category killers and specialty retailers, such as Old Navy and Dick's Clothing and Sporting Goods. Another trend was the demise of several retailers who were well entrenched in the area, such as Merry-Go-Round and Rudo's Sports (which historically had a strong presence in inner city Baltimore).

All in all, the market for apparel and footwear is hotly contested in the Baltimore-Washington, D.C., metropolitan area. DTLR faces considerable intra- and intertype competition in the area. This competition takes the form of national specialty clothing, athletic footwear, and sporting goods retailers, such as Footlocker, The Athlete's Foot, Champs Sports, Gap, Foot Action, Just for Feet, Abercrombie & Fitch, Eddie Bauer, and so on; and department stores, such as Hechts and Macy's. There is also a great deal of competition from stores representing local independent and chain retailers, such as Changes, Jean City, Sports Zone, Shoe City, Total Male, and Up Against the Wall. Key retailing statistics on a number of important Maryland regions are shown in Table 2. This EXCEL data must be downloaded from the student site:

DTLR'S RETAILING STRATEGY

DTLR's Target and Their Shopping Behavior

DTLR's decision to specifically target African-American males was not a deliberate one from the outset. Instead, it was one that has evolved with the success of the retailing chain. Recent research conducted for DTLR by a local HBCU indicated that over 85 percent of its customers were in their mid-teens to less than 35 years old. These shoppers were predominantly African-American males. While slightly over half of them reported shopping for urban/casual wear once a month or less, there is a hard-core segment of frequent shoppers (at least twice a month) who are of college age and in their late twenties. This target segment visits a variety of retailing formats when shopping for casual clothing and footwear. Specialty stores (clothing, footwear, and/or athletic gear) are the predominant shopping destination, followed by department stores and quite distantly by discount department stores.

Based on customer spotting research and focus group interviews, it is known that DTLR's customers were quite mobile and willing to travel considerable distances when it comes to shopping for urban wear. It is also common for customers to visit several stores in the chain. However, the spotting research indicates that DTLR's inner city stores have a more geographically concentrated customer base than the stores located in the central business district and suburban malls. Feedback from the stores, observations by company executives, and recent focus group research suggest that these inner city stores might be considered as destination stores. As Rick Levin notes, "We're a hangout". In contrast, the mall and central business district stores are more akin to being parasites, i.e., living off the traffic generated by the anchor department stores and the mall overall.

Many of DTLR's frequent shoppers are seeking "fashion forward" apparel. Often, they will purchase an entire color-coordinated ensemble (e.g., name-brand T-shirt, a pair of jeans, and sneakers) with a combined total purchase price of between $200 and $300. Others with less disposable income may try to emulate this coordinated look by buying items piece-meal. DTLR store personnel will often notify frequent shoppers prior to when new merchandise is received so they can be among the first to be sporting the latest fashion look.

Interestingly, the merchandise buyers for DTLR recognize that there is no single "look" in the Baltimore-Washington, D.C., region. Those from Baltimore tend to wear brighter colors, while those living in the District of Columbia prefer more subdued colors like tans, grays, and blacks. Fashion trends for young African-Americans are heavily influenced by urban culture and styles worn by favorite music artists. DTLR has come to recognize that local radio DJ's are important role models to young African-American consumers and serve as a reference group that validates new clothing trends.

Location Strategy

Until recently, DTLR had initiated little formal research to determine the trade areas of its existing stores and evaluate prospective store sites. Aside from anecdotal accounts coming from store personnel and regular visits to these stores, company executives did not know from where the chain was drawing its customers. In the late 1990s, it commissioned a local university to conduct customer spotting research for its Baltimore stores and later to make general site recommendations for the entire Baltimore-Washington, D.C., region. Prior to these research efforts, store siting was largely done by the "seat of the pants," based on anecdotal evidence, observations, spotting businesses with similar customer profiles (e.g., Murray's Steaks and pawnbrokers), and recommendations by commercial realtors.

In the city of Baltimore, DTLR has two stores in or nearby the central business district and another three in small neighborhood shopping centers located in inner city neighborhoods. It also has two stores in western Baltimore County, one in a smaller mall located in the southwest near the city boundary and a second in a large regional shopping mall located to the west. Additionally, it has two outlet-type stores operating under the name Athletic Warehouse located in business parks in Harford and Anne Arundel Counties. The Harford location is slated to close when its lease expires. DTLR has two stores located in shopping centers in Prince George's

County and four located in inner city neighborhoods in the District of Columbia. DTLR also has opened and closed a store in the fashionable Georgetown area.

Merchandising Strategy

Although DTLR does not cater exclusively to young African-American males, its merchandise mix primarily reflects the fashion orientation of this group. Its merchandise strategy is typical of specialty retailers: narrow and deep. The primary merchandise categories that are carried include men's, women's, and children's athletic footwear and boots, men's T-shirts, sweats, jeans and shorts, casual/athletic jackets, and related accessories. DTLR has been experimenting with stocking a limited amount of music CDs and tapes because of the many inquiries about the music playing in the background at its stores and is even test marketing a broader selection at one of its stores. Levin and Trantas view music as an "accessory" to the urban wear outfits they sell. This is an ideal cross-selling opportunity.

Carrying a wide array of national and designer brands is critical to DTLR's merchandise assortment. Its selection during the late 1990s included brands most closely associated with African-Americans, like FUBU, Mecca, Pelle Pelle, RP55, Sean John, and Maurice Malone, as well as those that are generally popular with teens and young adults, such as Iceberg, Nike, Polo, and Timberland. DTLR's buyers are constantly visiting stores, getting feedback from sales personnel, and visiting manufacturers and trade shows to stay abreast of emerging fashion trends. Levin and Trantas have observed that urban fashions tend to originate on the East Coast, often in New York, and then migrate west, moreso than a west-to-east trend.

Now that it has grown to 20 stores, LevTran finds it is becoming easier to "sell itself" to designers and national manufacturers to persuade them to distribute their products through the DTLR chain and to gain special deals and other concessions. However, they do not always succeed. For example, DTLR has been striving to carry the Hilfiger line for years, but has been rebuffed repeatedly on the grounds that the designer did not want to become over-exposed in the market and thus was concentrating its distribution with larger national chains, such as Hechts (part of the May Company). Recently, DTLR introduced its first private label merchandise, a line of high- quality fleece sweatshirts and pants.

DTLR features an extensive assortment of men's clothing and footwear in a variety of colors and sizes. For shirts, it only stocks sizes large (L) through triple extra large (XXXL). A limited variety of styles and size footwear for women and children is also carried.

Customer Service Strategy

DTLR prides itself on the high level of service it shows to its customers. The chain accepts major credit cards and offers layaways. Although not a formal policy, store personnel often develop a personal relationship with frequent shoppers and will give them advance notice of new merchandise deliveries. When a particular item or size is not available at a given store, the staff will call other stores to locate the desired merchandise and offer to have it transferred to their store for the customer. In many cases, the customer is not willing to wait the few days for the delivery, but will instead travel to the other store to purchase the item that same day.

DTLR places considerable effort behind recruiting store personnel from city neighborhoods. Often, sales clerks will develop a loyal following of customers who will seek assistance from them during each visit. The chain trains its store staff to have a general familiarity about all the merchandise and more in-depth knowledge about particular product categories. Because the staff is paid on a salary basis (with bonuses for achieving store sales goals) rather than by individual sales commissions, there is not the "vulture effect" of sales clerks pouncing on customers as they enter the store and the insincere "everything looks so-o-o good on you" hard sell tactics. Instead, it is common for the sales staff to acknowledge customers and offer assistance, and when necessary, hand the customer over to another employee who may have greater knowledge about a particular product.

Store Layout, Display, and Atmosphere Strategy

DTLR stores tend to range in size from 3,500 to 4,500 square feet. Typically, they are rectangular in shape. The inner city stores tend to have more width than depth, while the stores located in malls generally have relatively narrow storefronts but greater depth.

A notable aspect of DTLR's retailing strategy is the attention it pays to making its stores a comfortable, exciting place to shop. If you were to be blindfolded and escorted into one of DTLR's inner city stores, you would be hard-pressed to know that you were not in a mall store by virtue of the store's interior appearance. Carpeting and wood flooring, wall sconces and lots of lighting, and other visual cues that suggest "this is a quality, classy place" are incorporated as standard design elements. The background music is typically Hip-Hop in Baltimore and go-go in the District of Columbia, coming from CDs or local African-American-oriented radio stations where DTLR has developed close relationships with the DJs.

The stores generally have a free-form layout. They make use of a variety of fixtures, including rounders, four-ways, straight racks, and wall displays. Because of the extensive merchandise assortment being stocked, the stores have a somewhat busy look. Footwear is typically found on wall displays, located on the left towards the rear of the store to draw shoppers through the store and expose them to the clothing. Displays featuring color-coordinated ensembles are hung from the ceiling throughout the store. Otherwise, the bulk of the stock is found in style/item presentations. The sales register is typically located midway through the store on the right side or at the rear, depending on the configuration of the store. Smaller accessory items are displayed behind the register to promote cross-selling opportunities and impulse buys, as well as to curtail shoplifting.

Pricing Strategy

Because it is perceived as carrying fashion-forward merchandise, DTLR is able to command premium prices on much of the apparel it offers. In many cases, with items that reflect the latest fashion trends, the entire lot may be sold before any markdowns are taken. Clothing that is going out of style or season is moved to the rear of the store, where the marked-down merchandise is concentrated. If it is not sold in a reasonable period of time, the merchandise may be shipped to LevTran's two Athletic Warehouse outlet stores to be sold at a deep discount.

Promotion Strategy

By experimenting over the years, DTLR has come to regard publicity and word-of-mouth as being its most powerful promotional tools. It makes extensive use of radio, not only with spot ads, but also through the use of co-sponsorships, tie-ins, and remote broadcasts by key local radio stations whose listeners are primarily young African-Americans. DTLR has historically concentrated much of its promotional activities in publicity activities, such as donations to community organizations and sponsorships of community activities and staging store visits by music and sports celebrities such as the Baltimore-based group Dru Hill and heavyweight contender Hasim Rahman. The chain also makes use of outdoor advertising by periodically employing billboards that are strategically located along major traffic arteries. It makes limited use of TV advertising on local cable stations.

DTLR has also gained national attention through its strategic partnership with PepsiCo's Mountain Dew® brand of soft drinks to operate "street teams" manned by area DJs and music celebrities. Using a 1999 platinum-colored Lincoln Navigator that is emblazoned with the logos from Mountain Dew, DTLR, and other national clothing brands, the street teams travel throughout the region promoting goodwill and product among the locals, with stops at high schools and universities, grocery stores, and community events. "The street team is like the Pied Piper of the urban market," CEO Levin is quoted as saying. Because the music and clothing tastes in Baltimore and the District of Columbia are so different, DTLR actually employs two different teams, led by popular DJs from each city. Emulating the alternative, grass-roots approach to marketing that has propelled Hip-Hop/rap music to become a major music genre, DTLR initially planned to continue the street team experiment for three years. However, its immediate success is likely to make this effort a major component of DTLR's promotional strategy for the foreseeable future.

MANAGEMENT AND OPERATIONS

Organizational Chart

Overall, LevTran operates with few managerial layers. Levin and Trantas share the Office of CEO. To date, Levin has taken on the major managerial role, overseeing store operations, developing and executing the overall retailing strategy, along with promotion strategy and store location strategy. Trantas is in charge of merchandise buying. Recently, a third person, Glenn Gaynor, has been elevated to COO/President with overall responsibilities for distribution center operations, information systems, finance and accounting, and human resources. LevTran's organization chart is shown in shown in Exhibit 1.

Distribution/Logistics/Information Systems

LevTran presently operates a single distribution center located in Hanover, Maryland. Located in a business park near the Baltimore-Washington International Airport, this facility operates in the rear of the space leased by LevTran that also houses its corporate headquarters and one of its Athletic Warehouse stores. Company executives feel that the distribution operations are approaching full capacity. During times when inventory is built up, off-site warehouse space is also rented.

LevTran operates a sophisticated computerized inventory system that is also tied in with each store and the scanner-equipped sales registers. As merchandise is received from vendors, it is unpacked and verified, has bar-coded price tags attached, and is entered into the system along with the store destination. Thus, the company is able to monitor its inventory levels and sales trends with minimal time lags.

Store Staffing and Recruiting

Another sign of DTLR's local commitment to African-Americans and the inner city is the chain's policy of recruiting sales staff from local neighborhoods where their customers are found. It also prides itself on its longstanding policy of promoting from within. While some store managers have had prior experience in retailing management, a significant number have climbed the internal career ladder to become store and regional managers, after having originally started out as store sales clerks.

What the Future Holds

While Levin and Trantas feel that their venture has far surpassed their initial expectations, they are not smug about their success. They are vitally concerned with developing a strategic plan that will ensure the continued growth and profitability of their retailing chain. They recognize that, so far, they have made a number of wise decisions and no major errors from which they have not been able to recover. They also realize that the hands-on, intuitive, and less formal style of management they have practiced in the past is being replaced by more formal, systematic procedures and increasing delegation to others in the executive and middle management ranks.

Levin, Trantas, and others working with them are faced with the ongoing challenge of having to make crucial decisions, such as determining what growth strategies to pursue, re-evaluating their merchandise mix, and determining whether to make major capital expenditures related to their logistics infrastructure and information systems. What would you recommend if you were brought in as a consultant to assist with these issues?

Exhibit 1 Downtown Locker Room (LevTran Enterprises) Organizational Chart

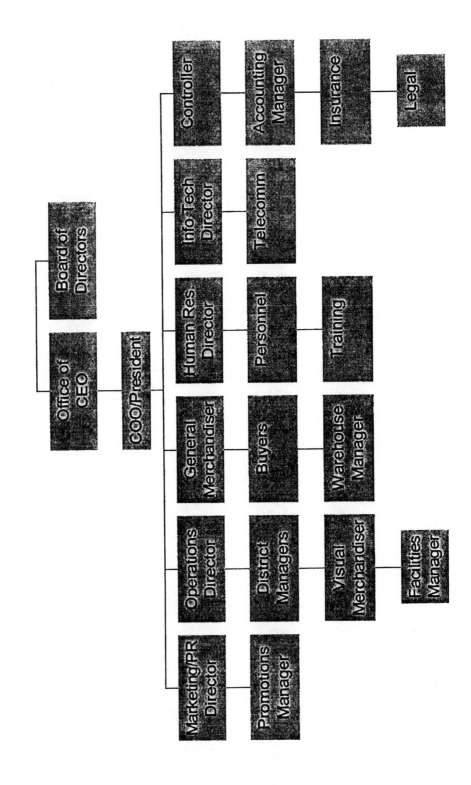

Exhibit 2
What Growth Strategy Should DTLR Pursue?

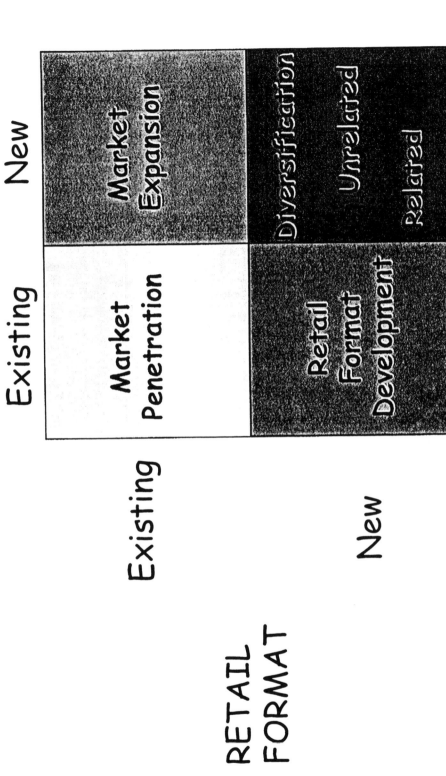

TARGET MARKET SEGMENT

New
- Market Expansion
- Diversification
  - Unrelated
  - Related

Existing
- Market Penetration
- Retail Format Development

RETAIL FORMAT

Existing

New

Questions:

1. Why are African-Americans and other minorities an attractive target for apparel retailers?

2. Discuss the advantages and disadvantages of inner city retailing.

3. Evaluate DTLR's retailing strategy.

4. Using the retailing variant of the Ansoff matrix, identify potential growth strategies DTLR might consider. See Exhibit 2.

5. Should DTLR add more stores in the Baltimore-Washington, D.C., metro region and/or expand elsewhere? If the latter, where would you recommend? What are the critical decision criteria to consider in making this decision?

CASE 7

Wal-Mart Stores, Inc.: Strategies for Continued Market Dominance

This case was prepared and written by Professor James W. Camerius, Northern Michigan University. It is intended to be used as a basis for class discussion rather than to illustrate either effective or ineffective handling of an administrative situation. All rights reserved to the author. Copyright ©1998 by James W. Camerius. Reprinted by permission.

INTRODUCTION

David Glass assumed the role of President and Chief Executive Officer at Wal-Mart, the position previously held by Sam Walton, the chain's legendary founder. Known for his hard-driving managerial style, Glass gained his experience in retailing at a small supermarket chain in Springfield, Missouri. He joined Wal-Mart as executive vice-president for finance in 1976. He was named president and chief operating officer in 1984. In 1998, as he reflected on growth strategies of the firm, he suggested: "Seldom can you count on everything coming together as well as it did this year. We believe we could always do better, but we improved more this year than I can ever remember in the past. If Wal-Mart had been content to be just an Arkansas retailer in the early days, we probably would not be where we are today."

A Maturing Organization

In 1998, Wal-Mart Stores, Inc., headquartered in Bentonville, Arkansas, operated mass merchandising retail stores under a variety of names and retail formats including Wal-Mart discount department stores; Sam's Wholesale Clubs, wholesale/retail membership warehouses; and Wal-Mart Supercenters, large combination grocery and general merchandise stores in all 50 states. In the International Division, it operated stores in Canada, Mexico, Argentina, Brazil, Germany, and Puerto Rico, and through joint ventures in China. It was not only the nation's largest discount department store chain, but had surpassed the retail division of Sears, Roebuck & Co. in sales volume as the largest retailer in the United States. The McLane Company, a support division with over 36,000 customers, was the nation's largest distributor of food and merchandise to convenience stores and served selected Wal-Marts, Sam's Clubs, and Supercenters. Wal-Mart also continued to operate Bud's Discount City, a small number of discount department stores.

The Sam Walton Spirit

Much of the success of Wal-Mart was attributed to the entrepreneurial spirit of its founder and Chairman of the Board, Samuel Moore Walton (1918-1992). Many considered him one of the most influential retailers of the century. Sam Walton (or "Mr. Sam" as some referred to him), traced his down-to-earth, old-fashioned, home-spun, evangelical ways to growing up in rural

Oklahoma, Missouri, and Arkansas.

Sam Walton said in an interview, "The reason for our success is our people and the way that they're treated and the way they feel about their company." Many have suggested it is this "people first" philosophy which guided the company through the challenges and setbacks of its early years, and allowed the company to maintain its consistent record of growth and expansion in later years.

There was little about Sam Walton's background that reflected his remarkable success. He was born in Kingfisher, Oklahoma, on March 29, 1918, to Thomas and Nancy Walton. He completed high school at Columbia, Missouri, and received a Bachelor of Arts Degree in Economics from the University of Missouri in 1940. "I really had no idea what I would be," he said, adding as an afterthought, "at one point in time, I thought I wanted to become president of the United States."

A unique, enthusiastic, and positive individual, Sam Walton was "just your basic home-spun billionaire," a columnist once suggested. "Mr. Sam is a life-long, small-town resident who didn't change much as he got richer than his neighbors." Walton had tremendous energy, enjoyed bird hunting with his dogs, and flew a corporate plane. When the company was much smaller, he could boast that he personally visited every Wal-Mart store at least once a year. A store visit usually included Walton leading Wal-Mart cheers that began, "Give me a W, give me an A..." To many employees, he had the air of a fiery Baptist preacher," Paul R. Carter, a Wal-Mart executive vice-president, was quoted as saying. "Mr. Walton has a calling." He became the richest man in America, and by 1991, had created a personal fortune for his family in excess of $21 billion.

Sam Walton's success was widely chronicled. He was selected by the investment publication, *Financial World*, in 1989 as the "CEO of the Decade." He had honorary degrees from the University of the Ozarks, the University of Arkansas, and the University of Missouri. He also received many of the most distinguished professional awards of the industry, like "Man of the Year," "Discounter of the Year," and "Chief Executive Officer of the Year," and was the second retailer to be inducted into the Discounting Hall of Fame. He was the recipient of the Horatio Alger Award in 1984 and acknowledged by *Discount Stores News* as "Retailer of the Decade" in December 1989. "Walton does a remarkable job of instilling near-religious fervor in his people," said analyst Robert Buchanan of A.G. Edwards. "I think that speaks to the heart of his success." In late 1989, Sam Walton was diagnosed to have multiple myeloma, or cancer of the bone marrow. He planned to remain active as Chairman of the Board of Directors.

THE MARKETING CONCEPT

Genesis of an Idea

Sam Walton started his retail career in 1940 as a management trainee with the J.C. Penney Company in Des Moines, Iowa. He was impressed with the Penney method of doing business and later modeled the Wal-Mart chain on "The Penney Idea," as reviewed in Table 1. The

Penney Company also found strength in calling its employees "associates" rather than clerks.

Following service in the U.S. Army during World War II, Sam Walton acquired a Ben Franklin variety store franchise in Newport, Arkansas. He operated this store successfully with his brother, James L. "Bud" Walton (1921-1995), until losing the lease in 1950. When Wal-Mart was incorporated in 1962, the retailer operated 15 stores. Bud Walton became a senior vice-president and concentrated on finding suitable store locations, acquiring real estate, and directing store construction.

Table 1
The Penney Idea: 1913

1. To serve the public, as nearly as we can, to its complete satisfaction.
2. To expect for the service we render a fair remuneration and not all the profit the traffic will bear.
3. To do all in our power to pack the customer's dollar full of value, quality, and satisfaction.
4. To continue to train ourselves and our associates so that the service we give will be more and more intelligently performed.
5. To improve constantly the human factor in our business.
6. To reward men and women in our organization through participation in what the business produces.
7. To test our every policy, method, and act in this wise: "Does it square with what is right and just?"

The early retail stores owned by Sam Walton in Newport and Bentonville, Arkansas, and later in other small towns in adjoining southern states, were variety store operations. They were relatively small operations of 6,000 square feet, were located on the town's "main street," and displayed merchandise on plain wooden tables and counters. Operated under the Ben Franklin name and supplied by Butler Brothers of Chicago and St. Louis, the retail strategy of these stores were based on limited price lines, low gross margins, high merchandise turnover, and concentration on return on investment. In 1992, the retailer, operating under the Walton 5 & 10 name, became the largest Ben Franklin franchisee in the country. The variety stores were phased out by 1976 so that the company could concentrate on developing Wal-Mart discount department stores.

Foundations of Growth

Sam Walton became convinced in the late 1950s that discounting would transform retailing. He traveled extensively in New England, the cradle of "off-pricing." After he had visited just about every discounter in the United States, he tried to interest Butler Brothers executives in the discount store concept. The first Kmart, a "conveniently located one-stop shopping unit where customers could buy a wide variety of quality merchandise at discount prices," had just opened in Garden City, Michigan. Walton's theory was to operate a similar discount store in a small community. Butler Brothers' executives rejected the idea. The first Wal-Mart Discount City opened in late 1962 in Rogers, Arkansas.

The retail strategy of Wal-Mart was to sell nationally-advertised, well-known brand merchandise at low prices in austere surroundings. Refunds, credits, and rain checks were also cheerfully given. Early emphasis was placed upon opportunistic purchases of merchandise from whatever sources were available. Heavy emphasis was placed upon health and beauty aids (H&BA) in the product line and "stacking it high" in a manner of merchandise presentation. By the end of 1979, there were 276 Wal-Mart stores located in eleven states.

The retailer developed an aggressive expansion strategy. New stores, ranging in size from 30,000 square feet to 60,000 square feet, were primarily located in towns of 5,000 to 25,000 population. The retailer expanded by locating stores in contiguous areas, town by town, state by state. When its discount operations came to dominate a market area, it moved to an adjoining area. While other retailers built warehouses to serve existing outlets, Wal-Mart first built its distribution center and later spotted stores all around it, pooling advertising and distribution costs. Most stores were located less than a six-hour drive from one of the company's warehouses.

National Perspectives

At the beginning of 1991, Wal-Mart became the largest retailer and the largest discount department store in the United States. In that year, there were 1,573 Wal-Mart stores in 35 states.

As a national discount department store chain, Wal-Mart Stores, Inc. offered a wide variety of general merchandise to the customer. The stores were designed to offer one-stop shopping in 36 departments which included family apparel, health and beauty aids, household needs, electronics, toys, fabric and crafts, automotive supplies, lawn and patio, jewelry, and shoes. In addition, some store locations had pharmacies, automotive supply and service centers, garden centers, and snack bars. Wal-Mart operated all of its stores with an "everyday low price" policy, as opposed to putting heavy emphasis on special promotions.

Although many of Wal-Mart's strategies were similar to those at its discount store competitors, there were many important differences. At Wal-Mart, employees wore blue vests to identify themselves, aisles were wide, apparel departments were carpeted in warm colors, a store employee followed customers to their cars to pick up their shopping carts, and the customer was welcomed at the door by a "people greeter" who gave directions and struck up conversations. A simple Wal-Mart logo in white letters on a brown background on the front of the store served to identify the retailer. In consumer studies, it was determined that the chain was particularly adept at striking the delicate balance needed to convince customers its prices were low without making people feel that its stores were too cheap. In many ways, competitors like Kmart sought to emulate Wal-Mart by introducing people greeters, by upgrading interiors, by developing new logos and signage, and by introducing new inventory response systems.

A "Satisfaction Guaranteed" refund and exchange policy was introduced to allow customers to be confident of Wal-Mart's merchandise and quality. Technological advancements like scanner cash registers, hand-held computers for ordering of merchandise, and computer linkages of stores with the general office and distribution centers improved communications and merchandise replenishment. Each store was encouraged to initiate programs that would make it an integral part of the community in which it operated. Associates were encouraged to "maintain the highest standards of honesty, morality, and business ethics in dealing with the public."

The Competitive Environment

Industry analysts labeled the 1980s and early 1990s as eras of economic uncertainty for retailers. Many retailers were negatively affected by increased competitive pressures, sluggish consumer spending, slower-than-anticipated domestic economic growth, and recessions abroad. In 1995, Wal-Mart management felt the high consumer debt level caused many shoppers to reduce or defer spending on anything other than essentials. Management also felt that the lack of exciting new products or apparel trends reduced discretionary spending. During this time period, Wal-Mart experienced fierce competition, which resulted in lower profit margins. By 1998, the country had returned to prosperity. Unemployment was low, total income was relatively high, and interest rates were stable. Combined with a low inflation rate, buying power was perceived to be high and consumers were generally willing to buy.

Many retail enterprises confronted heavy competitive pressure by restructuring. Sears, Roebuck became a more focused retailer by divesting itself of Allstate Insurance Company and its real estate subsidiaries. In 1993, the company closed 118 unprofitable stores and discontinued its unprofitable Sears general merchandise catalog. After unsuccessfully experimenting with an everyday low-price strategy, management chose to realign its merchandise strategy to meet the needs of its middle market customers, who were primarily women. The new focus on apparel was supported with the advertising campaign, "The Softer Side of Sears." A later companywide campaign broadened the appeal: "The many sides of Sears fit the many sides of your life." Sears completed its return to its retailing roots by selling off its ownership in Dean Witter Financial Services, Discover Card, Coldwell Banker Real Estate, and Sears mortgage banking operations.

The discount department store industry by the early 1990s had changed in a number of ways and was thought to have reached maturity by many retail analysts. Several formerly successful retailers such as E.J. Korvette, W.T. Grant, Atlantic Mills, Arlans, Federals, Zayre, and Ames had declared bankruptcy. Regional retailers like Target Stores and Shopko Stores began carrying more fashionable merchandise in more attractive facilities and shifted their emphasis to more national markets. Specialty retailers such as Toys "R" Us, Pier 1 Imports, and Oshmans were making big inroads in toys, home furnishings, and sporting goods. The drug and food superstores were rapidly discounting increasing amounts of general merchandise. Some retailers such as May Department Stores Company (with Caldor and Venture), and Woolworth Corporation (with

Woolco) had withdrawn from the field by either selling their discount divisions or closing them down entirely.

Several new retail formats had emerged in the marketplace to challenge the traditional discount department store format. The superstore, a 100,000- to 300,000-square-foot operation, combined a large supermarket with a discount general-merchandise store. Originally a European retailing concept, these outlets were known as "malls without walls." Kmart's Super Kmart Centers, American Fare, and Wal-Mart's Supercenter Store were examples of this trend toward large operations. Membership clubs emerged, using warehouse-like environments to reduce operating expenses. Home Depot combined the traditional hardware store and lumber yard with a self-service home improvement center to become the largest home center operator in the nation.

Some retailers responded to changes in the marketplace by selling goods at price levels (20 percent to 60 percent) below regular retail prices. These off-price operations appeared as two general types: factory outlet stores (such as Burlington Coat Factory Warehouse and Bass Shoes), and independents (such as Loehmann's, T.J. Maxx, and Marshall's) which bought seconds, overages, closeouts, or leftover goods from manufacturers and other retailers. Other retailers chose to dominate a product classification. Some super specialists, like Sock Appeal, Little Piggie, Ltd., and Sock Market, offered a single narrowly-defined classification of merchandise with an extensive assortment of brands, colors, and sizes. Some retailers, like Silk Greenhouse (silk plants and flowers), Office Club (office supplies and equipment), and Toys "R" Us were called "category killers" because they had achieved merchandise dominance in their respective product categories. Stores like The Limited, Limited Express, Victoria's Secret, and The Banana Republic became mini-department specialists by showcasing new lines and accessories alongside traditional merchandise lines. Still others, as niche specialists, like Kids Mart, a division of Woolworth Corporation, and McKids, a division of Sears, targeted an identified market with carefully selected merchandise and appropriately designed stores.

Kmart Corporation became the industry's third-largest retailer after Sears, Roebuck & Co. and the second-largest discount department store chain in the United States in the 1990s. This retailer was perceived by many retail analysts as a laggard. According to one industry observer, the original Kmart concept of a "conveniently located, one-stop shopping unit where customers could buy a wide variety of quality merchandise at discount prices," had lost its competitive edge in a changing market. As one analyst noted in an industry newsletter: "They had done so well for the past 20 years without paying attention to market changes; now they have to." Wal-Mart and Kmart's sales growth over the period 1987 to 1997 is reviewed in Table 2. A competitive analysis is shown of four major retailers in Table 3.

Some retailers, such as Kmart, had initially focused on appealing to professional, middle-class consumers who lived in suburban areas and who were likely to be price sensitive. Other firms like Target (Dayton Hudson), which had adopted the discount concept early, attempted to go generally after an upscale consumer who had an annual household income of $25,000 to $44,000. Some retailers, such as Fleet Farm and Menard's, served the rural consumer, while others, like Chicago's Goldblatt's Department Stores and Ames Discount Department Stores, chose to serve inner city residents.

In rural communities, Wal-Mart's success often came at the expense of local merchants and regional discount store chains. Hardware stores, family department stores, building supply outlets, and stores featuring fabrics, sporting goods, and shoes were among the first to either close or relocate elsewhere. Regional discount retailers in the Sunbelt states like Roses, Howard's, T.G.&Y., and Duckwall-ALCO, who once enjoyed solid sales and earnings, were forced to reposition themselves by renovating stores, opening bigger and more modern units, re-merchandising assortments, and offering lower prices. In many cases, stores like Coast-to-Coast, Pamida, and Ben Franklin closed upon a Wal-Mart announcement that it was planning to build in a specific community. "Just the word that Wal-Mart was coming made some stores close up," indicated a local newspaper editor.

Table 2
Competitive Sales & Store Comparison[1]
1987-1997

	Kmart		Wal-Mart	
Year	Sales (000)	Stores[1]	Sales (000)	Stores[1]
1997	$32,183,000	2,136	$117,958,000	3,406
1996	31,437,000	2,261	104,859,000	3,054
1995	34,389,000	2,161	93,627,000	2,943
1994	34,025,000	2,481	82,494,000	2,684
1993	34,156,000	2,486	67,344,000	2,400
1992	37,724,000	2,435	55,484,000	2,136
1991	34,580,000	2,391	43,886,900	1,928
1990	32,070,000	2,350	32,601,594	1,721
1989	29,533,000	2,361	25,810,656	1,525
1988	27,301,000	2,307	20,649,001	1,364
1987	25,627,000	2,273	15,959,255	1,198

[1] Number of general merchandise stores.

Table 3
An Industry Comparative Analysis
1997

	WAL-MART	SEARS[1]	KMART	TARGET
Sales (millions)	$117,958	$36,371	$32,183	$20,368
Net Income (thousands)	$3,526	$ 1,188	$ 249	$ 1,287
Net Income Per Share	$ 1.56	$ 3.03	$ .51	n/a
Dividends Per Share	$ .27	n/a	n/a	n/a
% Sales Change	12.0%	8.0%	2.4%	14%

Number of Stores:
WAL-MART AND SUBSIDIARIES
    Wal-Mart Stores - 2,421
    Sam's Clubs - 483
    Supercenters - 502

SEARS, ROEBUCK & CO. (ALL DIVISIONS)[1]
Sears Merchandise Group:
    Department Stores - 833
    Hardware Stores - 255
    Furniture Stores - 129
    Sears Dealer Stores - 576
    Auto/Tire Stores - 780
    Auto Parts Stores:
        Western Auto - 39
        Parts America - 576
        Western Auto Dealer Stores - 800

KMART CORPORATION
    General Merchandise - 2,136

Dayton Hudson Corporation
    Target - 796
    Mervyn's - 269
    Department Stores - 65

Source: Corporate Annual Reports.

Wal-Mart's Overall Domestic and International Retail Strategy

Wal-Mart's emerging retail strategy was based on a set of two main principles: a value orientation for its customers and a team focus for its employees. The value orientation meant that "customers would be provided what they want, when they want it, all at a value." The team focus evolved around management acknowledging its dependency on its employees, who were called "associate partners."

Wal-Mart's retail strategy also included aggressive plans for new store openings; opening new distribution centers; expansion to additional states; and upgrading, relocating, refurbishing, and remodeling of existing stores. The plan was to not have a single operating unit that had not been updated in the past seven years. For Wal-Mart management, the 1990s were considered "a new era for Wal-Mart, an era in which we plan to grow to a truly nationwide retailer, and should we continue to perform, our sales and earnings will also grow beyond where most could have envisioned at the dawn of the 80s."

In the 1980s, Wal-Mart developed a number of new retail formats. The first Sam's Club opened in Oklahoma City, Oklahoma, in 1983. The membership wholesale club was an idea which had been developed by other retailers earlier, but which found its greatest success and growth in acceptability at Wal-Mart. Sam's Clubs featured a vast array of product categories with limited selection of brand and model, cash-and-carry business with limited hours, large (100,000-square-foot) bare-bones facilities, rock bottom wholesale prices, and minimal promotion.

Wal-Mart Supercenters were large combination stores. They were first opened in 1988 as Hypermarket*USA, a 222,000-square-foot superstore which combined a discount store with a large grocery store, a food court of restaurants, and other service businesses such as banks or video tape rental stores. A scaled-down version of Hypermarket*USA, called the Wal-Mart SuperCenter, had similar merchandise offerings, but about half the square footage of hypermarts. These expanded store concepts included convenience stores and gasoline sales to "enhance shopping convenience." The company proceeded slowly with these plans and later on suspended its plans for building any more hypermarkets in favor of the smaller Supercenter. In 1998, Wal-Mart operated 502 Supercenters. It also announced plans to build several full-fledged supermarkets called "Wal-Mart Food and Drug Express" with a drive-through option as "laboratories" to test how the concept would work. The McLane Company, Inc., a provider of retail and grocery distribution services for retail stores, was acquired in 1991. It was not considered a major segment of the total Wal-Mart operation.

Several programs were launched to highlight popular social causes. Wal-Mart's "Buy American" program was initiated in 1985. In this program, the retailer tried to influence vendors to produce goods in the United States rather than import them. The "Buy American" program centered around producing and selling quality merchandise at a competitive price. The promotion included television advertisements featuring factory workers, a soaring American eagle, and the slogan: "We buy American whenever we can, so you can too." Prominent in-store signage and store circulars were also included. One store poster read: "Success Stories -- These items formerly imported, are now being purchased by Wal-Mart in the U.S.A."

According to the president of Gitano Group, Inc., a maker of fashion discount clothing which imported 95 percent of its clothing and now makes about 20 percent of its products here: "Wal-Mart let it be known loud and clear that if you're going to grow with them, you sure better have some products made in the U.S.A." Farris Fashion, Inc. (flannel shirts), Roadmaster Corporation (exercise bicycles), Flanders Industries, Inc. (lawn chairs), and Magic Chef (microwave ovens) were examples of vendors that participated in the program.

Wal-Mart was one of the first retailers to embrace the concept of "green" marketing. The program offered shoppers the option of purchasing products that were ecologically superior in terms of their manufacture, use, and disposal. To initiate the program, 7,000 vendors were notified that Wal-Mart had a corporate concern for the environment and to ask for their support in a variety of ways. Wal-Mart's television advertising showed children on swings, fields of grain blowing in the wind, and roses. Green and white store signs, printed on recycled paper, marked products or packaging that had been developed or redesigned to be more environmentally sound.

As the nation's largest retailer, Wal-Mart exerted considerable bargaining power in its negotiation with vendors in terms of price, delivery terms, promotion allowances, and continuity of supply. Many of these benefits of its power could be passed on to consumers through lower prices. As a matter of corporate policy, management often insisted on doing business directly with the manufacturer rather than going through a wholesaler. As a representative of an industry association representing a group of sales agencies suggested, "In the Southwest, Wal-Mart's the only show in town." An industry analyst added, "They're extremely aggressive. Their approach has always been to give the customer the benefit of a corporate saving. That builds up customer loyalty and market share."

Another key factor in its overall retail strategy was an inventory control system that was recognized as the most sophisticated in retailing. A high-speed computer system linked virtually all the stores to Wal-Mart's corporate headquarters, as well as its distribution centers. The system electronically logged every item sold at the checkout counter, automatically kept the warehouses informed of merchandise to be ordered, and directed the flow of goods to the stores down to the shelf level. Most important for management, it helped detect sales trends quickly and speeded up the retailer's market reaction time. According to Bob Connolly, Executive Vice-President of Merchandising, "Wal-Mart has used the data gathered by technology to make more inventory available in the key items that customers want most, while reducing inventories overall."

On the international level, Wal-Mart management sought to be the dominant retailer in each country it entered. With the acquisition of 122 former Woolco stores in Canada, Wal-Mart exceeded expectations in terms of sales growth, market share, and profitability. Wal-Mart also gained a controlling interest in Cifra, Mexico's largest retailer. Cifra operated stores with a variety of concepts in every region of Mexico, ranging from the nation's largest chain of sit-down restaurants to a soft goods-based department store. Plans were also proceeding with start-up operations in Argentina and Brazil, as well as China. The acquisition of 21 "hypermarkets" in Germany at the end of 1997 marked the company's first entry into Europe, which management considered "one of the best consumer markets in the world." These large stores offered one-stop shopping facilities similar to Wal-Mart Supercenters. The international expansion accelerated management's plans for the development of Wal-Mart as a global brand along the lines of Coca-Cola, Disney, and McDonald's. While some changes in Wal-Mart's overall retail strategy were necessary to meet local tastes, much planning was centralized. For example, Wal-Mart's stores in different international markets would coordinate purchasing to achieve great bargaining power. Technology planning was also centralized. At the beginning of 1998, the International Division of Wal-Mart operated 500 discount stores, 61 Supercenters, and 40 Sam's Clubs.

Decision Making in a Market-Oriented Retailer

One principle that distinguished Wal-Mart from other retailers was the unusual depth of employee involvement in company affairs. Employees of Wal-Mart became "associates," a name borrowed from Sam Walton's early association with the J.C. Penney Company. Input was encouraged at meetings at the store and corporate level. The retailer hired employees locally, provided training programs, and through a "Letter to the President" program, encouraged employees to ask questions, and made words like "we," "us," and "our" a part of the corporate language. A number of special award programs recognized individual, department, and division achievement. Stock ownership and profit-sharing programs were introduced as part of a "partnership concept."

Wal-Mart's "store within a store" concept, as a corporate policy, trained individuals to be merchants by being responsible for the performance of their own departments as if they were running their own businesses. Seminars and training programs also enabled Wal-Mart's associates to grow within the company.

Wal-Mart's human resources program was recognized by the editors of the trade publication, *Mass Market Retailers*, when it recognized all of Wal-Mart's 275,000 associates as a group for the award of "Mass Market Retailer of the Year." "The Wal-Mart associate," the editors noted, "in this decade, that term has come to symbolize all that is right with the American worker, particularly in the retailing environment and most particularly at Wal-Mart."

The Growth Challenge

Wal-Mart Stores, Inc. had for over 25 years experienced tremendous growth and as one analyst suggested, "been consistently on the cutting edge of low-markup mass merchandising." Much of the forward momentum had come from the entrepreneurial spirit of Samuel Moore Walton. The company announced on Monday, April 6, 1992, following Walton's death, that his son, S. Robson Walton, Vice-Chairman of Wal-Mart, would succeed his father as Chairman of the Board. David Glass would remain President and CEO.

And what of Wal-Mart without Mr. Sam? "There's no transition to make," said Glass, "because the principles and the basic values he used in founding this company were so sound and so universally accepted." "As for the future," he suggested, "there's more opportunity ahead of us than behind us. We're good students of retailing and we've studied the mistakes that others have made. We'll make our own mistakes, but we won't repeat theirs. The only thing constant at Wal-Mart is change. We'll be fine as long as we never lose our responsiveness to the customer." Management identified four key legacies of Sam Walton to guide the company's "quest for value" in the future: (1) everyday low prices, (2) customer service, (3) leadership, and (4) change.

A number of new challenges, however, had to be met. It had been predicted as early as 1993 that Wal-Mart's same-store growth would likely slip into the 7 percent to 8 percent range in the near future. Analysts were also concerned about the increased competition in the membership club business and the company's move from its roots in Southern and Midwestern small towns to the more competitive and costly markets of the Northeast. Wal-Mart "supercenters" faced more resilient rivals in the grocery field. Unions representing supermarket workers delayed and, in some cases, killed expansion opportunities. Some analysts said: "The company is simply suffering from the high expectations its stellar performance over the years has created."

Questions:

1. Identify and evaluate the marketing strategies that Wal-Mart pursued to maintain its growth and marketing leadership position. What factors should a firm consider in the development of its marketing strategy?

2. Discuss the importance of changes in the external environment to an organization like Wal-Mart.

3. What conclusions can be drawn from a review of Wal-Mart's financial performance?

4. Speculate on how much impact the "absence" of Samuel Moore Walton had on the forward momentum of the organization. What steps have been or should be taken by management to continue Mr. Sam's formula for success?

5. What evidence is there to suggest that the marketing concept was understood and applied at Wal-Mart?

SHORT CASES

CASE 1

An Ace Hardware Store: Can It Compete in a Changing Retail Environment?

This case was prepared and written by Professors Algin B. King and William P. Darrow, Towson University. Reprinted by permission.

After graduating from college, James Brown worked as a purchasing agent for a large corporation in the Baltimore, Maryland, area. His company was seriously considering closing its Baltimore operations and consolidating all of its operations to Louisville, Kentucky. Since his company did not anticipate closing its Baltimore operations for at least a year, Brown had ample time to consider several options.

Recently, Brown had given serious consideration to becoming an entrepreneur. He felt that being his own boss would be more satisfying than being an employee. In addition, he would have the potential of earning substantially more than his current salary. Brown also decided to give preference to a business located in a small town environment in preference to an urban one.

Through a mutual friend, Brown learned that the owners of an Ace Hardware store in Frederick, Maryland, were planning to retire after owning their store for close to 40 years. James Brown began to gather and study economic data on the Heilburners' store. Frederick, Maryland, a town with a population of about 58,000, is located about 40 miles west of Baltimore. Some demographers have predicted that Frederick is on its way to becoming a "satellite town" to the metropolitan Baltimore area. Frederick's economy is currently growing at a rapid pace due to construction of both single-family houses and multi-family complexes and the large number of young families that have either relocated or plan to relocate to this area.

The Ace Hardware is located in a secondary retail district adjacent to Frederick's Main Street. The store has approximately 9,000 square feet of floor space and is housed in an old building with old store fixtures and a wooden floor. The store is viewed by community residents as a "mom and pop" operation with a strong base of loyal customers, a good reputation for customer service, and a reasonably convenient location.

Brown did some analysis on the hardware store industry. Based upon data from the National Retail Hardware Association (NRHA), there are three segments to the hardware store industry: hardware stores, home centers, and do-it-yourself (D-I-Y) lumberyards. The hardware stores are commonly small, average 8,000 square feet to 20,000 square feet of floor space, and are typically independently owned. Most hardware stores are members of large retail cooperatives, such as Ace Hardware Stores, Servistar, and True Value. The home centers are larger stores, typically with 80,000 square feet to 120,000 square feet of floor space in a warehouse format. Examples of home centers are Home Depot and Lowes. Many home centers serve as the anchor store in shopping centers. The D-I-Y lumberyards are traditional lumberyards with lumber stored in sheds or buildings. Data on dollar sales, number of stores, and market share for each of these segments is shown in Table 1.

Table 1
Do-It-Yourself Retail Industry Structure (1999)

Industry Category	$ Sales (Billions)	# of Stores	Percent of Sales
Hardware Stores	23.4	21, 100	14.7
Home Centers	79.9	10, 300	50.0
D-I-Y Lumber Yards	56.4	11, 700	35.3

Brown also talked to personnel at the Frederick Chamber of Commerce and Retail Merchants Association to learn more about the Fredrick area. According to members of the chamber of commerce, downtown Frederick and several nearby shopping centers were thriving. Annual population growth for Frederick was forecast at between 2 percent and 3 percent over the next ten years. The town's economic base was also diversified.

The Heilburners shared with Brown some relevant financial data for the most recent year, 1999. The store's sales for 1999 were $983,000, with a gross margin of 38.5 percent. The store's net profit was a healthy 10 percent. Included in the store's operating expenses was Mr. Heilburner's drawing account of $2,500 a month. The operating expenses also include the store's current rental costs. The store's lease was due to expire in late 2000, but was renewable. Table 2 shows the major components of the store's 1999 income statement.

Table 2
Heilburner Ace Hardware Store
1999 Income Statement

	Dollars	Percent of Total Sales
Net Sales	$ 983,000	100.0
Cost of Goods Sold	604,545	61.5
Gross Profit	378,455	38.5
Operating Expenses	278,189	28.3
Net Profit	100,266	10.2

The Heilburners' asking price for the store is $675,000. As part of the purchase agreement, James Brown would have to agree to assume all obligations under the current lease agreement. Brown is able to cover the purchase due to his savings, monies received from an inheritance, and proceeds from a long-term loan at a favorable rate obtained by a local savings bank.

A retired neighbor and friend with significant experience in the retail hardware store field filled Brown in on the benefits of retail hardware cooperatives, such as Ace. One, retail hardware cooperatives have sufficient buying power to compete with home centers due to their purchasing goods in large quantities. Two, the co-ops provide private label products that help its members obtain store loyalty. Three, the regional distribution centers operated by the cooperatives enable retailer members to receive goods twice each week. This enables member stores to reduce their inventory needs, as well as to reduce the probability of stockouts. Four, the cooperative manages a successful cooperative advertising program at the local and national level for its members. In addition to the retail cooperatives, independent hardware stores, such as the Heilburners' Ace store, receive important market research and financial data from their trade association, NRHA, which provides its members with timely market research and cost data. NRHA's Home Center Institute also provides its members with a broad array of training in store operations, product knowledge, accounting and financial controls, and retailing techniques.

The current retail competitive environment in Frederick was tough. A Lowes home center is located on Buckeystown Pike about three miles south of the center of Frederick. Lowes also has a Contractors Yard outlet about ½ mile from the main store, just off Buckeystown Pike. In addition, Home Depot has a home center on Urbana Pike, about one mile north of the town center.

Brown has not only heard of both Lowes and Home Depot, the two industry leaders in the hardware/home center industry, but he also has frequently shopped at Home Depot. He is aware that many retail analysts consider Home Depot as being on a par with Wal-Mart. While he has less personal experience shopping at Lowes, he realizes that Lowes' overall retail strategy is quite similar to Home Depot's. Brown also studied the web sites for both Home Depot and Lowes (www.homedepot.com and www.lowes.com). He developed a table to summarize the services provided by each store. See Table 3.

Brown is also aware of the buying power of both Home Depot and Lowes. For example, he learned that soon after Home Depot opened its unit in Frederick, the Ace Hardware store was forced to discontinue selling power tools since Home Depot's regular retail price was lower than the wholesale price Mr. Heilbruner could obtain through Ace. In addition to price competition, Home Depot and Lowes compete with Heilbruner for talented employees. Both Home Depot and Lowes seek employees with building trades experience. This enables home centers to provide in-store consulting for their do-it-yourself customers. The strategy of the two industry leaders is simple and very powerful. It is based upon low prices, a selection of between 40,000 and 50,000 items, and superior customer service. Home Depot refers to its strategy in terms of a three-legged stool.

James Brown knows that he quickly needs to decide as to whether to pursue this opportunity. If he plans to purchase the store, he knows that there are additional points for him to consider.

Table 3
Services Available at Home Depot and Lowes

Services Provided	Home Depot	Lowes
Kitchen Design	Yes	Yes
Custom Color Matching (paint)	Yes	Yes
Low Price Guarantee	Yes + 10% of price difference	Yes + 10% of price difference
Loading Assistance	Yes	Yes
Delivery Service	Nominal Fee	Nominal Fee/Free
Hourly Truck Rental	Yes	No
Tool Rental	Yes	No
Free Do-It-Yourself Clinics	Yes	Yes
Credit	Home Depot and Major Credit Cards	Major Credit Cards
Store Hours	Mon.-Sat: 7am-10pm and Sunday: 9am-6pm	Mon.-Sat. 7am-10pm and Sunday: 9am-6pm
Special Orders	Yes	Yes
Cutting Lumber	Yes	Yes
Glass Cutting	No	Yes
Assembly	No	Yes
Installation Services	Yes	No
One-Year Plant Guarantee	Yes	No
No-Hassle Return Policy	Yes	Yes

Questions:

1. What other information about Frederick, Maryland, does James Brown need to obtain?

2. Consider Home Depot's and Lowes' strategy for (1) price, (2) selection, and (3) service. How can a small independent hardware store compete? Consult Ace Hardware's Web site (www.acehardware.com) and the National Retail Hardware Association (www.nrha.org) Web site to get additional information.

3. Assuming that James Brown purchases the Heilburners' Ace Hardware Store, should he (a) continue to operate the store in its present location, (b) relocate to one of the three medium-sized shopping centers, or (c) choose a neighborhood convenience center? Support your choice.

4. Would you recommend that Mr. Brown purchase this Ace store? Why or why not? Support your decision.

CASE 2

Amazon.com: The Customer-Centric Company

This case was prepared and written by Professors Marianne C. Bickle and Antigone Kotsiopulos, Colorado State University. Reprinted by permission.

During 1994, the World Wide Web grew by 2,300 percent. As a hedge-fund executive, Jeff Bezos knew very little about c-commerce. He did, however, have an intense fascination and belief in its fixture. In 1995, Bezos borrowed $1 million from family and friends and started Amazon.com. After viewing over twenty products, books were selected as the initial product based on the vast number of available titles.

Amazon.com's initial merchandising strategy was to offer over 100,000 books, at a discounted price of up to 30 percent, from those offered by brick-and-mortar stores. Bezos instinctively knew that low prices alone would not keep customers loyal. Lower prices may bring the consumers to the electronic retailer; however, it was the excellent customer service and value that would keep them loyal. Examples of exemplary customer service included the following:

• Viewers' unsolicited comments about titles were given.
• A 1-800-number was shown for those who were uncomfortable ordering via the Internet.
• Popular books were shipped within three days. Similar to brick-and-mortar-retailers, special order books required a four to six week delivery period.
• A confirmation notice via E-mail was sent once the merchandise was shipped.

Traditional direct marketers' sales have grown 7 percent, whereas Amazon.com's sales have been increasing 3,000 percent annually. By 1999, Amazon.com was serving 85 percent of the

The material in this case is drawn from: "Amazon Adds Home Improvement Goods," *Industrial Distribution* 88 (June 1999), 26-27; *Amazon.com 1998 Annual Report; Amazon.com 10Q for the Fiscal Year Ending September 30, 1998*; Dan DuFon, "Amazon.com: On-Line Books and Music Sales," *International Tax Review E-Commerce Taxation Supplement* (1999), 17-18; *Direct Marketing Association Statistical Fact Book* (NY: Direct Marketing Association, 1999); Robert D. Hof, "Jeff Bezos," *Business Week* (May 31, 1999), 137 ff.; Jennifer Hunter, "Amazon's Kingpin," *Maclean's* (June 21, 1999), 30-31; and Margie Slovan," Bound for the Internet," *Nation's Business* (March 1997), 34-35.

Web book market including more than 13 million customers worldwide. Today, the expanded product offerings include 18 million items in CDs, videos, DVDs, computer games, books, and toys, generating over $355 million in net sales.

The majority of retailers (c-commerce and bricks-and-mortar) have became successful by focusing on a specific market niche. Amazon.com is challenging this strategy. Bezos' goal is to make Amazon.com the most customer-centric company in the world, being everything to everyone. Eventually, the goal is to offer consumers Internet shopping experiences ranging from items such as groceries, apparel, pharmaceuticals, and car repair equipments, and more simply by accessing an Amazon.com Internet site. These are four examples of Amazon.com's expansion efforts during 1999:

- Expanding into the hard goods industry, Amazon.com purchased Tool Crib of the North. As the largest tool and equipment retailer, Tool Crib is consistent with Amazon.com's goal to dominate the market. The more than 6,000 items offered at a 30 percent discount over the catalog and retail outlet list pricing parallels that of Amazon.com's pricing strategy.
- Focusing on the family, Amazon.com opened an electronic Toy Store. Within months of opening the virtual store, Forrester Research and MSNBC recognized the Toy Store as the best toy store on the Internet.
- The company features zShops, whereby consumers can sell any type of merchandise via the Internet. Amazon.com Payments is a credit card payment system for use on items purchased through zShops.
- It offers Amazon.com Anywhere, whereby a wireless c-commerce reference base allows consumers to verify the status of auction items without being at their computers.

Amazon.com is considered to be the most successful Internet retailer in the world. Some industry analysts predict that its success will not continue. Amazon.com has never made a profit; its comprehensive net loss has reached $206 million. The aggressive expansion into new markets has placed a strain on the company's cash flow. Other concerns have included changing consumer trends, seasonality of merchandise, increased competition, international expansions, and the combination of businesses. Despite the obvious trend-setting actions of this retailer, the ambitious consumer-centric goal and numerous limitations may pose serious long-term problems for Amazon.com.

Questions:

1. Explain the relationship between Amazon.com's desire to be consumer-centric and the characteristics of the World Wide Web.

2. Describe consumers' characteristics contributing to Amazon.com's growth.

3. Discuss the pros and cons of Amazon.com's rapid growth rate.

4	What features make Tool Crib of the North, Toy Store, and zShops consistent with the features of Amazon.com booksellers?

CASE 3

International Expansion Of A U.S. Apparel Retailer: Assessing South American Markets

This case is prepared and written by Assistant Professor Karen Hyllegard and Associate Professor Molly Eckman, Colorado State University. Reprinted by permission.

A U.S. specialty retailer of casual apparel is considering expanding operations to the South American market. The retailer's U.S. target market is well-educated young professionals (20 to 35 years old), who lead fast paced lives, appreciate good customer service, enjoy athletic and social activities, and are knowledgeable about and confident in purchases of quality apparel. The product mix is men's and women's high-end private label apparel designed to complement the firm's fashion-forward image. The retailer controls production and sale of private label goods, thus the firm makes all decisions concerning price, product, promotion, and distribution. Private label goods are less subject to price competition than are national brands because distribution of goods is limited to that specific retailer.

The firm recognizes the need for economic, competitive, technological, social, and governmental information on South American markets to assist in their decision to enter either Argentina or Brazil. Research indicates that both markets are potentially viable for U.S. specialty retailers. Argentina and Brazil share positive characteristics, such as improving economic stability, relatively less competitive retailing environments, competent senior managers, young populations, increasing discretionary incomes, increasing spending for apparel, consumer preference for traditional retail stores, positive attitude toward American culture and brands, and desire for upscale retail assortments. Shared characteristics that may pose difficulties for expansion include low gross national product, unstable gross domestic product, periods of high inflation (Argentina's economy has stabilized since 1993, Brazil's since 1996), slow adoption of technology, and national cultures and languages that differ from those in the U.S. Additional characteristics to consider are discussed below and summarized in the table.

Characteristics that make Argentina attractive include gross national product, annual per capita clothing expenditures, and media subscriptions and viewer-ship. Argentine consumers tend to be more highly educated than are Brazilians and therefore may be less likely to purchase national brands. Argentina is among the fastest growing apparel import markets worldwide and ranks third among importers of U.S. apparel goods. While managers in Argentina are perceived to have more international experience, they are less customer-oriented than those in Brazil; Argentine managers and workers also receive higher compensation.

Brazil's population far exceeds Argentina's and it is predicted to grow considerably (by approximately 50 million) over the next 25 years. Stabilized inflation rates have contributed to more consumer buying power. Domestic national brands are more common in Brazil than they are in Argentina and fewer private label goods are sold in these markets than in European or U.S. markets. Sourcing apparel in Brazil may be easier and less expensive than it is in Argentina because of its well developed manufacturing sector. Brazil's advertising agencies are well established, with sophisticated standards and creativity. Television advertising plays an important role in promoting consumer goods.

Questions

1. What are the advantages and disadvantages to the apparel specialty retailer of expanding to Argentina?

2. What are the advantages and disadvantages to the apparel specialty retailer of expanding to Brazil?

3. Which market would you recommend to the apparel specialty retailer for expansion? Why?

4. What additional information, not included in the case, would be helpful in making the expansion decision?

Table 1
Selected Economic Characteristics for Argentina and Brazil

Characteristics	Argentina	Brazil
Population millions, 1997	36.1	165.2
Higher education % of 20 – 24 year olds enrolled	40.5	11.5
Age (% of population) 0 – 14 years 15 – 64 years 65+ years	29.3 61.4 9.3	33.6 61.2 5.2

GDP $U.S. per capita, 1997	9,950	6,240
Inflation in consumer prices average annual percent growth 1990-1996	361.5	1074.5
Total retail sales $U.S. per capita, 1996	1,933	1,026
Expenditures on clothing $U.S. per capita, 1997	819	138
Specialty apparel retail outlets number per 10,000 residents, 1997	6.1	2.2
Unemployment % of labor force, 1997	17.3	5.2
Daily newspaper distribution per 1,000 people, 1995	135	45
Television per 1,000 people, 1996	347	289
Internet hosts per 10,000 people, 1997	5.3	4.2
International telephone rates avg. price for 3 minutes $U.S., 1995	7.37	4.99
Official language	Spanish	Portuguese

CASE 4

Assortment Planning and Inventory Management

This case was prepared and written by Mary Bartling, Mount Mary College. Reprinted by permission.

**This case is to be used in conjunction with an EXCEL worksheet
(ASSORTPLANWORKSHEET) which needs to be downloaded from the student site—
http://www.prenhall.com/bermanevans.**

John Smith is an assistant buyer working for a large centrally bought Midwest retailer. Having recently graduated from the company's Management Training Program, he was placed in a high-volume area, the Crystal Buying Office. Since his buyer is often gone on market trips, the running of the buying office is left to him.

One of Smith's responsibilities is to create assortment plans in preparation for his buyer's market trips. The assortment plan is a vehicle which helps his buyer quantify selling capabilities of potential purchases at market, as well as manage inventory by accurately placing the correct quantity of goods in each store according to its sales volume profile.

The assortment plan that Smith is currently working on is for a group of promotional crystal impulse items. These items are reasonably priced (the average retail price is around $19.99) and will be merchandised not only in the Crystal Department, but outposted on tables near wrap stands throughout the store. Smith's buyer will be buying these impulse items for the Fall season, specifically as Christmas gift ideas. Smith will need to address the following factors when creating his assortment plan:

- Quantities must be sufficient to supply stores with enough inventory for an initial setup of goods, as well as fill-in orders which will be used to replenish stocks throughout the holiday season. The buyer has informed John Smith that she wishes to purchase goods with the intention of four delivery periods. An initial order is to be used for setup in September, followed by three fill-in orders with deliveries in October, November, and December.
- Smith's buyer purchased similar promotional items last year; therefore, last year's Fall season selling history of 28,311 units should be used as a sales plan basis. The buyer has informed Smith that she wishes to meet a sales plan of 32,004 units this year.
- Since the vendor will assume responsibility for packing the merchandise by store, the assortment must coincide with vendor pack and ship specifications. For example, the retailer must adhere to the vendor's pre-pack size of 12.
- The Crystal Department is currently housed in 48 stores. The buyer wants all stores to receive, at a minimum, 132 total units. The buyer feels this quantity should be sufficient to make an adequate merchandise presentation in the Crystal Department, as well as the outpost locations.

Assortment Plan Requirements
The assortment plan is used in the following ways:

Volume Group Cluster
- Eligible stores are listed by store number and grouped together in A-J clusters according to similar last year sales volume history. The number of stores included in a cluster is determined by their sales volume and the percent that the average store in each cluster represents to total selling. (Please note that each cluster has at least 1 member but no greater than 9 members. When assigning quantities to stores, one must remember that each member of the cluster must receive the same quantity as the other members included in the cluster.)

Store Distribution
- Merchandise description and styles are listed on the left portion of the sheet. In this case, the style is listed by delivery dates.
- Total quantities that the buyer intends to purchase per style are listed on the right portion of the sheet.
- Store breakouts must coincide with the designated pre-pack, i.e., if the merchandise is pre-packed in groups of 12, store breakouts must be listed in multiples of 12.

- Target quantities and percent contributions by store cluster are listed across the top of the sheet. Each cluster will receive a portion of the total buy based on its percent contribution. The actual units which the buyer intends to buy and their corresponding percent contribution must coincide with the suggested target units and percent contribution per store cluster. It is important to note that because of specific pre-pack requirements or merchandise presentation requirements in smaller stores, it is difficult (and sometimes impossible) to meet the actual target quantity; therefore, one should attempt to come as close to the target quantities as is possible. The actual percent contribution may be determined by dividing a cluster's total unit contribution by the total units purchased. For example, if the "A" cluster's total unit contribution is 1,752 units, dividing that number by the total unit buy of 32,004 units will result in a 5.47 percent unit contribution in the "A" cluster.
- Total store distribution of a style must adhere to the total quantity purchased of a style. The total distribution quantity of a style can be obtained by adding the number of stores (48) by the store distribution per cluster and comparing that to the total number that the buyer intends to buy.

Questions:

1. Adhering to the rules listed above, use the downloaded worksheet (AssortPlansWorksheet) to assist John Smith in formulating an assortment plan.

2. Do you agree with the buyer's suggested target units and merchandising strategies? Explain your answer.

CASE 5

Avon's Search for New Customers

This case was prepared and written by Professor Jack Eure, Southwest Texas State University. Reprinted by permission.

Avon Products, Inc., founded in 1886, is the world's largest direct seller of beauty and related products. With $5.1 billion in annual revenues, the company ranks 308th on the *Fortune 500* list of America's largest companies. It markets to women in 135 countries through nearly 2.6 million independent sales representatives. Avon is among the world's largest-selling single brands of cosmetics, fragrances, and toiletries, including such recognizable brands as Anew, Avon Skin Care, Skin-so-Soft, and Avon Color. In addition, the company is one of the world's largest manufacturers of fashion jewelry. It also markets an extensive line of apparel, gifts, collectibles, and family entertainment products.

Today, Avon's direct selling system is one of the world's most powerful distribution channels. Every year, Avon representatives fill over 650 million orders, generating more than $2 billion in commissions for themselves and their families. In the U.S. market, almost 90 percent of American women have purchased Avon at some time in their lives, and 50 percent have bought at least one product from Avon in the past year.

Avon pursues a three-fold growth strategy for business growth: expanding geographically, leveraging the direct selling channel, and expanding access.

1. Expanding Geographically -- While Avon has been expanding overseas for decades, today it is emphasizing expansion into countries with emerging or developing economies. The company has entered 18 new markets since 1990. Avon's operations in Latin America, Asia, Central and Eastern Europe, and Russia are the company's most entrepreneurial. Not only does it adapt the direct selling channel to local conditions, but it also creates innovative approaches for serving Avon representatives and new customers. Approximately two-thirds of Avon's sales come from international markets.

2. Leveraging the Direct Selling Channel -- Approximately 61 percent of Avon's revenues come from the direct sale of cosmetics, fragrances, and toiletries (CFT). But the direct selling channel is also a mechanism for generating additional sales or products which complement the company's core beauty business. Examples include jewelry, apparel, gifts, collectibles, health, home, and decorative categories.

3. Expanding Access -- Avon's third strategy is to make its direct selling channel more contemporary and relevant to women in established markets such as the United States, Canada, and Europe. Put another way, some potential customers either don't know an Avon representative to purchase from or prefer to buy company products using another method. Other methods being used to reach new customers include:

    *   An online Web site (www.avon.com) that provides information and allows customers to order products online.
    *   A direct mail catalog, "Avon Beauty and Fashion by Mail," that generates an average order almost double that of Avon reps.
    *   A 1-800 telephone number (1-800-FOR-AVON) to get the names of local representatives or to request a direct mail catalog.
    *   Avon Running--Global Women's Circuit, designed to appeal to all levels of physical fitness by conducting clinics in 11 cities in the United States and international markets.
    *   Avon Retail Express Centers in Tampa and San Francisco, previously designed to serve Avon reps with faster fulfillment of their customer's orders, that now allow direct consumer purchases.
    *   The Avon Centre, located in the Trump Tower on 5th Avenue in New York City, that will showcase Avon's global brands, sell select Avon brands, and offer beauty, salon, spa, and other services to women.

- Avon kiosks, being tested to retail company products in an upscale Atlanta-area shopping mall.

Avon's vision is to be the company that best understands and satisfies the product, service, and self-fulfillment needs of women globally. This vision influences the company's research, product development, marketing, and management practices as it positions itself for growth and entry into the next century and new millennium.

Questions:

1. What are the advantages and disadvantages of each of the three company growth strategies?

2. What risks does Avon run, if any, of alienating its representatives by letting consumers buy direct through catalogs and retail outlets?

3. Should Avon continue expanding its retail operations by opening additional stores? Explain your answer.

4. What other possible strategies could Avon use to secure increase sales?

CASE 6

Bagels, Breads, & More: Is It Price or Location?

This case was prepared and written by Professor Kathryn L. Malec, Manchester College; and Edward Heler, Heler² Consultancy, LLC. Reprinted by permission.

Between the mid-1980s and the late 1990s, the retail bagel industry underwent impressive growth. During this time, the lowly bagel became a staple of the American diet as bagel bakeries and shops found their way into the storefronts and strip malls of major American cities. Initially, a product offered by independent bagel bakeries predominantly in cities such as New York and Chicago; franchise operations with the names of Einstein, Bruegger, Chesapeake, Big Apple, and Great American, and others became established across the retail food landscape. Dunkin' Donuts and other coffee-related food service operations added bagels to their product lines of doughnuts, muffins, croissants, and so on. Supermarket offerings grew from the initial product line offered under the Lender's brand to more than a dozen other brands found among the frozen and fresh bakery items. Independent "mom-and-pop" bagel bakeries and stores continued to increase in numbers as manufacturers of bagel forming and baking equipment offered training and support to new entrepreneurs who preferred not to pursue the franchise route. By the end of the 1990s, growth in the retail bagel industry slowed as competitive forces among all lines of bagel products began to take its toll; both franchise and independent operations across the United States began to close as their operations became financially nonviable.

Bagels, Breads, & More, an independent bagel bakery, was located in a mid-western community, Vale. Historically a college town with some light industry, during the decade of the 1990s, Vale became a bedroom community for workers who commute to the businesses and industries of Chicago. In 1996, when Bagels, Breads, & More opened, Vale's population was just over 26,000 persons and it had been estimated that over the next ten years, more than 2,500 new residents could be expected with the growth in new housing that was underway and planned.

Bagels, Breads, & More was operated by Hiram Nielsen and his wife, Dorothy. Mr. Nielsen, a retired educator, had viewed the bagel bakery business as a good outlet for his energies during his retirement years and offered the potential of a reasonable return on their investment. Although Mr. Nielsen did not have any experience in the bakery business, he had attended a one-week training session at the American Institute of Baking and had researched the business thoroughly. He believed that his growing community could support a bagel bakery, that the community was too small to attract the interest of a franchise operator, and that it would be possible to secure financing from a local bank for the equipment the bakery would need. Upon further investigation, all of his suppositions turned out to be reasonably accurate.

Bagels are a simple product to manufacture, consisting of high gluten flour, yeast, malt, water, and flavored toppings. There are variations in the recipe, usually dough-conditioning additives depending on the degree of shelf life desired. There is almost no handwork; forming and baking is done by specialized equipment. In addition to the bagels, Mr. Nielsen added gourmet breads, muffins, and cookies to the product line. Bagels, however, were the principal product line. In addition to selling bagels by the dozen, half-dozen, and individually, bagels were sold as a sandwich item with flavored cream cheese, hummus, and other fillings. Although the equipment manufacturers advised Mr. Nielsen that it would cost him fifteen cents to make and sell a bagel, experience proved that the realistic costs were running around 26 cents a bagel.

The retail price for Mr. Nielsen's bagels was 55 cents each, $5.25 for a baker's dozen (13 bagels), and $2.75 for a half-dozen. Bagel sandwich prices ranged from $1.50 to $2.95, with the price varying by the type of filling. Bagels were also wholesaled to the local college and other food service operations at 40 cents each. By the end of the first six months of operation, just over 60 percent of the business' revenues were derived from wholesale and retail bagel sales, almost 25 percent from sandwich sales, and the remainder from sales of breads, cookies, and muffins.

Bagels, Breads, & More was located in a strip mall shopping center at the busiest intersection in uptown Vale. Within a half-mile of the location were three branch banks, six fast-food restaurants, two full-service restaurants, the community's principal shopping center with Kmart as the anchor store, and four supermarkets. Available data from his bank informed Mr. Nielsen that two-thirds of the community's adult population drove by his location at least once a week.

The principal disadvantage of the location was the speed of the traffic going by the strip mall center and the fact that turnover among the strip mall's tenants was extremely high. Being at the most visible end of the strip mall and with a drive-up window to serve customers, Mr. Nielsen felt he could overcome the traffic disadvantage.

Mr. Nielsen observed that almost all of his business occurred during the morning, principally during the morning drive time; during "coffee-break" time, 9:30 A.M. to 10:30 A.M.; and at lunch, 11:30 A.M. to 1:30 P.M. After 1:30 P.M., business noticeably slacked off. During the evening drive time, there was almost no business except for those few customers who called in orders for bagels and breads.

By the end of the eighth month of operation, Bagels, Breads, & More was beginning to break even. In the subsequent month, Mr. Nielsen began to notice that his sales, except for lunchtime sandwiches, were beginning to drop off. He anticipated some slight reduction in sales when the Dunkin' Donuts store began to sell bagels; however, since he produced a higher quality bagel, Mr. Nielsen expected to recover those lost sales after a short period of time. That did not happen. When a good customer came in who normally purchased a dozen bagels at a time and only bought a loaf of bread, Mr. Nielsen inquired if there was a problem with his bagels. The customer informed him that the supermarket located a block away was selling fresh bagels at a half-dozen for 99 cents.

Checking out the two major supermarkets closest to him, Mr. Nielsen learned that what his customer had told him was true. In fact, what he learned was that both supermarkets were now offering both fresh and frozen bagels at retail prices less than what it cost Bagels, Breads, & More to make up, bake, and sell its bagel products. Further, Mr. Nielsen observed that the supermarket price for fresh bagels was not a loss-leader price; it was able to sell at that price because all it had to do was bake off formed, frozen bagel dough that had been mass- produced at a commissary bakery.
Three months later, Bagels, Breads, & More closed.

Questions:

1.   If you were Mr. Nielsen, how would you react to your competition? Would Bagels, Breads, & More be able to compete on a price basis with the supermarket? Dunkin' Donuts?

2.   Is this a question of pricing or location? What other variables should Mr. Nielsen have evaluated before he chose his current location? Would you have opened your business at this strip mall? Explain your answer.

3.   What other "things" could Mr. Nielsen have done to remain in business?

CASE 7

Basically Bagels: Promotion Mix Planning to Grow and Strengthen a Business

This case was prepared and written by Professor Anne Heineman Batory, Wilkes University; and Professor Stephen S. Batory, Bloomsburg University. Reprinted by permission.

Ron and Kathy Lieberman decided to open a bagel bakery/restaurant after being unable to find freshly-baked bagels and fresh appetizing supplies (such as cut-to-order smoked white fish and homemade cream cheese) near their home. After more than three years of planning, they opened their store, Basically Bagels, in a Wilkes-Barre, Pennsylvania, suburb. Although Ron and Kathy both knew the retail site they chose was poor (in terms of pedestrian and vehicle traffic and road visibility), they chose it based on the low rent. The Liebermans realized they would need to devise and enact an effective promotional program to generate and sustain store traffic at the site.

The initial promotional strategy for the store's grand opening fully met its goals. The local cable TV station and the local newspaper provided excellent coverage. As a result, the store was very busy during its first three weeks of operation. Unfortunately, sales soon slackened off. The owners attributed this to two factors: a reduction in the novelty effect for a new store and the store's air-conditioning system being inadequate during the hot and humid summer season.

For two years, the Liebermans' attempts to expand sales were unsuccessful. This was despite running coupons (such as "Buy 12 bagels, get 6 free") and using the shop as a broadcast site for a popular local radio station. However, the coupons did not generate added revenues because most redeemers were current customers. While the Liebermans were initially excited about the on-site broadcast that featured a popular disk jockey, it had virtually no effect on store traffic or sales.

Two key events occurred during the third year of Basically Bagels' operation that led to the successful turnaround of the firm. First, the Liebermans began selling a line of gift baskets (as an alternative to fruit baskets), besides their usual bagels and appetizing products. The gift baskets consisted of special bagels (with a long shelf life), cream-cheese spreads, specialty coffees, and other gourmet products housed in an attractive wicker basket. The baskets were promoted via a one-page, three-fold flyer that was mailed to community residents and businesses.

The second positive event was a bartering agreement negotiated between the Liebermans and WKRZ, the area's leading radio station. Through this agreement, the radio station received bagel baskets and other merchandise (primarily for use in listener contests) as full payment for Basically Bagels' spot advertising. The long-term use of these ads and contests resulted in continued reinforcement of the store and its high-quality products.

After being at their original location for over eight years, the Liebermans still advertise on WKRZ and participate in contests aimed at the station's listeners. Basically Bagels has also begun to use local cable TV advertising (with spot commercials on general news and business news programs) and to run a commercial on an early-morning news program of a local TV network affiliate.

Although Basically Bagels no longer offers coupons or price promotions, it gives its customers its own form of a "Baker's Dozen" (14 bagels for the cost of a dozen) to increase sales volume. It has instituted a frequent-buyer club for specialty coffee and bagel products to raise consumer loyalty. In this program, customers receive the eleventh cup of coffee or the eleventh specialty bagel free of charge. Recently, Basically Bagels expanded its hours of operation by having an "After Hours" evening cafe with specialty coffees and pastries.

Basically Bagels has begun to refine the promotion of its gift baskets. The gift basket catalog is now a glossy, full-color catalog that is professionally prepared. And the gift baskets are to be marketed on the firm's new Web site. With these promotional vehicles, Basically Bagels plans to sell its gift baskets beyond its normal trading area. Basically Bagels also now promotes its bagel baskets as a bereavement token in tactful ads placed in the obituary section of the town's paper.

The success of Basically Bagels has not gone unnoticed. Several competitors, including both local bakers and units of nationally-based franchises, have entered the Wilkes-Barre suburban market. Ron and Kathy Lieberman know that it is time again to re-examine their store's overall promotional strategy.

Questions:

1. Evaluate Basically Bagels' overall promotional strategy.

2. What additional promotional media should now be considered? Explain your answer.

3. What is the role of public relations for Basically Bagels?

4. How should Ron and Kathy revise their promotional strategy based on the emergence of competitors?

CASE 8

Beverages and More!: Devising and Enacting an Integrated Retail Strategy

This case was prepared and written by Professor Howard W. Combs, San Jose State University. Reprinted by permission.

Founded in 1994, Beverages and More! is a rapidly growing and successful chain of category killer beverage and gourmet snack food stores in the San Francisco area. The heart of each of its 18,000-square-foot stores is the superior wine and beer selection.

While a traditional California supermarket carries 30 or so Chardonnay wines, Beverages and More! carries over 300 (from a variety of vineyards and vintages). Wines account for 40 percent of the chain's total sales. And beers and spirits comprise another 40 percent. The typical Beverages and More! store stocks over 300 microbrews, 300 imported beers, and over 1,200 spirits. Gourmet food, nonalcoholic beverages, and general merchandise make up 15 percent of sales; the other 5 percent is from cigars. Four-foot-high glass cases equipped with humidifiers display the cigars near each store entrance. Most of them are imported from the Caribbean.

Several new product categories are being added to the Beverages and More! product mix. These include some 500 types of cheeses, fresh pasta, olives, deli salads, dips, and gourmet deli meats. A test of frozen appetizers and desserts is in process. These new items are expected to boost the proportion of overall revenues attributed to food to around 25 percent.

Prices at Beverages and More! have remained relatively low due to the chain's low purchase costs and low overhead. Because the firm purchases huge amounts of its goods, it is able to take advantage of quantity discounts and its buying clout with vendors. Furthermore, Beverages and More! generates additional savings by insisting that most vendors deliver their goods directly to the chain's stores, as opposed to a distribution center. Direct store delivery reduces costs due to the elimination of certain warehousing and shipping expenses.

The chain's primary market is 35- to 54-year-olds, who are affluent and college educated. Males presently account for 60 percent of the firm's total revenues. In contrast, 90 percent of the customers of a typical liquor store customer are male. Beverages and More! appeals both to consumers who shop the store regularly and seek a wide selection and low prices, and those who visit the stores to stock up for parties and holiday gatherings. The average transaction size at a Beverages and More! store is over $30.

Beverages and More! recently launched Club Bev, a frequent shoppers program. With Club Bev, each purchase by a member is scanned; and the chain then enters the information into its data base. The data base is used to develop targeted newsletters that reflect individual consumer purchase histories. Thus, the newsletter for a cigar smoker has a different editorial content than a newsletter oriented toward a cheese buyer.

Even though the chain is very young, Beverages and More! has ambitious expansion plans. It hopes to enter other areas of California in the near future. After that, it will consider other markets -- possibly the East Coast.

Questions:

1.   What are the competitive advantages and disadvantages of Beverages and More! in comparison with traditional beverage stores? In comparison with traditional gourmet food stores?

2. Do you think that Beverages and More!'s retailing strategy is well integrated? Explain your answer.

3. Present a five-year plan for Beverages and More! to expand into other regions of the United States. What potential risks does it face? How would you overcome them?

4. Describe a customer-service vertical retail audit for Beverages and More!

CASE 9

Buying Lesson Activity

This case was prepared and written by Professor Sharon S. Pate, Illinois State University. Reprinted by permission.

INTRODUCTION

Fashion students will compile sample market surveys that will be sent to high school classrooms in selected market areas via the Internet. The college fashion students would use spreadsheets, interactive video conferencing, E-mail, and communication presentation software to compile surveys from retailers. This survey of apparel and accessories would preview upcoming season lines and produce sampling surveys through culturally diverse teen population groups. Students will improve their technology skills and learn more about potential careers in the fashion industry through participation in this course.

Goals

1. Students will gain knowledge about fashion careers by exploring fashion buying, logistics, and marketing analysis. Understanding about the fashion industry will be expanded through interaction with retail professionals. University-to-work partnerships will be provided.
2. Competency in technology skills will enhance the curriculum through the compilation of the surveys that are sent/received and the use of spreadsheets, E-mail, and communication presentations.
3. As the faculty member in charge of the distance learning, the university fashion professor and the high school instructors will master the newer method of classroom instructional delivery.
4. Retailers will collaborate with Western Illinois University by developing test market training for students.

5.   The fashion merchandising students will survey the teen market to determine its buying preferences through a weekly survey to be developed and distributed via a Web-site or interactive CD.

PROCEDURES

<u>What Is Intended</u>

Fashion merchandising students will compile sample market surveys of upcoming seasonal lines that will be sent to high school classrooms, in selected market areas via the Internet. The high school instructor collaborating with the fashion instructor at the university will assist in the delivery of instructions and course content to their students.

<u>When and Where the Project Will Be Implemented</u>

The teen market will be studied by university fashion merchandising students to determine teens' clothing purchases. Clothing styles from fashion retailers would be sent to freshman college and high school students who would do simulated test market buying. This information for the high schools' students compiled as a weekly power point slide for each retailer will contain ordering information, i.e., price, color, and size. These power point slides will be combined, burned on computer disks, and mailed to the target market or would be sent via the Internet with an order form. These simulated purchases sent to the teen market weekly, when sent back to the university, will allow the fashion students to compile results.

While surveying is not a new concept, it can be extended into newer research with computerized systems so that the results will have fewer erroneous conclusions. This type of survey will be beneficial for the small and large retail markets.

<u>Timeline for the Project</u>

1.   Identify participating schools and retailers.
2.   Develop lesson plans for programming.
3.   Do a test with the high schools to train teachers about the program.
4.   Train university students on the use of technology.
5.   Send pilot programming to the high schools.
6.   Send weekly scheduled program.
7.   Program evaluation.

CASE 10

Crucial Technology: Reinventing the Marketing Channel

This case was prepared and written by Professor David C. Houghton, Northwest Nazarene University; and Bridgette Shields, Crucial Technology, a division of Micron. Reprinted by permission.

Crucial Technology was founded in 1996 with the goal of providing consumers with the ability to purchase the same computer memory products that the major personal computer manufacturers installed in their systems. Demand for increased computing power at the consumer level played a large role in the strategy. It was hoped that the consumer that balked at $1,000 or more to purchase a new computer could be persuaded to spend approximately $100 to upgrade his or her current computer by adding computer memory.

Preliminary research indicated that the target customer was between the ages of 20 and 40, had an annual household income of at least $45,000, and had two or more years of college. To reach this customer, Crucial was considering the use of an electronic kiosk that would be placed at several retail locations. By answering questions at the kiosk, a consumer could determine exactly what kind of memory was required for his or her system and computing needs. With a credit card, the consumer could then purchase the memory through the kiosk. After the order was placed, the memory would arrive at the consumer's home in two to three working days in most cases.

In order to place the kiosk at a retail location, Crucial would most likely have to rent the space for the kiosk or provide the retailer with a percentage of the memory sales. Since the concept was untested, it was believed that most retailers would desire a fixed rental fee at first. For some retailers, Crucial Technology's kiosk was a way to sell a new product category without maintaining an inventory since Crucial shipped the product directly to the end user. For retailers that already carried computer memory for consumers, the kiosk was a way to expand their current product offering. Another advantage to the retailer was that the kiosk permitted memory to be sold with a robust memory selector. If a salesperson was unavailable to answer a consumer's questions, the kiosk essentially provided the same level of expertise when used properly. The presence of the interactive kiosk might also cause some consumers to make an impulse purchase of computer memory.

Crucial Technology was evaluating three types of retailers in which to place its kiosks. Costco, a wholesale club, did not currently sell computer memory to its customers. Thus, Crucial Technology faced no direct competition within the store for its products. Although it had not yet approached Costco with the opportunity, Crucial felt that the kiosk would be attractive to Costco since it required no inventory on Costco's part and allowed it to offer a new product category to its customers. Wal-Mart, the discount store, already carried some computer memory in its electronics department. Crucial's kiosk would allow the discounter to expand its computer memory offering. Importantly, the kiosk would allow the Wal-Mart associate to focus on other, more profitable, electronics products. Finally, Crucial considered deploying its kiosk in Future Shop. Future Shop, a specialty store, carried a wide variety of computer memory products. More than the other retailers, Future Shop's customers matched Crucial Technology's target market. Unfortunately, Future Shop's current offering also represented the most competition for Crucial's memory products. It was hoped that if Future Shop accepted the kiosk, that it would decrease its current memory offerings and shift its inventory burden to Crucial Technology.

In May 1998, Crucial Technology was trying to determine which retail site made the most sense for the deployment of its kiosk. More importantly, Crucial Technology was wondering if the kiosk concept, in its current form, was the best way to reach the consumer. Would the consumer that had not planned on purchasing memory see the kiosk and make an impulse purchase? What about the consumer that had come to the store seeking computer memory? Would the consumer be willing to wait two to three days to receive a slightly discounted computer memory product?

Questions:

1.   What are the advantages and disadvantages of the kiosk concept?

2.   Assuming that the consumer would purchase computer memory through Crucial Technology's kiosk, in which of the three retail stores mentioned above should Crucial attempt to launch its kiosk? Why?

3.   What other types of retail sites should Crucial Technology consider as potential candidates for the kiosk?

4.   In your opinion, should Crucial Technology move forward with the kiosk? Why or why not?

CASE 11

Custom Ski Pants: New Technology on the Selling Floor

This case was prepared and written by Professor Doris H. Kincade, Virginia Tech University; and Professor Ginger Woodard, East Carolina University. Reprinted by permission.

In June, Randy Barbar, the active sports-athletic wear buyer for Specialty Sportswear stores, met with Sam Tando, the sales representative of the Fast Track Ski Products company, to discuss the upcoming Winter line. For a change, Tando had a really new product line including a computer kiosk with a body-scanning booth. The equipment was called the Custom Fit Unit (CFU) and was designed to measure a person and take information about color and style to create an order for custom-made ski pants. Measurements and color/style preference would be transmitted directly from the store to the Fast Track Ski Products sewing plants and each pair of custom pants, when completed, would be directly shipped to the customer. From order to shipping should take only a few days. The customer would have custom-made pants in less than one week.

Barbar knew that custom-made ski pants had great potential. With more and more people becoming active with winter sports, fitting all body types with those tight-shaped ski pants was impossible. As Barbar listened to Tando's sales pitch, images of piles of messy stock, hundreds of returns of pants with broken seams and sprung knees, and lines of dissatisfied customers began to disappear. Instead, she envisioned the ringing of the cash register, happy employees, and smiling customers. After watching a video of a customer using the CFU and a few more minutes of listening to Tando, Barbar was enchanted with the idea of body scanning and custom fit ski pants.

As part of the negotiations for the product line, Sam Tando offered two deals. Option A required the Specialty Sportswear stores to make a deposit with Fast Track of $22,000 per store to receive the CFU. The deposit would be returned, minus some service fees, when sales of the custom pants passed $80,000 per store. In return for the deposit, each Specialty Sportswear store would receive a full installation of the equipment and 320 hours of training for employees in each store. Option B required a guarantee of $45,000 in sales per store, no deposit, and one day (eight hours) of training for each store manager.

Randy Barbar immediately chose Option B. Lack of cash flow and a belief that the custom pants would be an immediate sales success fueled her decision to take Option B. Knowing the number of ski pants sold in one winter season, Barbar was confident that the guaranteed minimum sales amount would be easily surpassed. As for training, she thought, "How hard could it be to punch a few buttons on the computer screen and stand in a dark booth? Besides, the stores had already spent $1.5 million on training sales staff on the new electronic cash registers and everyone knows about computers. Right?" Barbar signed the Option B contract.

In mid-September, a CFU was delivered to ten Specialty Sportswear stores. Each store manager received the eight hours of training during the last week in September. The CFU was introduced to the sales staff at the following Monday morning staff meetings. The corporate plan at Specialty Sportswear was that each manager would train one assistant manager who would be responsible for the kiosk and booth and would do any additional training of sales staff as needed. During the first of October, the manager in Store #1 left the company, and the manager from Store #5 was promoted to a district position. The assistant manager in Store #1 was promoted to manager, and the assistant manager in Store #3 was transferred to Store #5 as manager. With the Founder's Day sale on October 8th and the series of absences due to the flu, no training was done for assistant managers or sales staff.

The sales staff was told that they would not receive the usual 10 percent commission on sales generated by the CFU, but would instead receive a 3 percent commission. The reasons for the reduced commission were the reduced time in stock handling and the reduced time in bagging the purchases. Sales staff were told to greet customers looking at the CFU with the usual store greeting but to assist customers only if they had specific questions. The managers decided in their quarterly meeting that the custom process with body measurements was a personal issue and that too much attention by the sales staff would be embarrassing to the customers.

Early November officially starts the peak sales period of skiwear. Although the region had had a few snowfalls and plenty of cold weather, sales of ski pants through the CFU were minimal. The Specialty Sportswear stores had included a promotion about the CFU and the new custom-made ski pants in the bills for their store charge customers. The promotion had included an explanation of the process and a coupon for $10 off the purchase of a pair of custom ski pants or $5 off the purchase of any new skiwear item in the store. Throughout the stores, 100 coupons had been collected but the register transactions showed that none of them were used for purchase of the custom pants.

In early December, Randy Barbar rechecked the sales of the custom pants relative to the other ski pants. Sales of the regular pants were on schedule with previous seasons. Barbar was alarmed to find that the custom pants had sales that calculated to one-third of the necessary $45,000. She knew that fast action was required. The week after Thanksgiving was past and with it, the maximum sales potential time for the entire season. If sales of the custom pants did not double in the next two weeks, she was doomed. Instead of happy customers and ringing cash registers, Barbar had visions of unpaid bills and her boss yelling. Her first thought was to blame the sales staff. They were probably ignoring the customers and were not pushing the CFU. She thought that anytime a product line failed to sell, the sales staff could be blamed for the poor sales performance. "They are the people on the front line. Why don't they make people buy the products that I so carefully select?" She shook her head in wonder.

Overnight, Barbar devised a plan. She thought, "I will catch those lazy sales staffers. I'll send out the secret shoppers." She talked with security and hired two people that were recommended as secret shoppers. Each shopper was assigned five stores and given a charge card with instructions to shop for and order custom pants in each of the five stores. A report to Barbar was due in two days.

On the morning of December 6th, the two reports were stacked neatly in the center of Barbar's desk. Armed with a cup of coffee and sweet roll, she began to read. Store #1 was the flagship store for the company. The report was dismal. The secret shopper had found an out-of-order sign taped to the computer screen. When the shopper asked a sales staff employee about the CFU, the reply had been vague and noncommittal, something about the buttons not working since the computer was installed. The story for Store #2 was similar. The secret shopper had tried to use the computer but found that the order form was hard to read and the program had no way to correct errors so her address, which should have been 123 Smith Lane, was 231 Lane Street. She doubted that the package would ever reach her and was not sure that the order had really been transmitted. The tale about Store #5 was even worse. The secret shopper thought she had been shocked when she pushed the button to start the scanning process. When she called out for help, nobody came. After she came out of the booth, she approached a sales staff employee and complained but was told that the sales staff could not assist with the personal aspects of the fitting process.

Randy Barbar put down the report. Her sweet roll was untouched and her coffee was getting cold. She held her head in her hands and wondered what she should do. What had gone wrong? Who should she call and what could be done to salvage this disaster?

Questions:

1.   What were the pros and cons of each original option to the retailer?

2.   What training methods should have been used? Why? Who should have received the minimal training that was provided with Option B?

3.   How do you train and motivate sales personnel to help the customer when their commission on these sales has been cut from 10 percent to 3 percent?

4.   How should sales personnel have been supervised to assure that sales on the CFU would have been achieved?

5.   Should the buyer have the authority to make this type of decision above for a company? What organizational format would have helped to work through these problems before they occurred?

CASE 12

Deep Water Diving

This case was prepared and written by Professor Michele M. Granger, Southwest Missouri State University. Reprinted by permission.

As the buyers of The Clothes Horse are seated in the conference room, the new merchandise manager of ladies' apparel, Carl Bedell, is sharing both his assessment of the chain store's current marketing strategies and his suggestions to improve the company's bottom line through more effective merchandising techniques. Mr. Bedell believes that the merchandise assortment has been too fragmented and too diverse in the past. He states that the buyers have been overly cautious by purchasing small quantities of an excessive number of styles from an overabundance of vendors. "The breadth of the inventory has been too extreme," he asserts. "The resulting stock," Bedell continues, "looks like an end-of-the year closeout at the beginning of a new season." He recommends that the buying staff jointly determine important seasonal trends in advance and take a stand on these looks through more in-depth purchases. He explains that the customer decision-making process is simplified with more consistent stock. "When the consumer sees a clear fashion statement in quantity, she concludes that she must have that look to be fashionable," Bedell summarizes. He adds that an inventory with greater depth makes visual merchandising and advertising efforts clearer and more effective. Finally, he suggests that quantity purchases give the buyer more negotiating power with the reduced number of chosen vendors.

Virginia Nelson is the misses' swimwear buyer for The Clothes Horse. She has been a buyer at the store for the past ten years. Although she likes Carl, she is wary of his new approach to merchandising the store. Nelson suspects that Bedell's merchandising philosophy is a result of his years of working with mass-merchandising chains, rather than specialty store organizations. Because of her long-term experience with The Clothes Horse, Virginia Nelson believes that her customer is extremely selective and does not want to see others coming and going in the same garment. "This will be a turnoff to our customers." It's for a mass-marketing operation, not for a specialty store," she thinks. She decides to continue writing her orders the way she always has done, but she now must receive approval from the new merchandise manager before actually placing an order. Additionally, Nelson thinks about the manufacturers that she has used for her department over the past decade. Each one, she decides, fills an important niche in the total swimwear stock.

Mr. Bedell slowly reviews the stock of orders that Nelson has prepared and then leans back in his chair. "Virginia, you must not have heard what I said about in-depth purchasing. I see nothing in this pile of orders that reflects a major trend statement. You will need to revise these before I can approve them," he declares. Nelson leaves Bedell's office in frustration.

Questions:

1.   If you were in Virginia Nelson's position, what would you do next?

2.   What alternatives should Nelson consider? Identify specific criteria to evaluate vendors.

3.   If you were in Mr. Bedell's position, what would you do to convince Virginia Nelson that in-depth purchasing is a successful strategy for The Clothes Horse?

4.   As the merchandise manager, what specific directions can you give the buyers to implement this merchandising strategy?

CASE 13

Dolphin Bookstore: Development of a Goods/Services Category

This case was prepared and written by Professor Carolyn Predmore, Manhattan College. Reprinted by permission.

Dolphin Bookstore was founded in 1946 in Port Washington, New York, an affluent Long Island suburb. The store, located on the town's main shopping street, was purchased in 1972 by Dorothea Vunk, an employee of the store's original owners. She ran the store with the part-time assistance of her husband and two daughters.

Although Vunk was able to pay off the loan for the store after five years of ownership, it was never a financial success. Much of the reason for the store's continued existence was the long hours worked by Dorothea Vunk and her family members. Yet, she had little understanding of the basics of buying, cash flow management, promotion, and strategic planning. She ran the store primarily to "make friends and sell a few books along the way."

In January 1982, after 10 years of ownership, Patty Vunk purchased the store from her parents upon their retirement. Unlike her parents, who had an eclectic selection of titles, Patty Vunk sought to rationalize the store's stock. All goods purchased had to fit into one of four basic categories: a personalized selection of book titles, children's books, distinctive cards and stationery items, and specialized gift items that convey feelings. Patty Vunk sought to only stock book titles that she could recommend to customers. She reasoned that if she read and then liked a particular title, she could better communicate its contents to her customers. She also planned to have a strong selection of children's books, an area neglected by many large chain-based bookstores. In addition to children's books, Patty stocked plush toys that coordinated with very popular books. This strategy enabled Vunk to receive higher profit margins from the sale of toys, to attract additional customers, and to increase customer purchases. A third focus was on a hand-picked, unique selection of greeting cards, holiday items, and correspondence items. Lastly, Patty Vunk wanted to sell gift items that conveyed emotional thoughts or feelings. The store's atmosphere was renovated to reflect its products and new target market.

Unfortunately, the building was sold just as Patty Vunk was completing renovation on the store's interior. The new owners informed her that they would not renew the lease and that they did not understand why she was doing all this work when her lease expired in a little over two years. Vunk then knew she had a little over two years to build her business to the point where the profits could sustain a significant increase in rent at another site. She began to focus her energies on finding a new store location in Port Washington.

It took close to two years for Patty Vunk to find new retail space in town that met her criteria regarding minimum store size, pedestrian traffic, parking facilities, and rental costs. When she found saw the new space, she immediately envisioned how the new store should be laid out. She moved to the new location, which was three blocks from her original store, in 1989, just as the lease on the original store expired.

Patty Vunk's current store builds on the goods/services of the previous store. In addition, she has instituted a well thought-out promotional strategy that consists of regular advertising in Port Washington's local weekly newspapers, the hosting of book signings and author discussions, and direct mail promotions. For example, she runs four special promotions per year to a targeted group of customers. This approach is so successful that it results in purchases from 7 percent to 8 percent of the targeted population. Patty is now thinking of developing a Web site.

Patty Vunk has been so successful that she has expanded her store twice (it is now three times as large as it was in 1989 and ten times larger than the original location). The store has also managed to withstand the competition from both a discount bookstore and a Barnes & Noble chain store unit (that features a wide selection of books, discounted prices, an in-store Starbucks coffee bar, and a "stay and read for as long as you want" philosophy).

Questions:

1. Evaluate the appropriateness of the Dolphin Bookstore's four-point goods/service category definition.

2. How can Patty Vunk lower the time demands associated with her running a bookstore?

3. How can Dolphin Bookstore better compete against a Barnes & Noble store that offers low prices, long store hours, and an in-store coffee bar?

4. Should Patty develop a Web site? Explain your answer.

CASE 14

Duds for Dudes: Dual Distribution

This case was prepared and written by Professors Karen Hyllegard, Jennifer Paff Ogle, and Antigone Kotsiopulos, Colorado State University. Reprinted by permission.

Duds for Dudes (DFD) is a Colorado-based manufacturer of Western wear for men and women. DFD's products are sold through specialty stores in the western United States and selected international markets. Historically, the company's success has stemmed from the sale of boot-cut style jeans, a key component in its well-known men's line. Two years ago, in an effort to break away from its traditional look, DFD entered the women's fashion market. The new line includes Western-style apparel in designer colors, fabrics, and trims. The company's success with the men's label and logo prompted DFD to use the same label and to rely upon similar promotional strategies for the women's line. The target market for this line is female ranchers, horseback riders, rodeo goers, and country western music and dance enthusiasts. Many of DFD's domestic customers are time-starved shoppers who do not live in close proximity to major retail centers. The majority of them are ages 30 to 55.

During the first year in the fashion market, DFD learned that retailers were having difficulties turning inventories. The merchandising team attributed lagging sales to marketing efforts, rather than to the design of the women's line; prior testing and evaluation indicated consumer satisfaction with product design and fit. To improve promotion and generate sales, the company hired a marketing consultant to assess the situation. Although the consultant agreed with the assessment that the fashion line was meeting the needs of the target market, she expressed concern that the new fashion look may be inconsistent with consumers' impressions of DFD as a male-oriented, Western wear company or brand. Thus, she urged the company to develop a separate image for the women's fashion line, including a new brand name and logo.

To improve retail sales, the consultant recommended that the company engage in dual distribution of the new women's line to domestic and international consumers by using a direct marketing strategy: catalog, Web site, or strategic alliance. The consultant was confident that direct marketing would increase the company's sales and profits; however, she acknowledged that manufacturers who use such strategies may encounter some challenges. First, the use of direct marketing by manufacturers may create additional competition for retailers who stock the same products, thereby straining relationships with retailers. This type of vertical integration changes the manufacturer's relationship with retailers from that of strictly a supplier to a supplier/competitor. Second, it is sometimes difficult to provide strong customer service through direct marketing. This can lead to consumer dissatisfaction with the product manufacturer -- dissatisfaction that may otherwise be directed toward an independent retailer. For example, in a store setting, consumer dissatisfaction due to the stock-out of a product is generally directed toward the retailer rather than toward the manufacturer.

To date, DFD has not used catalogs and does not employ personnel with expertise in catalog design and distribution. Nor does the company have experience in Web site development. However, the potential to increase sales through this technology is ripe; the number of female online shoppers is growing (they currently account for 40 percent of online customers). To avoid straining relationships with retailers, DFD could enter into strategic alliances (i.e., partnerships related to distribution of goods) designed to support retailer-based Web sites. This option is less expensive than maintaining a company-owned site and allows for the development of cooperative sales programs. The manufacturer takes responsibility for the distribution of the product, which maximizes efficiency and profitability for both partners and may provide customers with improved availability and lower prices.

Questions:

1.   What factors should DFD consider if it should either engage in direct marketing or focus on assisting retailers in the sale of its goods?

2. Should DFD engage in direct marketing activities? Why or why not?

3. What factors warrant special consideration to generate sales in international markets through direct marketing?

4. If DFD engages in direct marketing, which format (e.g., catalog, Web site, strategic alliance) should it choose? Why?

CASE 15

Eastern Financial Federal Credit Union

This case was prepared and written by Professor Jonathan N. Goodrich, Florida International University; John Callahan, Eastern Financial Federal Credit Union; Patrick Kemp, Medic Aid Communications, and B. John D'Auria, Metro-Dade County. Reprinted by permission.

INTRODUCTION

In 1937, Eastern Airlines established a credit union for the benefit of its employees. The credit union, then named Eastern Airlines Employees Federal Credit Union, provided a variety of typical financial services for Eastern Airlines' employees: savings and checking accounts, and loans to purchase homes, cars, and other consumer products. In February 1989, however, Eastern Airlines filed for bankruptcy, and in January 1991, went out of business. This case is a classic example of how a credit union fought for survival and eventually became one of the great success stories in credit union history, after its parent organization (Eastern Airlines) went out of business. Crisis management, retailing strategies, and other aspects of marketing are described.

Eastern Airlines

Eastern Airlines was formed in 1937. Its name emanated primarily from the fact that its major routes were along the eastern parts of the United States (e.g., round trips of Miami-New York City, Miami-Chicago, Boston-Miami, New York-Philadelphia, and so on). Eastern also had flights to eastern Canada, Bermuda, Jamaica, Puerto Rico, the Virgin Islands, and Mexico. During its heydays of the 1970s, it had a fleet of over 220 jet aircraft, assets of over $1 billion, and employed 40,000 people nationwide. At that time, it was the largest company employer in South Florida, employing 7,000 people in South Florida alone. The association and name recognition of Eastern Airlines, originally a marketing asset for its credit union, became a marketing liability when Eastern Airlines declared bankruptcy in 1989, and closed operations in 1991.

Crisis Management

The Eastern Airlines bankruptcy and eventual cessation of operations adversely affected the credit union initially. For example, many credit union members, unemployed as a result of the closing of Eastern Airlines, withdrew all of their savings from the credit union to support themselves and/or through fear that the credit union would also declare bankruptcy and they would lose their savings in the credit union. This run on the credit union depleted its reserves and assets tremendously. Bad publicity about all of this ensued in the local news media (radio, television, newspapers, and magazines). The credit union's marketing and management team responded admirably to this situation. Meetings of the credit union membership were held to quell fears about the variability and solvency of the credit union. Flyers and letters were sent to members, telling them that their money was safe, and not to panic or withdraw their savings. Management also helped members in job search and placement. The situation eventually calmed down, but many marketing challenges remained, and had to be confronted if the credit union was to grow and survive.

Marketing Challenges

In the late 1980s, after "riding the coattails" of Eastern Airlines for many years, the association between the two organizations became a burdensome liability. Although the credit union had always been a totally separate institution, the many years of national association with the airline had caused the public to get the impression that both companies were experiencing financial difficulties. This proved to be one of many marketing challenges Eastern Financial faced as a result of the failure of Eastern Airlines. Others were:
- Public perception associating a failed airline with its credit union.
- The loss of income and, therefore, payroll deductions from an Eastern Airlines work force that once numbered 40,000.
- Loss of merchant confidence in Eastern Financial's checks.
- The dilemmas of how to service the now displaced workers, how to attract new members and charter companies, how to keep unemployed and newly-employed members, and how to reverse the downward trend in assets.
- Possible future changes in federal credit union laws that would constrict their markets.

MARKETING STRATEGIES

How did Eastern Financial deal with the aforementioned challenges? Brilliantly! In response to the public's negative perception of Eastern Financial because of its association with a failed airline, Eastern Financial sent out news releases to the news media about its financial strength, autonomy, and separateness from the defunct Eastern Airlines. Around 1990, the credit union also changed its name from Eastern Airlines Employees Federal Credit Union to Eastern Financial Federal Credit Union (EFFCU), thus shedding any perceptual association with the defunct Eastern Airlines. All stationery and the logo were changed and updated to reflect the name change. The new name of the credit union was also put on all credit union (retail) outlets where customers did business. Letters were also sent to the credit union members informing them of the name change and of the positive things that EFFCU was doing to strengthen itself.

In response to the loss of income and payroll deductions from an Eastern Airlines work force that once numbered 40,000, EFFCU began to market itself aggressively to other companies in Florida and other states to become a member of EFFCU, through payroll deductions, and so on. This strategy was successful. For example, in 1992, EFFCU had a membership of 145,000 people, and total assets of $1 billion. Today, its membership is over 500,000 from 600 member companies, and it has total assets of $2 billion. Some of these companies include Avis Rent-A-Car, NEC Home Electronics, Norwegian Cruise Line, System One, and many retail stores.

EFFCU is now the largest credit union in Florida and one of the top ten credit unions in the United States. It has over 34 branch locations, mainly in South Florida; Georgia; and Louisville, Kentucky. Additional branches are located in Lake Success, New York; Clark, New Jersey; Boston, Massachusetts; Washington, D.C.; and Villa Park, Illinois. Through this branch network, EFFCU provides a full range of financial services nationwide. It is interesting to note that EFFCU accomplished what the commercial banking industry in the United States has coveted for years -- interstate banking without the formation of separate holding companies.

Until banking deregulation legislation of 1987, credit unions could only market their service to the employees of the host company. Deregulation allowed other companies to petition existing credit unions to provide the same service to their employees. Consequently, independent companies willing to provide payroll deductions and doing business within 75 miles of a credit union location could join existing credit unions. EFFCU, unlike many other major credit unions, actively pursued additional companies to serve. As a result, it now serves over 600 companies.

EFFCU was aggressive in its marketing and lobbying practices. Even before deregulation, it pushed the National Credit Union Administration (NCUA), the federal agency that regulates credit unions, to allow it to serve not only the employees of Eastern Airlines but also their relatives by blood and marriage. Aunts, uncles, cousins, nephews, nieces, grandparents, brothers, and sisters were all encouraged to join. Additionally, EFFCU adopted the policy, "Once a member, always a member." Legislation and EFFCU policy had defined the market; it consisted of the employees and relatives of the former Eastern Airlines, and those of over 600 other charter companies. EFFCU marketed to all stages of the family life cycle, from custodian accounts for young children to Individual Retirement Accounts (IRAs) for retirees. New and enhanced financial services were marketed to potential members, as well as to current members.

Recall that around 1989, when Eastern Airlines declared bankruptcy, merchants began to lose confidence in Eastern Financial checks. By mid-1991, this was no longer the case, as EFFCU won accolades for its turnaround, growth, and community confidence.

While EFFCU has grown larger over the years, its objective remains the same -- providing customers with a broad selection of up-to-date services and maintaining a strong financial institution. In keeping with this objective, several new products and services were introduced in 1999. They include Eastern Online Internet Banking, expanded Bank-by-Phone services, the

Home Equity Visa Platinum Credit Card, and new tiered rate options with the Money Market Plus Account.

EFFCU also publishes a monthly newsletter, called *Lifestyles*, which provides timely and interesting financial information to the membership. Such information may be about IRAs, Roth IRAs, mortgage rates, home equity loans, online banking, investment advice, and so on.

EFFCU had one other marketing challenge cited earlier: anticipating future changes in federal credit union laws that would constrict EFFCU's market. EFFCU responded to this challenge by hiring an attorney with expertise in banking and credit union laws, by hiring a lobbyist, and by constantly gathering industry information from the NCUA and from appropriate Internet sites.

Questions:

1.   Identify EFFCU's competitors.

2.   Is EFFCU a retailer? Explain your answer.

3.   What are some of the strategies that EFFCU implemented to turn itself around after its parent organization, Eastern Airlines, declared bankruptcy in 1989, and ceased operation in 1991?

4.   What are some of the newer services that EFFCU has offered since 1999?

CASE 16

Flushing Fine Furniture

This case was prepared and written by Professor Larry Goldstein, Iona College. Reprinted by permission.

Thirty-three years ago, Alex Brewster, a master carpenter who specialized in building custom-made furniture, bought a three-story warehouse in Flushing, New York. He renovated the ground floor as a showroom, the middle floor as a storage area, and the top floor as a cabinetry shop. Brewster and his carpenters initially concentrated on making custom-made cabinets, living room display cases, and bookcases; later on, they added custom-made dining room and bedroom sets.

Despite the lack of a detailed promotional plan or a high level of promotional expenditures, Flushing Fine Furniture (FFF) was popular from the onset. Most shoppers were repeat customers or came on the basis of recommendations of friends and relatives. For its first fifteen years of business, FFF's sole advertising efforts consisted of occasional small ads in a local shopper paper and a simple listing in three local Yellow Pages directories.

In 1980, Brewster realized he needed to reposition FFF away from custom-made furniture due to long lead times and high costs. The lead time from ordering to delivery had reached 12 weeks. This was longer than many customers were willing to wait. Producing custom-made furniture was also costly since mass production technology could not be used. Brewster concluded that what people now wanted was high-quality, stylish furniture that was sold in a pleasant environment. He also reasoned that by stopping production of custom-made furniture, he could expand his retail showroom from one to three floors.

After selling all of its existing inventory, FFF reopened as a retailer of branded bedroom, living room, and dining room sets. It represented more than 400 furniture manufacturers, displayed furniture in room settings, and offered free decorating advice to customers. Between 1980 and 1990, sales doubled from $10 million to $20 million. Brewster's daughter Susan joined FFF in 1988 as an interior design consultant and his son Robert joined as a part-time salesperson, while earning his bachelor's degree at a local college. After completing his master's degree in marketing in 1995, Robert became director of marketing.

After examining the store's sales figures, Robert discovered that between 1990 and 1995, furniture sales were pretty flat, at $22 million per year. He also believed that major furniture was a high-involvement shopping good and people were willing to travel long distances to find what they wanted. The household furniture business also had become much more competitive with the opening of an Ikea, a Huffman-Koos, and an Ethan Allen furniture chain store within several miles of FFF. In addition, FFF's competition included several major department stores with excellent furniture departments, such as Macy's and Bloomingdale's. Virtually all of these firms have large advertising budgets and regularly advertise furniture sales in daily newspapers (sometimes with freestanding inserts) and use local radio and TV commercials.

As a result, Robert questioned his father's resistance to media advertising and FFF's lack of a promotional plan. He decided to develop a tentative promotional plan for his father for review. In developing the plan, Robert deliberately sought to avoid traditional print and broadcast media because they were extensively used by FFF's larger competitors. He wanted to consider using innovative media such as the World Wide Web, video catalogs, and CD-ROMs.

Robert wanted to explore several Web-based promotional alternatives. These included joining a home-based shopping mall that would lead to sharing advertising costs and site visits with appliance, lighting, and kitchen and bath renovators. Another possibility would be for FFF to develop its own Web site by retaining a professional Web expert.

Robert also considered devising a catalog in either a VHS or CD-ROM format. He estimated the development cost of an attractive VHS video catalog at between $25,000 and $50,000; and copies would run between $1 and $2 each, depending on quality and length. While Robert did not know the development and per copy costs of a CD-ROM catalog, he was intrigued by its long shelf life and the high trial rate among computer owners who have multimedia capabilities.

This group also has very favorable demographics for FFF.

Questions:

1. What promotional opportunities did Alex Brewster overlook? How could he have capitalized on these opportunities?

2. Do you think FFF was correct to avoid using the broadcast and print media for advertising? Explain your answer.

3. Is going online appropriate for FFF? Explain your answer.

4. Evaluate the concept of video and CD-ROM catalogs for FFF.

CASE 17

Focus Group Strategy: Ineffective Use in Consumer Research

This case was prepared and written by Professor K. Denise Threlfall, Old Dominion University. Reprinted by permission.

Katherine Connors owns a small women's specialty boutique in the downtown area of a mid-sized city on the eastern seaboard. Although there is a tourist draw to this area due to museums and historic sites, Katherine's boutique, *K.C.'s*, is not doing as well as she projected in her initial business plan. There is a steady draw during lunchtime when the business districts' employees are on their break, and she does have some repeat clientele from ladies who venture to the area for shopping or to frequent one of the many downtown restaurants. Her dilemma, then, is how to increase traffic to her store from the tourist population and other potential area patrons. To determine her options, she decides to hold a focus group and see what suggestions are made that would be useful in growing her business.

Connors hires a marketing consultant, Michael Oliver, from the local downtown business association to conduct the focus group. Not wanting to see *K.C.'s* move from the downtown area, he asks her what she would like to see evolve from the research. Connors admitted that she really wanted to hear that all areas of her business were a success and that things would pick up once she was established in her location for a longer period of time. The marketing consultant, then asked her for a list of questions she would like to have answered during the session. Connors developed the questions for the focus group relative to current advertising strategies, store image, product mix, and store location. She provided Oliver with a list of twenty of her best customers and asked that they be the core of her focus group session. Oliver contacted the customers and asked them to attend a luncheon at one of the downtown restaurants. No mention of the research portion of the meeting was provided in advance and the stage was set for client-driven outcomes!

At the beginning of the luncheon, the ladies were presented with a gift certificate to *K.C.'s* as a token of their participation in the research (in addition to the free lunch). As Michael Oliver asked the questions, one by one, Katherine Connors was there to record all of the comments. She was pleasantly surprised by all the compliments she received during the session. She did notice, however, that when a certain question wasn't really following Oliver's agenda, he would refocus the participant and lead her to the desired answer. Connors thought this was odd but enjoyed the very positive comments made by all her customers. The participants thanked her for the luncheon and the gift certificate, happily promising to shop at *K.C.'s* in the near future.

Upon reflection of the focus group process, Katherine Connors realized that she did not learn anything new on how to increase patronage, particularly from the tourist segment, for her store. She felt the money and time invested in the focus group was a waste. She concluded that focus groups are an ineffective method in conducting consumer research and vowed never to go that route again. Connors found herself right back where she began.

Questions:

1. What types of things did Katherine Connors and Michael Oliver do that are contrary to the effective use of focus groups in consumer research?

2. What suggestions would you provide Katherine Connors in developing future focus group sessions?

CASE 18

The Food Zone: Identifying and Understanding Consumers

This case was prepared and written by Professor Brian R. Hoyt, Ohio University. Reprinted by permission.

The Food Zone is a University Food Service operation with 25 onsite locations. The Food Zone has an expertise and niche as a specialized food service operation for regional campuses of major universities and other nonresidential campuses located in the Midwest. A recent trend on many campuses includes the review of subcontracted food operations and evaluating the financial impact on the campus's bottom line. Many food operations are prime targets for takeover opportunities and converted to a university-owned profit center. Presently, the Zone's university customers receive a percentage of sales revenue. Recently, The Food Zone's largest account has given them one year to develop a detailed plan to grow business or they will take over the food service operations. If the Zone does not respond with a complete review of its market and a growth plan, it may not just lose this client; many of its other customers will not be far behind.

The industry outlook in food service for all segments (restaurant, institutional, corporate, and university) is bright with the overall food service industry projected for healthy growth. Each separate segment within the overall industry is projected to grow individually. The National Restaurant Association reported just under 50 percent of all food purchases were made away from home and will grow to 53 percent with the total amount reaching $577 billion dollars. Real growth for the industry is projected to be 3 percent in the year 2000 and continue to increase. Any slowdown in sales growth is expected to be a move down in food service outlets, not a move back home (i.e., fine dining to casual dining). Two-income families and longer working hours will keep food service operations busy at some level. These growth numbers demonstrate a subtle industry move from special occasion as the primary use of food service to everyday home meal replacement planning. The food service consumer base is strong but the basis for that shift is changing. The Baby Boomers who drove the growth for the second half of the century are aging and their requirements for food service are changing. In addition, the generations behind the Boomers (Gen X and Gen Y) are dramatically influencing the home-meal replacement purchase. Restaurant consultant Reynolds Design Group observes that all generations are eating out more because it fits their high-speed, consumer-mad lifestyle rather than the traditional special occasion. Food service in this next millennium will be defined by innovations beyond drive-through and delivery. Food Service outlets, in all segments, will service more people, have a higher technology environment, and do explosive takeout and delivery business. The National Restaurant Association predicts that food quality will become more important to consumers as they become more aware of nutrition and biotechnology issues. This observation indicates a trend toward customization of food service, food and service that fits individual customers' tastes. John Weiss, a financial analyst at Thomas Weisel Partners, forecasts an above-average rise in demand for food away from home, but there will be more emphasis in quality and less on low absolute price points.

The Zone's District Marketing Manager has assembled a high-performance team to begin growth-planning activities. This team decided to focus on the specific university customer who initiated the growth ultimatum. After a brief visit to this regional/commuter campus, a profile of the operation was drafted: The food court operation has two components including a grill/counter and a large vending area. The court is centrally located among the campus buildings, has high traffic counts, and is positioned on the lower floor of the main academic building. The food court has adequate room, plenty of tables, new furniture, a big-screen TV, computer stations, and quiet decorum. Operating hours are Monday through Thursday from 8:00 A.M. until 4:00 P.M. for the counter/grill and access to the large vending area (including microwave ovens) from 7:00 A.M. until 11:00 P.M. The menu for the food court is limited (only one hot entrée per day and one sandwich per day) and with minimal changes (averages menu change every 24 weeks) to the overall menu. The food court (both grill and vending) averages about $100,000 gross revenue per quarter. The profit margins are in part protected by an employment contract with a state-supported program for the vision impaired. This contract requires hiring vision-impaired employees and supervisors with a percentage of their wages subsidized by the state. Perhaps the subsidy reduces pressure or concerns for the Zone's bottom line but the university receives a percentage of revenue, not profits. While the high-performance team visited, it discovered a university-sponsored survey (general satisfaction in all areas of student experience) that ranked the food service as the worst area of students' experience.

Taking a "zero-based" approach, the Zone's growth team redefined the market by first estimating demand for its services. The balance of the team's review included new gross revenue projections, a full segmentation analysis (including segment labels, benchmarking, growth analysis, and segment attractiveness assessment), competitive analysis, market share projections (including any adjustments to primary and secondary market targeting), and finally culminating in any adjustments to the overall marketing plan (product/service adjustments, price adjustments, promotion adjustments, and distribution adjustments). The initial demand estimate revealed population numbers of 4,080 full-time students, 2,720 part-time students, 152 full-time faculty, 520 part-time faculty, 152 full-time staff/administrators, 40 part-time staff, and 444 different groups using the university facilities (22,279 individuals, some of the groups are repeat facility users) including conference rooms, labs, auditoriums, classrooms, and so on. Their initial segmentation analysis revealed the information shown in Table 1 about the users of university food courts.

The Zone's high performance team commissioned a business professor and a team of students to survey students, faculty, and facility users to measure overall satisfaction and customer service levels, desired features and services, and purchasing patterns. This information would be used to identify product/service opportunities and project revenue growth. In addition to the survey, they were asked to analyze growth of each segment and then assess the attractiveness of each segment. The Zone's team will then complete the competitive analysis and put together its final marketing plan.

Questions:

1.   How might you "re-label" the segments for this university food service provider changing them from Gen Y, Gen X, and Baby Boomer?

2.   After re-labeling the segments and using your own experiences/observations at your college, add to the segment description by including characteristics in needs area, demographic area, and purchasing patterns?

3.   Describe the decision making process for one of the segment's customers relative to making food or meal purchases during an academic semester. Identify the customer by segment label. Make sure you start with need stimulus and finish with any post-purchase cognitive dissonance.

Table 1
Restaurant and Institutions Trends Study Summaries

Generation Y (5-22 years old)
- 76% of food purchases by this group was spent on meals prepared outside of the home.
- 36% watch TV more than 10 hours per week, 25% listen to radio over 10 hours per week, 2% read magazines more than 10 hours per week, and 1% read newspapers more than 10 hours per week. Use of the Internet by this group is rapidly increasing.
- Exposure to diversity (including food) is strong – 90% of this group indicated they have friends of a different race.
- College campuses report a demand for variety and shorter menu change cycles of between 4 and 6 weeks.

Generation X (21-34 years old)
- There is a greater interest in a broader range of food types .
- This group is not fanatic about health (80% frequent a variety of fast food venues).
- Gen Xers want excitement and entertainment in food service including theme eateries.

Baby Boomers (36-55 years old)
- This group comprises the largest share of frequent eat-out customers (45%).
- This well-educated group is sophisticated and concerned with healthy diets.
- The boomers search out good casual dining to fill a void (home cooked meals and sense of families) while demand for time increases.
- 58% frequent fast-food venues at least once per week, 37% frequent casual dining, and 14% frequent fine dining at least once per week.

Food Management Study on Trends on Campus
- "Grab it and Go" food service outlets are growing in leaps and bounds.
- Students demanded expanded menus at these quick food outlets.
- Expanded hours were demanded to meet flexible and fast-paced schedules of students.
- Meals and offerings that can be taken to another place to eat also has increased.
- All three meals are requested for "quick grab and go."
- Although variety is desired and pressed, it continues to lag behind convenience as the most important need (This group wants broader menus but not at expense of speed and convenience.)
- Menu cycle changes are important.
- Participation in variety choices is important – self help opportunities that make it a grab, pack, and go.

Restaurant and Institutions Study on Commercial/Corporate/Catering Segment
- Menu turnover is important.
- Expanding health/nutritious offerings desired.
- Designation of health information is desired.
- Quick kiosk offerings are expanding.
- There is growth of full operation catering for onsite and offsite events (booking, preparation, serving, and clean up).

CASE 19

The Golden Fleece

This case was prepared and written by Professor Doreen Burdalski, Philadelphia University (formerly Philadelphia College of Textiles). Reprinted by permission.

Lucky Stores is a discount store chain located in the northeast region of the United States. It currently has 25 stores located in Pennsylvania, New Jersey, and Delaware. Lucky's assortment includes hardlines and softlines merchandise. National brands like Hanes, Carter's, Hoover, West Bend, and Fieldcrest are an important part of its merchandise mix. Forty percent of its mix is national name brands. Approximately 25 percent of its merchandise is private label. Lucky's competitors include Kmart and Wal-Mart. Lucky has been in the Philadelphia area for over 30 years. It was established for 25 years before Wal-Mart came into the area. The chain prides itself in the cleanliness of its stores. It considers itself a "step above" the national discounters in terms of quality and presentation of merchandise.

Ima Spender is the junior sportswear buyer for Lucky Stores. She is responsible for purchasing junior pants, tops, and coordinates for the chain. This merchandise is targeted toward pre-teen and teenage girls. The sizes run small/medium/large and from size 3 to 13. Her department does about $10 million a year in sales and the gross margin is 45 percent.

Late last November, Spender received a phone call from a jobber who offered her 9,000 dozen basic fleece pants at a cost of $2.00 each. This merchandise became available because a regional sporting goods chain in the northwest went out of business and could not commit to the order. Spender's sales were sluggish at the time and she was overbought; but she recognized what a great deal was being offered to her. These fleece pants normally retail for $7.99. Spender went to her divisional merchandise manager with the deal. Together, they contacted the store managers to get their feedback. The managers were excited about the purchase and promised to merchandise the fleece pants on promotional tables throughout the main aisle of their stores. Ima Spender purchased the fleece pants and retailed them for $5.00 each. They came packed in cartons of five dozen. The colors and sizes were assorted. There were men's and women's sizes mixed together in the cartons.

The stores complained about the mix of sizes and colors, particularly the gold color. They also complained about the amount of manpower it took to keep the promotional tables straightened up and neat looking; but by January, the stores had sold out and were getting customer requests for more fleece pants. Customers wrote letters to the president of Lucky Stores telling how much they liked the $5.00 fleece pants.

Ima Spender increased the sales in her department that year by $500,000 over the previous year. She sold $520,000 worth of $5.00 fleece pants. She needed $20,000 in markdowns on the fleece parts to sell out her inventory. These sales actually made the difference in the ready-to-wear division, making its sales plan for the year. Spender's divisional merchandise manager attributed the success of the season to the $5.00 fleece pants sales. The president of the company was very pleased with the happy customers; however, the store managers complained about being left with promotional tables filled with gold fleece pants in January that needed to be marked down to $2.00 retail.

It is now March and Ima Spender is in the process of developing a six-month forecast and budget for the coming fall that will include August through January. Upper management is looking for a 3 percent sales increase over last fall and a 10 percent increase in gross margin percent. Spender's 5 percent increase last fall was totally attributed to the sales of the $5.00 fleece pants. The jobber that she purchased the fleece pants from cannot guarantee the merchandise will be available for sale this year. She has concerns about being able to make the same advantageous purchase this fall. In her ten years of buying experience, Spender has never seen any department plan less sales than it did the previous year.

Questions:

1.   What important factors are determined in the forecasting and budgeting process?

2.   What must the retailer consider when forecasting sales for the upcoming season?

3.   What are Ima Spender's key concerns with forecasting and budgeting sales for this fall?

4.   Should Spender plan the 3 percent sales increase that upper management is asking for this fall? Explain your answer.

CASE 20

Green and Growing Nursery

This case was prepared and written by Lynn Samsel, doctoral candidate, University of Nebraska-Lincoln; and Dean Raymond A. Marquardt, Arizona State University-East. Reprinted by permission.

Clay Dickinson is the owner of Green and Growing Nursery, a retail garden center located in Collegevale, a midwestern city of 200,000. Three years ago, Dickinson moved to Collegevale to purchase the garden center from its retiring owner. When he bought the nursery, it had an adequate supply of annuals, perennials, shrubs, and seeds, as well as a good assortment of house plants. Although Dickinson had many good ideas to revitalize the center's overall appearance and improve its product mix, he got so busy running the store that many of these plans have not been implemented.

Now, Clay Dickinson is faced with increased competition from other nursery stores, in addition to several specialty and discount retailers. According to a retail analyst familiar with the Green and Growing Nursery, "if only the firm's profits were as green as its plants!"

Collegevale has three other nursery retailers: Cameron's, A Daisy A Day, and Fisk's. Each has a different overall retail strategy. Cameron's is a three-store chain that focuses on quality products, has a well-trained staff, and offers a broad assortment of merchandise, including the largest tree nursery in the region. Cameron's is well-regarded in the community, but has a reputation for charging somewhat higher prices. A Daisy A Day, part of a national chain, has two outlets in Collegevale. Unlike Cameron's, A Daisy A Day focuses its offerings on popular plants and products, and sells them at low prices. Lastly, while Fisk's specializes in supplying horticultural products to professional landscapers, it also sells nursery products to final consumers. As a consequence of its target market strategy, Fisk's is located in an out-of-the-way site, is open at times and days to accommodate its professional customers (for example, it is closed on Sunday), and rarely advertises in mass media.

Besides these garden centers, several specialty and discount retailers (including a local hardware store, a Kmart, and a Wal-Mart) sell plants and gardening supplies (such as vegetable seedlings and fertilizer) on a seasonal basis. Though Clay Dickinson is confident that his merchandise and services are of better quality, Kmart and Wal-Mart offer lower prices, one-stop shopping, and the convenience of being open seven days per week.

A recent report sponsored by the American Association of Nurserymen's Horticultural Research Institute (HRI), on consumer perceptions of garden centers, has given Dickinson a lot to think about. The HRI report indicates that people visit nurseries an average of ten times a year, and while they mainly go to browse, two-thirds of them purchase something on their average visit.

For final consumers, garden centers/nurseries are the major sources of supply for annual plants, perennial plants, house plants, trees, shrubs, and chemicals and fertilizer applied by someone in the household. On the other hand, sod, landscape design advice, landscape installation and maintenance, and yard improvement items were purchased less often, meaning that these areas represented unrealized opportunities for garden centers. The HRI study found that although consumers said they made some transactions for the latter products in garden centers, the average amount purchased was lower than through some other channel (such as hiring a service firm). Garden centers were also poorly evaluated as sources of lawn mowing and fertilizer application services. The study suggests that expanded offerings in these areas would not only increase dollar volume sales, but also permit a center to offer one-stop shopping for yard products and services. Lastly, the study found the most important factors that people consider in the purchase of garden products and services are product quality, product prices, a large assortment or selection, knowledgeable salespeople, and excellent customer service.

After reviewing the HRI report, Clay Dickinson met with Carol Stacey, his store manager. He remarked: "How can we use the findings of this report to improve traffic and increase profits? We need to do something to recapture market share." Ms. Stacey suggested they analyze their merchandise mix in light of the competition and the report findings. She had also been thinking about adding landscape services to their offerings for some time and thought this would be the ideal point to suggest it to Clay Dickinson.

Questions:

1.   Identify three different market segments that exist for gardening and landscape services. How well does Green and Growing Nursery appeal to each segment?

2.   Explain how the consumer decision process can be applied to the purchase of nursery products and landscape services. Include "what" and "where" in your answer.

3.   What types of nursery products can be most effectively sold in a Wal-Mart? Explain your answer using the extended, limited, and routine decision making processes.

4.   How can Green and Growing Nursery increase its impulse sales of vegetable seedlings? Develop specific strategies using the concepts of completely unplanned, partially unplanned, and unplanned substitution.

CASE 21

Haddonfield: Planning Within an Historic CBD

This case was prepared and written by Andrew Cullen, Senior Consultant, The Pennmor Group; and Professor Carol Felker Kaufman, Rutgers University, Camden, New Jersey. The casewriters would like to acknowledge the participation and assistance of the Haddonfield government, community leaders, and business professionals in providing valuable insight in the preparation of this case. Reprinted by permission.

Haddonfield, New Jersey is known as one of the premier residential communities in southern New Jersey. *Philadelphia* magazine recently named Haddonfield as the "best place to live" in the region. Although the magazine did not rate Haddonfield on specific attributes, retail experts generally cite the community's charm (based on the successful preservation of its historic homes), the area's unique shopping opportunities, and its sense of community as major positive attributes. An additional attraction to Haddonfield is its linkage with surrounding areas through several highways and a high-speed mass transit system that connects the community to downtown Philadelphia.

While historic Haddonfield was originally settled by English immigrants in 1682, efforts to preserve the town's colonial heritage have gained momentum during the last 30 years. The Haddonfield Preservation Society, organized in 1966, was instrumental in passing an ordinance forbidding the alteration of historic buildings unless the changes were in keeping with the town's original architecture. Partly as a result of the group's efforts, Haddonfield became listed in the National Register of Historic places in 1982.

Downtown Haddonfield now has over 150 retail stores, in addition to a number of lawyers, accountants, and other professionals. Most of these retail businesses cater to the needs of upper-income individuals who live and work within a ten-mile radius of the town. Some of Haddonfield's merchants specialize in luxury-type goods (such as fine jewelry, designer fashions, and fine art), others in meeting the convenience needs of the local population (such as hardware and film processing stores), and a third group caters to consumers who visit Haddonfield as part of a day trip. Most merchants are independents, but the area also has some national retail chains.

Retail space in Haddonfield is generally scarce. Stores that are vacant are usually in transition between owners. Retailers generally state that they are attracted to the area because of its high density of affluent consumers. While most customers live within a short distance of the shopping area, others travel longer distances due to the area's charm and specialized retailers.

Despite the overall attractiveness of the retail environment in Haddonfield, there are areas of concern. Almost all the merchants in Haddonfield would agree that parking is an issue that needs further attention. Strict ordinances that limit new construction, as well as a store's expansion and the use of sidewalk displays and signs, are also viewed as restrictive by some merchants. Lastly, as in any shopping district, retailers exercise autonomy in setting their own store hours. This affects the ability of an area to draw shoppers during early evening hours on weekdays, and on weekends when not all stores are open.

The Haddonfield retail community is polarized about how to best attract more shoppers. One group of retailers has sponsored such activities as craft shows, sidewalk sales, and carriage rides as a means of increasing sales to the mass market. These merchants have promoted the events in several ways, including ads on cable TV, a Web site (featuring ads from selected merchants, as well as a classified section), and brochures placed in the Philadelphia convention center. This merchant group has financed the promotions through the collection of dues from members, depending on each retailer's business and location. On the other hand, another group of merchants is advocating a less aggressive marketing effort. This group credits Haddonfield's historic preservation efforts with the revitalization of its shopping district. The group also wants to maintain the quietness of the community and its appeal to upper-income shoppers.

Questions:

1. Classify downtown Haddonfield as a planned or an unplanned business district. Support your answer.

2. What are the pros and cons of Haddonfield for a national retail chain? What could a national chain like McDonald's do to enhance its ability to operate in historic sites like Haddonfield?

3. Given the opportunity to shape their marketing efforts, what would you suggest Haddonfield do next? (These can be discussed as alternative courses of action.)

4. Figure 10-8 in the text contains a checklist for location and site evaluation. Using the criteria in the checklist, evaluate downtown Haddonfield's attractiveness as a potential site. Discuss the benefits and the limitations of using this scale.

CASE 22

The Hiring Dilemma

This case was prepared and written by Professor Gale A. Jaeger, Marywood University. Reprinted by permission.

A major New York City flagship store is the venue for this case study. Several thousand people in many different capacities are employed at this location. The store is an old and well-regarded retailer that continues to do well through its innovative merchandising, marketing, and operating techniques.

It is mid-September and recently, several sales managers have been promoted, one has retired, and one has resigned. It is important to hire some promising talent to fill these vacancies, particularly because the holiday season is fast approaching. Geri Jennings, the Director of Executive Personnel/Human Resources, expects to have several new managers in place soon in order to have them properly trained by the start of the busy and most important season of the retail year. She is counting on her employment manager, John Mack, to do whatever it takes to get these positions filled.

According to the most recent vacancy report, four of the openings have been filled through promotion from within. A candidate with an excellent background in retail management has been hired and begins training next week for the fifth position. There are two candidates being considered for the sixth position.

The employment manager is relatively new to his position and needs some assistance in making a hiring decision. The position to be filled is in the furniture gallery adjacent to china, silver, and gifts. In addition to some fine quality furniture and decorative accessories, the trim-a-tree shop is set up in this area for the holiday season. It is followed by the garden shop which is set up from March through September. The area grosses between $15 and $20 million annually and has been trending upwards.

There are 26 employees in this large department including full-time, part-time, and sales support people. A few of the full-time people have been with the company for over 20 years and, while excellent at product knowledge, customer service, and sales, they are rather "set in their ways." Some of the part-timers have been very dissatisfied of late because the previous manager showed partiality to the full-time staff and there were a number of unpleasant incidents that had to be written up.

The morale of the department is low and it is affecting performance and productivity. Several employees say it is the fault of the previous manager who had been new and lacking in the ability to motivate and manage people, in spite of being a talented and creative merchandiser. Though mature and with a good experience base in the industry, he had poor people skills and did not pay attention to the needs and wants of his staff.

Knowing all of this in advance, John Mack is having a difficult time deciding which of the two remaining candidates he should recommend for this position. The candidates are Janet Guiterez and Joseph Bianco.

Janet Guiterez is a 34-year-old woman of Hispanic background who holds a Bachelor of Business Administration Degree with a concentration in retail and marketing. She has excellent experience, having worked in an up-scale, privately owned gift emporium, as well as a large furniture and accessory chain. Clearly, Guiterez has a strong track record in sales and in product knowledge. She understands the industry and is ambitious and confident. The problem is that she

117

may be too confident and comes across as being somewhat argumentative and, at times, arrogant. She does have experience in managing people and says that in no way does she let her people "manage her." She is in "full charge at all times." She indicates to John Mack that, if hired, she will have the department up and running "full speed ahead" for the holidays and that she will get the employees "in hand." She is familiar with the lines carried and is creative and excellent at merchandising the selling floor. At the end of the interview, Guiterrez mentioned that she has a back problem due to an injury that occurred at her last place of employment as a result of lifting heavy merchandise.

Joseph Bianco is the second candidate. He is a 25-year-old white male who holds a bachelor's degree in Business Administration with a concentration in management. He seems exceedingly mature and well spoken with an appealing manner of getting his point across. He is a good listener, yet seems decisive and competent. Bianco did an internship for a major furniture chain during his last year of college at Texas A&M. He enjoyed his work in the furniture industry and learned a great deal from it. He was offered a position at the company, which he accepted, and has worked there for three years. He has now been offered a promotion at his current position in Texas. Bianco wants to relocate to Manhattan because, as he puts it, it is where "the action of the Big Apple takes place." Bianco's recommendation letters speak of his excellent analytical abilities coupled with strong management potential and "people skills." He acknowledges that he is not totally familiar with all of the lines shown on the selling floor, but also mentions that he is a fast learner and eager to get to know the business. He also is eager to relocate as soon as he secures a position and has indicated to this current company that he plans to do so.

Questions:

1. What are the advantages and disadvantages of each candidate?

2. If you were the Director of Executive Personnel/Human Resources, what are the major issues you would need to consider?

3. If you were the Merchandise Administrator for this area, what are the major issues you would need to consider?

4. From an EEOC perspective, what concerns might you have?

5. What recommendation do you think John Mack should make to Geri Jennings? Explain your answer.

CASE 23

The J. Peterman Company: Stretched Beyond Limits

This case was prepared and written by Sangeeta M. Sarma and Professor Leslie Stoel, University of Kentucky. Reprinted by permission.

J. Peterman Company – The Lexington, Kentucky-based purveyor of off-beat and pricey merchandise, a name known to almost all Americans after the hilarious sitcom "Seinfeld," has recently changed owners and resurfaced with a new zest and a slightly changed approach. After a decade into business and a year into an over-ambitious expansion plan, John Peterman sought refuge under Chapter 11 on January 25, 1999. His kitschy but unique concept was salvaged by Paul Harris, a retail chain from Indianapolis.

"The J. Peterman concept is a moneymaker if run properly," said Charlotte Fischer, Paul Harris CEO, Chairman, and President. The new owners have decided to focus on the retail outlets instead of revamping the catalog. As a first step, they moved the J. Peterman headquarters to Indianapolis and opened the first new J. Peterman store there. The J. Peterman staples (1903 cologne, Otavalo mountain shirts, and men's vintage T-shirts) remain, but the $3,000 pewter candlesticks have gone. The signature style remains, but the store interiors have changed. Fischer foresees at least 100 "great" J. Peterman stores all over the United States.

John Peterman's stroke of genius started with his chance purchase of a canvas horseman duster on a trip to Wyoming. People liked it so much that they tried to buy it off his back. This formed the basis for a new business. In 1986, he met Don Staley, the man behind the lyrical prose in his catalogs. The two decided that Peterman should purchase more of the dusters and Staley would advertise them in *The New Yorker* with some enticing text. This strategy was so successful that in 1987, they sold 2,500 dusters. Soon, people wanted to know what else the company sold. Peterman added three more items to his merchandise list: the New York Fireman's Coat, the Baker Street Coat with Cape, and the Alternative Coat. Thus, his first catalog was born in 1988.

The J. Peterman Company broke all the rules of direct marketing by making its catalogs more artistic and descriptive than advised by experts. But instead of spelling disaster for Peterman, Bob Hagel's illustrative watercolor renderings and Don Staley's exotic, lengthy descriptions proved to be key factors for success. The reason for this unconventional business decision was John Peterman's belief that people were looking for something different. He said, "If you're not doing anything different, why should people buy from you?" People found the difference not only in his selling style, but also in his product range, pricing, and quality. His catalogs were filled with products evoking a sense of fantasy and nostalgia. The company's unusual merchandise and strong emphasis on customer service helped the business skyrocket within a very short time span. Revenues grew from $560,000 in 1987 to $45 million in 1992.

That was the year Peterman opened the doors of his first full-price store in Lexington, Kentucky. His store maintained the aura and image created by his catalogs. Sales increased and so did Peterman's ambition, resulting in three outlet stores in Manchester, Vermont; Chattanooga,

Tennessee; and Camarillo, California. Sales kept increasing. In 1995, Peterman received a tremendous publicity boost from the sitcom "Seinfeld." The sitcom exposure gave J. Peterman 25 percent brand recognition among American adults. Peterman recognized the growing demands on his brand and decided to expand. In July 1997, he hired Arnold Cohen, a former J. Crew employee, to assist with the expansion.

Peterman and his staff believed that their customers were a unique segment of the market and should be treated with special care. Each store was unique, to differentiate from chain retailers who strive to achieve uniformity. The stores were designed and built to evoke feelings of romance, fantasy, a multifaceted past, somewhere between the two World Wars, and sometimes slipping into an Edwardian style. The mood in the stores was enhanced by the décor, accented with touches like worn suitcases, photographs, history books, and 1950s movie posters.

The merchandise and price combination at the Peterman stores was an interesting mix. They carried everything from horseman dusters to yellow rubber boots to movie memorabilia. They had men's and women's clothes from the 1920s, but redesigned so as to be classically stylish for any decade. They sold an Otavalo mountain shirt for $29 and a coat for $1,000. Some amazing items were the Sheffield sterling silver tea service for $12,500, a bronze post and plaque from Babe Ruth Plaza for $25,000, and a "Queen's umbrella" for $235. Some of the moderately priced items included beaded purses, vintage hats, leather jackets, beads, and scarves. Mid-price range items included a woman's French-style lambskin duster for $850; Frederica's Jacket, a military inspired coat, for $225; and the men's Kansas City Duster for $375. In addition, Peterman also carried housewares and goods for the tabletop.

Arnie Cohen and Peterman planned a rapid expansion program. They decided to open 50 full-price stores and 20 outlet stores in five years. Peterman didn't want to flood the market or give a hackneyed impression of his brand. "At 70 stores, you're still a destination and not a mass marketer," said Peterman. Plans also included taking the company public, offering a Web site, and developing two new catalogs. They put their expansion plans into action and in April 1998, opened their second full-price store in the Somerset Collection in Troy, Michigan, and the third store in Fashion Island Mall in Newport Beach, California. Peterman planned to open five more full-price stores and five outlet stores by the end of 1998. The full-price stores included New York in Grand Central Terminal on August 27, Pacific Place in Seattle on September 30, and Market Street in San Francisco on October 30. The outlet stores included Woodbury Commons in Harriman, New York, on May 22, The Stateline Mall in Primm, Nevada, on July 15, and the Rentham Mall in Rentham, Massachusetts, on August 15. Peterman picked upscale locations for his new stores to tie in with the image of his customers: well read, well traveled, and well paid.

The year of massive expansion didn't prove to be a year for massive sales. In 1997, annual sales amounted to $65 million with one full-price store, three outlet stores, and catalog sales. In 1998, annual sales barely reached $74 million even with the addition of nine stores. In 1998, the company lost $24.7 million and another $2 million within the first three weeks of 1999. Consequently, the J. Peterman Company sought bankruptcy protection from its creditors under Chapter 11. At the time of its filing, its debts exceeded its assets by $14 million.

Retail experts summarize the causes for the company's tragic end as mismanagement, lack of direction, and inflated sales projections. "That's really what the only problem was with Peterman. They just spent too much money. Their problem wasn't in margins; it was in expense control," said Charlotte Fischer. She has decided to create a prototype for the new stores she plans to open. Such a "cookie cutter" approach will help in controlling expenses, as they won't need to draw up plans for every new store. Fischer also has plans for expansion, but at a gradual pace. She plans to expand and not stretch too far.

Questions:

1. What objective(s) was J. Peterman pursuing prior to its takeover by Paul Harris? What was J. Peterman's overall retail strategy?

2. What target marketing technique was J. Peterman using prior to its takeover by Paul Harris? Explain your answer.

3. Prior to the takeover by Paul Harris, was J. Peterman a "power retailer?" Explain your answer.

CASE 24

J.C. Penney: Putting the Dot Com in JCPenney.com

This case was prepared and written by Professor Deborah M. Moscardelli, Central Michigan University. Reprinted by permission.

The J.C. Penney Company began in 1902 as a dry goods store owned by James Cash Penney. Over the years, Penney has emerged as one of America's largest department store chains operating more than 1,230 department stores in the United States, Puerto Rico, Mexico, and Chile. Occupying more than 115 million square feet of retail space, the company generates $26 billion in retail sales each year and another $4 billion in catalog sales. In 1956, five years before the Internet was even conceptualized, James Cash Penney understood the value of maintaining a personal relationship with the customer, a core benefit of the online retail environment. The emergence of the Internet created what Penney viewed as an opportunity to leverage sales and corporate stock value. In addition, Penney saw the Internet as a medium that could capitalize on the strength of its existing catalog distribution infrastructure. The first Penney catalog, distributed in 1963, was serviced by a sole distribution center located in Milwaukee, Wisconsin. As the success of the catalog became certain, Penney continued to build its catalog business by adding additional distribution centers over a period of 14 years including Atlanta, Georgia (1969); Columbus, Ohio (1974); and Lenexa, Kansas (1977). One year later, Penney officially began operating nationwide with the opening of the Reno, Nevada, distribution center generating catalog sales exceeding $1 billion.

Within only 18 months of the Reno distribution center's grand opening, J.C. Penney had increased its catalog revenues by 50 percent, bringing annual catalog sales to $1.5 billion in 1980. During the 80s, the catalog division continued to prosper and in 1993, Penney had much to celebrate: the catalog's 30-year anniversary marked a milestone for the 1993 Fall/Winter "big book." It had become the biggest catalog ever in sales volume. During this same year, Penney was recognized as the largest catalog retailer in the United States. How could it leverage the success of the catalog business against the opportunities of the Internet?

Strategic decisions would prove critical to the success of JCPenney.com. First and foremost, Penney had to commit to an online corporate strategic initiative. In 1994, the same year the Internet became an official commercial medium, Penney purchased the JCPenney.com domain name and formulated a Web site with two objectives in mind. First, the company realized the only way to learn to conduct business in an environment with no commercial history was to garner first mover advantage and pave the way to success, a strategy used successfully by Amazon.com. Second, executives at Penney quickly realized they needed to buy time to work on systems and technologies needed to conduct business online, commonly referred to as the *back end* -- systems that are crucial to business but not seen by the customer. The solution, it became apparent, was to create a corporate Web site -- slowly adding merchandise from the catalog as technology and systems were created. Over the next three years, Penney continued to test the Internet market and gauge customer response in order to leverage the trusted Penney name and existing distribution infrastructure, two strengths considered crucial to the online opportunity.

A setback occurred during the Christmas season of 1998, however, just as J.C. Penney was making strides toward becoming *the* premier online retailer. Customers began to complain about the lack of merchandise available for sale on the Penney Web site. The media soon followed, criticizing Penney for not moving quickly enough to get *all* catalog products added to the Web site in time for the 1998 Christmas season. In January 1999, executives met at the Dallas, Texas, headquarters to discuss implementation of a five-year plan for competing in the fast-moving, ever-changing, Internet environment. On the agenda were three key questions:

- Can JCPenney.com continue to service the customer successfully while under the catalog division of the company?
- Will Penney cannibalize its retail store sales by continuing to compete in the online market and if so, should it segment and specialize its current market offering online?
- What are the primary strengths of the J.C. Penney Company that can be leveraged for future success online?

Questions:

1.   Can JCPenney.com continue to service the customer successfully while under the catalog division of the company? Explain your answer.

2.   Will Penney cannibalize its retail store sales by continuing to compete in the online market? If so, should it segment and specialize its current market offering online? Explain your answer.

3.   What are the primary strengths of the J.C. Penney Company that can be leveraged for future success online?

CASE 25

J.T.'s General Store

This case was prepared and written by Professor Michael R. Luthy, Bellarmine University. Reprinted by permission.

Carlisle, Iowa -- A 2-year-old J.T.'s General Store here may be getting an electric bill from the Carlisle Municipal Utilities for about $40,000 in back charges. The charges are the result of an electrical meter that was not installed properly when the store at 1005 Iowa Highway 5 was built two years ago, said Jack McCuen, electrical superintendent of the city utility.

McCuen said the store's electric bills have averaged around $230 a month since it opened in December 1992. In the month since the problem with the meter was discovered and corrected, electrical usage totaled $1,800. If that amount can be tracked back to the store's opening, J.T.'s could owe the utility more than $40,000. During the same period, a second J.T.'s store at 105 Iowa Highway 5 was paying about $2,000 a month. McCuen told the City Council last Monday that his department was investigating the meter problems. He said the Iowa Utilities Board will be contacted to determine how far back the city can go to collect fees. He also said the city would study the meter and the usage for two to four more months before it attempts to collect from J.T.'s.

Eli Wirtz, J.T.'s corporate attorney, said that J.T.'s had confirmed that the meter was not recording the electrical usage correctly. He said that the store is now waiting to hear from the city. The problem with the meter was discovered six weeks ago when Pat Brehse, deputy clerk at City Hall, brought the difference in usage between the two J.T.'s stores in town to McCuen's attention. "There was quite a difference in the bills," Brehse said.

McCuen stated that the three-phase meter, which is for commercial use, was not measuring the usage correctly. One phase of the meter was not measuring at all, another phase was going forward, and a third phase was measuring backward. The result was a significantly lower reading of kilowatt hours used and a lower electric bill. McCuen says the fault for the wiring lies with the city and with the meter's manufacturer. "When it was installed, it was installed wrong," McCuen said. "One phase was our fault and one phase was the company's fault."

As the city continues to investigate the J.T.'s problem, McCuen said it will also look at some other meters in town to see whether similar problems exist.

Questions:

1. Leaving aside the legalities, what would you propose is fair and ethical as a settlement of the bill if you were:
   a. The owner of the store receiving the small power bills?
   b. The owner of the store at 105 Iowa Highway 5 who read about this?
   c. Carlisle Municipal Utilities?

2. How would your response to Question 1 change (if at all) if it was discovered:
   a. The owner of the store in question tampered with the wiring when the store was being built?
   b. The owner of the store in question knew that he was receiving an inordinately small bill compared to the amount of power he was using?

CASE 26

The Joburg Health and Fitness Center

This case was prepared and written by Professor Jonathan N. Goodrich, Florida International University; and Dean Cohen, Quantum Storage Systems. Reprinted by permission.

Johannesburg has a population of 2.5 million people, about 70 percent are African, 25 percent are Caucasion. The city has many gyms and health and fitness centers similar to those in the United States, such as Gold's Gym, Bally Total Fitness (previously Scandinavian Gym), and Olympia Gym. This case demonstrates service retailing, market segmentation, and the growth of the health and fitness trend in Johannesburg and the United States.

The Facilities

The Joburg Health and Fitness Center (JHFC) is one of the most modern gyms and fitness centers in the world. It consists of over 10,000 square feet of space and is filled on three levels with top-of-the-line equipment and weights for building muscles (body shaping), muscle toning, weight reduction, cardiovascular training, and general fitness. Some of the equipment includes treadmills, stair climbers, bicycles, rowing and skiing machines, barbells, dumbells, pulley machines, and thousands of pounds of free-standing weights for exercises such as bench press, military press, leg press, squats, leg curls, abdominal crunches, and so on. Each piece of equipment or machine is strategically placed so that its user will have a clear, unobstructed view of one of the six big television screens displayed in the area. So, patrons can work out, as well as listen to and watch, local news programs, talk shows, sporting events, educational programs, and so on.

JHFC also has modern and beautiful facilities for racquet ball, tennis, squash, basketball, track, and swimming. Therefore, JHFC members have a variety of fitness activities in which to participate. After the workout, or before, one can go to the juice/snack bar and order fresh juices (e.g., orange juice, grapefruit juice, tomato juice) or smoothies made from different fruits (e.g., bananas, oranges, strawberries), and yogurt. JHFC also sells multi-vitamins, high protein powder, and various other nutritional supplements to its members.

You can also have an individualized instructor to help you do aerobic, stretching, and yoga exercises, as you desire. These exercises help to relax the body and mind. The sauna also helps you to relax, and lose weight. Leaving the gym, one feels stress free and content.

Price

The price for membership is approximately $400 per year. Some executives who are passing through Johannesburg sometimes stop at JHFC for a workout. JHFC may offer them a free workout or a workout at a small, nominal fee, such as $15. If you are going to be in Johannesburg for a few weeks or months, you may also arrange special deals with JHFC management for use of the facilities.

Promotion

Presently, JHFC spends about $250,000 annually for marketing and promotion. Media used to promote JHFC include television, radio, newspapers, flyers, and lighted "neon" signs on the property. But, perhaps, the most effective method of promoting JHFC has been through word-of-mouth. Family members, relatives and friends, and executives of many companies spread the word about the excellent facilities, programs, and services. JHFC is also developing its own Web site.

Market Segments

JHFC promotes itself to adult males and females. The age of members ranges from 18 to 75 years, with the predominant age group being 21 to 65 years. There are over 1,000 regular members, about 70 percent male and 30 percent female. People from various walks of life attend JHFC: executives, regular workers, professional athletes, housewives, politicians, entrepreneurs, students, and professors.

Services

In addition to the exercise facilities, JHFC provides other ancillary services, such as yoga classes, aerobics classes, simple medical checkups (e.g., blood pressure, heart rate, blood sugar level), massages, diet classes run by dieticians, and classes/workshops on general wellness and keeping fit physically and mentally. Management also stresses courteous treatment for all its members.

Questions:

1. What services does JHFC sell?

2. What retail positioning themes do you think JHFC should use in any attempt to attract and keep its customers?

3. What market segmentation variables is JHFC using?

4. Comment on the future of fitness in the United States.

CASE 27

L & T Enterprises

This case was prepared and written by Professor William R. Swinyard, Brigham Young University. Reprinted by permission.

It was a month before the spring semester ended, and Lara Daly was thinking about summer jobs while waiting for her retailing class to begin. Daly turned to Tyler Morgan, a classmate and close friend and said, "I'm tired of the usual summer job where I don't get anything out of it except a few dollars an hour. I've only got one summer left before I graduate. This year, I want to be my own boss, get some real work experience, and make more money, too." "That's a great idea. Maybe we can do something together. Let's talk about it after class," Morgan replied.

The in-class discussion that day was on the strategic profit model. That material was so interesting that Daly and Morgan talked about it after class and continued their dialog through lunch together. They knew the strategic profit model concept was an important tool for evaluating a potential business opportunity. Morgan agreed to come up with an interesting retail opportunity which they would further review after the next retailing class.

So, Daly and Morgan met again two days later to discuss a proposed business venture. Daly noted that although she had $500 in the bank, this was her expense money for the fall semester; and she needed to be sure this money would be available at the beginning of the fall semester. Morgan also had $500 to invest; and he could secure a loan for up to $10,000 from his parents (at an interest rate of 6 percent per year), if necessary. Morgan explained to Daly that they both would be equally responsible for repayment of the $10,000, even if the business did not work out. With the loan and their personal savings, they had up to $11,000 for investing in a retail business.

One retail opportunity that seemed particularly attractive to Daly and Morgan was the resale of used cars. Morgan was aware of a local auto auction that specialized in repossessed cars (due to nonpayment of loans). If they were to pursue this venture, the partners would have to obtain a used car dealer's license (at a cost of $300). Regardless of the business venture they would undertake, Lara Daly and Tyler Morgan agreed to name their business L & T Enterprises.

Daly and Morgan planned to purchase cars at the auction for an average amount of $3,000 and then to quickly resell them via classified ads (costing an average of $200 per car for a two-week ad) for $4,500. While they would "detail" (thoroughly clean, polish, and wax the interior and exterior) the cars and do some of the minor repairs themselves, they agreed to budget an average allowance of $500 per car for necessary parts and repairs.

Daly and Morgan decided to attend each of the four auto auctions held in their area over the summer. They would only bid on cars that were rather easy to sell (such as vans, 4-wheel-drive vehicles, and station wagons), had low mileage (less than 10,000 miles per year), and were "clean" (with only minor dents and pings) -- and that had not been involved in a major accident. They also planned to concentrate their bidding on 20 to 30 cars per auction, and to stop bidding on any car when its price was more than two-thirds its average retail value. Morgan thought they would be able to purchase between three and four cars at each of the four summer auctions.

The partners intended to detail, test, and repair each car within a week of taking title, and then to resell each car within two weeks of placing a classified ad for it. Thus, the expected turnaround time for selling each car would be three weeks after the auto's purchase. They could then go to the next auction with additional working capital.

Daly and Morgan wanted to have no more than four cars in inventory at any point in time. This meant that if they sold only two cars between auctions, at the next auction, they could purchase two additional cars. They both felt that restricting the number of cars they bought would assure that they could properly store all cars. This restriction would also facilitate the closing of L & T Enterprises before the start of classes and paying off their loan.

Questions:

1. Evaluate the auto brokerage business based on the strategic profit model.

2. Develop a projected profit-and-loss statement for L & T Enterprises based upon the data presented in this case.

3. Are the financial assumptions used by Daly and Morgan realistic? Explain your answer.

4. Should Daly and Morgan pursue this business opportunity? Explain your answer.

CASE 28

Demands of Large Retailers Alienate Small Manufacturers

This case was prepared and written by Professor Suzanne G. Marshall, California State University, Long Beach. Reprinted by permission.

The ability of manufacturers and retailers to negotiate the terms under which they conduct business has eroded over the past two decades due to the power of the retailer increasing and the power of the supplier decreasing. Vera Campbell, President of Design Zone, a manufacturer of misses and junior knit wear with sales of $15 million annually and Susan Crank, CEO of Lunada Bay, a women's swimwear and activewear licensee for Mossimo and others, with sales of $60 million annually, speak of the power shift in the apparel industry and its negative impact on small manufacturers.

Prior to the 1980s, apparel manufacturers held a high degree of channel power due to the fact that the demand for their products exceeded the supply. This is described as a "push" system -- whereas whatever goods are produced are pushed through the system to buyers who had limited choice options. In the 1980s, department stores began to merge together into large ownership groups such as Federated Department Stores (Macy's, Bloomingdale's, Rich's, Sterns, Goldsmiths, Burdines, and Jordan Marsh). As a result, buying became more centralized. Buyers bought in large quantities to supply inventory for large groups of stores all over the country rather than for a small chain in one city. Simultaneously, apparel manufacturing companies grew at a rapid pace which increased competition. As a result of the merge of retailers into fewer but more powerful conglomerates, and the increased competition among a larger number of apparel manufacturers, channel power shifted to those retailers with the "big pencils."

Realizing their higher elevation on the power channel, retailers began to shift some of the responsibilities that have traditionally been that of the retailer to the manufacturer. Manufacturers, especially smaller ones, felt that they had little power to negotiate, knowing if they refused to comply with large retailers' demands, there were plenty of other manufacturers who would supply the larger retailers. Crank and Campbell cite several examples of demands by retailers that cut into manufacturers' already narrow profit margins:

- Chargebacks -- Each of the major retail ownership groups write a routing guide which sets forth rules of shipping to which the manufacturer must strictly comply. The rules cover areas such as where to attach the address label, whether the invoice goes inside or on the outside of the box, and whether shipments should be consolidated or broken down and sent to individual stores. Each notebook of rules is complex in its details and each retailer has its own notebook of rules. "I'd have to hire MBAs to work in my warehouse to understand this," complained Crank, knowing if she did not strictly comply, she would be levied a heavy "chargeback" fee (a deduction from the invoiced amount) from the retailer for having to correct the problem.

- Merchandise Preparation -- Manufacturers are now responsible for tagging merchandise which involves not only price tagging, but also care labels and promotion-related tagging (which indicates the maker of certain fibers such as Dupont's Lycra). Crank was pressed to purchase both a hanging rack system and a bagging system for her warehouse, costing thousands of dollars, so that she could ship her swimwear on hangers and in bags making them "floor ready."

- Merchandisers and Specialists -- Manufacturers (Quiksilver, St. John, Liz Claiborne) now hire merchandisers whose main job is to visit the manufacturer's retail accounts and insure their product is being given visibility and is visually appealing. Merchandisers also work with the receiving department to insure the goods are placed on the floor in a timely manner. Similarly, many manufacturers hire retail specialists and place them in their key retail doors to sell only that manufacturer's merchandise.

- Profit Cutting Demands -- There are several common retail practices that cut into the potential profit of their suppliers:
  1. Advancing the season -- Campbell explained that retailers are breaking price (taking a markdown) on goods earlier and earlier each year, which eliminates the potential of a sell-through at the original retail price. Retailers explain that if they have a sale on January 15, 2000, they must "anniversary" that sale the next year to make their figures.
  2. Markdown guarantees -- The retailer expects the manufacturer to share the loss of profit from any markdowns, regardless of how early the markdown was taken in the season.

3. Automatic deduction for damages -- Several retailers automatically deduct a percentage from the manufacturer's invoice to cover potential damages. Crank explains that she has only .3 percent damages and resents having to pay for the poor quality of her competitors.

In summary, both Campbell and Crank feel increased pressure from their retail customers. On one hand, they want to sell to the power retailers because of the larger orders, but on the other hand, they feel these retailers "own you."

Questions:

1. Take the side of the retailer and make an argument supporting each demand.

2. Take the side of the manufacturer and respond to the retailer.

3. Develop a compromise strategy that might work for both sides. What would the strengths and weaknesses of your strategy be?

4. What do you think is the future for small manufacturers? How can they remain competitive?

CASE 29

Larry's Barber Shop

This case was prepared and written by Professor Jonathan N. Goodrich, Florida International University. Reprinted by permission.

INTRODUCTION

Miami has over 200 beauty salons and/or barber shops. They cater to the hair needs of the city's cosmopolitan population (such as Caucasians, African-Americans, and Hispanics), as well as provide manicures and pedicures. Every neighborhood has a few barber shops and salons.

Larry's Barber Shop (LBS) is located in the neighborhood of U.S. 1 and S.W. 174th Avenue (U.S. 1 is a prominent highway in Miami). The immediate neighborhood is occupied 30 percent by African-Americans. Many of the commercial firms in the area are owned by Caucasians and include restaurants, car washes, automobile dealerships, automotive parts stores, movie theaters, law firms, supermarkets, pharmacies, adult video stores, gas stations, furniture stores, automotive paint and body shops, and kindergarten schools.

LBS is an African-American barber shop. This case describes the marketing of LBS, and shows the importance of service quality to small business success. It also indicates that African-American barber shops also serve as social clubs and political forums for African-American customers, and as a respite from the pressures of everyday life.

Layout

LBS is located in a strip joint with seven other stores. These stores include a record shop and an antique dealer. LBS itself occupies an area 15 feet wide by 60 feet long. It has five barber chairs spaced along the length side of the barber shop, twelve chairs for customers along the wall facing the barber chairs, and a large sofa near the entrance of the shop. LBS also has a large Coca-Cola vending machine beside the sofa, which contains a variety of soft drinks for purchase. The two "length" sides of LBS are occupied by mirrors which begin at four feet from the ground and end at the ceiling, for customers to admire themselves.

Personnel

Larry is the owner of the barber shop and the main barber there. There are also two other barbers: a woman and a young fellow who is about 25 years old. Another woman comes in two days per week, Friday and Saturday, to provide manicures and pedicures to customers.

Services

LBS provides haircuts and styles for men and boys, shampoo and conditioning treatment, manicures, and pedicures.

Prices

The price of a typical haircut is $10. Trimming the beard is an additional $5. Shampoo and conditioning treatment costs an additional $15. The price of a special haircut with words "carved" in the head varies from $15 to $25, depending on the extent and difficulty of the job. A complete manicure costs $15 and includes cleaning and clipping the fingernails.

Promotion

Promotion of LBS is done primarily through word-of-mouth and signage at the shop. Larry also passes out business cards to clients and potential clients at LBS, and has T-shirts with the name and address of the barber shop.

Place

Distribution of LBS services is through LBS.

Plaques/Signs/Photos

There are a few signs on the wall of the barber shop that reflect Larry's concern for safety, and God, as well as his love of football. For example, one sign reads, "No Playing in the Work Area," and another reads, "Try God, He's Real." There is also a two-foot square photograph of Dan Marino in his Miami Dolphins uniform on one wall of the barber shop. Other African-American barber shops in the area have pictures of famous African-American athletes, such as Michael Jordan, Bill Russell, Muhammed Ali, Charles Barkley, George Foreman, Jesse Owens, Carl Lewis, Tiger Woods, and Arthur Ashe.

Music

Larry loves music, especially jazz and soul music. Soft music is always playing at LBS, especially by famous African-American singers, such as James Brown ("The Godfather of Soul"), Aretha Franklin, Barry White, Whitey Houston, B.B. King, Sam Cooke, Jackie Wilson, The Temptations, The Four Tops, The Spinners, The O'Jays, The Drifters, Marvin Gaye, The Supremes, Fats Domino, and Bobby Womack.

Social Place

LBS is similar to many African-American barber shops. It is a place where men and boys not only go for haircuts, but discuss sports, politics, the news, world affairs, and things of interest. LBS, therefore, acts as a social gathering place for some African-Americans in the neighborhood.

Competition

There are about six other African-American barber shops within a 5-mile radius of LBS. These include Richmond Heights Barber Shop and Don's Barber Shop. Other well-known African-American barber shops in the Miami area include Just Right, Green and Fort Barber Shop in Overtown, Jacky Jackson Relax Barber Shop in Little Haiti, and Band Box Barber Shop in Liberty City.

Famous Customers

African-American barber shops in America have groomed top performers and athletes, such as Michael Jordan, Muhammed Ali, Tiger Woods, Carl Lewis, Sammy Sosa, Sammy Davis, Jr., and Arthur Ashe. Many local African-American politicians also find these barber shops to be places to listen to the pulse of the community on issues as varied as racism, drugs, education, crime, jobs, and the President Clinton/Monica Lewinsky scandal.

Challenges

LBS has several challenges. They include:
- Overcrowding on Saturdays
- Sparse business during mid-week.
- Few qualified barbers.
- Most of the customers wanting Larry, not the other barbers, to cut their hair.

Questions:

1. What retail services does LBS provide?

2. How can LBS overcome overcrowding on Saturdays?

3. How can LBS get customers to want their hair cut by barbers other than Larry?

4. What segmentation method is LBS using?

CASE 30

Licensing: The Licensee's Perspective

This case was prepared and written by Professor Suzanne G. Marshall, California State University, Long Beach. Reprinted by permission.

Licensing has become an increasingly important method for a well-known name (designer, cartoon character, athlete) to increase visibility and build the name into a "brand." Licensors "sell" the right to use their name by charging a royalty on the sales of products featuring their name. Licensees increase their earnings by the profit made from producing and selling these products. If the product is successful, both the licensee and the licensor win; at least, that's the way it looks at first glance. Typically, the licensor does win as the majority of the risk is born by the licensee. If the licensee does his job -- makes a quality product, promotes, sells, and supports it adequately -- the licensor earns royalties. But what about the licensee? How does the scenario play out for him or her?

The licensee in this case is Lunada Bay, which produces women's swimwear for Mossimo and, until 1997, for Ocean Pacific (OP). It also produces a line under its own label called Runaway Bay.

Let's examine some of the pitfalls of licensing arrangements from the licensee's perspective. Lunada Bay employees spoke of several areas that cause concern for the licensee which are grouped under four main categories:

1. Lack of control/power: In short, in a licensing agreement, the licensee's success is tied to the decisions made by the licensor.

    - Distribution decision changes: In the mid-1990s, OP executives decided to change their product distribution from specialty stores to low price point department stores. Lunada Bay was opposed to this change of strategy. Lunada Bay's president, Susan Crank, felt that this new policy would alienate OP's customer base and weaken the cache factor of their product. She reasoned that if customers can find a product anywhere, they see it as less valuable. In discussing this issue with OP, Lunada Bay sales reps pressured her not to lose the OP account because a large percentage of their income came from the commissions from the sales of OP-labeled swimwear.

    - Licensor decides to lower product quality (This issue is a corollary to the one above. Typically, changes in distribution to lower price stores necessitates reducing the wholesale cost of the product.): In order to sell to lower price point stores, the product would need to be priced at a lower wholesale price. OP informed Lunada Bay that the suits must cost $7 or less. Lunada Bay had built its reputation on a high quality product and said it could not produce a suit for this price point.

    - Promotional differences: Mossimo's preferred method for promoting his name is to feature head shots with no product. Lunada Bay prefers product shots, as do the department stores who purchase his product. In addition, for one of its catalogs, Macy's wanted to put Mossimo swimwear on the front. This privilege came with a hefty charge -- a move that Mossimo resisted. When Macy's pressured Lunada Bay to comply with its request, Lunada Bay had to support its licensor, whether or not they were in agreement.

    - IPO: In the mid-1990s, Mossimo made the decision to go public. He called to inform Lunada Bay's president. She had misgivings about both the decision and the timing. She felt that part of the appeal of Mossimo's products were the result of his cache factor built from having a product that stores were always chasing, rather than one that was so widely distributed that the original customer base felt alienated. Crank knew that once Mossimo went public, stock managers would increase the pressure to expand the number of Mossimo retail stores and to sell to more department stores. She knew that for her company, it would have to increase production to meet the increased product demand. As she was unsure of the longevity of this increased product demand, increasing production was risky.

2. Lack of visibility

- Not promoting own brand: As a licensee, you are always promoting another's product -- not your own brand. Thus, if you are replaced by the licensor, your business is lost because you are unknown in the marketplace. The licensee finds it difficult to insure its own longevity.

- Licensee's designers feel invisible: When Mossimo swimwear won the Dallas Fashion Award, the Lunada Bay designer, Becky Fortune, who designed the swimwear, went to the award show but sat at the table while Mossimo accepted the award. "It's hard on Becky to have only Mossimo accept the award. She gets to go but Mossimo gets the credit. She's invisible. No one knows she did the designs." Another Lunada Bay designer explained that he increased business for their licensor by 4 percent but still feels unappreciated and invisible. He said, "We're creating an illusion. They told me when I interviewed for the job, I'd be invisible. We promote Mossimo. He has input into the product but to the world, he does it all. We are nothing. We perpetuate his ideas to the world for him."

3. Increased expense

- Royalties: The licensee pays the licensor a percentage of the selling price of each garment sold. Royalties range from a low of 3 percent to 5 percent to as much as 20 percent for avant garde products. The added expense for the licensee necessitates an increase in the wholesale price. Often, the licensor requires the same royalty on the sales of marked down products as well, which is frustrating to the licensee.

- Advertising/promotion: The licensee is required to pay a fee for advertising and promotion of the products to the licensor. Often, the licensee disagrees with the promotional strategy. For example, Lunada Bay disagreed with some of the media placements of OP and some of the sporting events it supported. Lunada Bay felt that this was not the best use of its money.

- Staff duplication: Occasionally, the licensees' employees do not meet the expectations of the licensor and thus, additional staff must be hired to work with a specific licensor, resulting in a duplication of effort and expense.

4.   Multiple "masters"

- Two showrooms: At the CalfiorniaMart (http://www.californiamart.com) where both OP and Mossimo show the products during market weeks, the Lunada Bay staff must set up both showrooms before the market opens, as well as continually run from one floor to another answering questions, working with models, selling, negotiating, and working with sales reps -- a tiring experience for all.

- Differing images: In licensing for several brands, the licensee must kept the images distinct for each licensor. This occasionally presents a problem for the design staff. Distinct products must be developed for distinct target groups. They must promote them in unique ways and sell them to a buyer from different retail store types and target customer groups.

- Various leadership styles: A licensee must please each of its licensors. Some licensors have a "hands-off" policy and allow the licensee to do business as it sees best. Others want total authority -- a voice in every decision. A licensee must juggle the demands of both.

Questions:

1.   What general advice would you give a manufacturer who is considering adding a licensed product to its offerings?

2.   How would you advise the manufacturer to address each of the pitfalls mentioned in the case?

CASE 31

The Lines-R-Too Long

This case was prepared and written by Professor Michelle Smoot Hyde, Brigham Young University. Reprinted by permission.

Barbie Nintendo is the manager of a 22,000 square foot toy store known as a "category killer." The Toys-R-Us store is located in Salt Lake City, Utah, and is the tenth largest store in the company in sales per square foot. Nintendo manages 35 sales associates and ten stockers. She has two assistant managers and one customer service specialist. The volume for her store for 1999 was just over $12 million, an increase of 3 percent over 1998 sales.

It's November 18, 2000, and Nintendo is considering her sales goals (set by corporate headquarters) for the following week. Typically, the Friday after Thanksgiving is the biggest shopping day of the season for her store. Last year's sales for that day alone were just under a half-million dollars. This year, sales are expected to be even bigger. The corporate office has planned a large-scale promotion for the day after Thanksgiving. It has sent a sample of the promotional ad that will run in Thanksgiving papers throughout the country and the prices are unbelievable, especially on the "door busters." The 12-page ad also includes a "will match any price guarantee" that applies to all of its competitors, even discounters like Kmart and Wal-Mart. The ad encourages shoppers to pick up everything they need at Toys-R-Us and guarantees the best deal in town.

As Barbie Nintendo considers her sales goals, she reflects on the chaos that the sale created last year and begins to worry if her store can handle the demand and make the set goal. In 1999, the store opened at 6:00 A.M. with a full parking lot and a bunch of bargain hungry shoppers eager to begin their shopping spree. The door busters were mostly gone by 6:15 A.M. and customers waited in lines for over two hours to make their purchases. The twelve cash registers were all being used, yet lines formed to reach the back of the store. The ringers were slow because they had to match the price of ads from various retailers and checking the competitive ads took extra time. Numerous customers complained and left the store without purchasing their cart-load of goods. Many, although, of the bargain hunters waited patiently to save the additional money on their Christmas purchases. However, Nintendo has no way of knowing if customers returned to her store for repeat sales or if the endless lines scared them away for the season.

The Christmas season is a "make or break" time of year for toy stores, considering that the majority of their sales occur during this time. Some toy stores do up to 80 percent of their annual volume during November and December. There is considerable pressure on Nintendo to have a "Green Friday." Her divisional manager has set Nintendo's sales goals at a 10 percent increase over 1999 due to the expected demand created by the Thanksgiving ad. This worries her because the ad prices are low on many of the sale items and she only has twelve registers to accommodate crowds similar to 1999.

Questions:

1.   How could Barbie Nintendo better accommodate the demand of the Christmas shoppers?

2.   Suggest ways to help Barbie Nintendo achieve her 10 percent sales goals.

CASE 32

Mall Anchors Away! The Franklins Discover Online Shopping

This case was prepared and written by Professor Terence L. Holmes, Murray State University. Reprinted by permission.

Drew Franklin put the box back on the shelf to the protests of his son, Ian. "But Dad! I really want that one, please!" Drew knelt and looked into the pleading face of his six-year-old. He took a deep breath and exhaled slowly, wondering whether buying a model ship was a good idea after all. He and Ian had visited four stores in the past two hours. From Toys "R" Us to Wal-Mart and now this specialty store, Hobby Lobby, the story had been the same -- limited selections and seemingly unlimited prices. In the discount stores, only a model of the *Titanic* was available. Ian and his grandfather -- mostly his grandfather -- had built that model during the summer. In fact, that work was what had triggered Drew's interest in building a model with Ian.

"Ian, this is the fourth store we've been in today. I just think . . ." Drew looked at the box he had just replaced, $30 for a small model of a World War II-era destroyer. "I know this is too much to pay. We just started looking." "You never do anything I want to do!" Ian pouted. Drew thought for a moment. For a marketing professor, he felt at a loss about what to do. Then he remembered the electronic commerce material he had begun gathering in preparation for a new class for the next school year. Many consumer products companies were jumping into direct sales on the Internet after seeing the success of Amazon.com and Dell. He picked up the destroyer model again and read the manufacturer's information. It was made by Tamiya of Japan, but there was no Internet address. He picked up a model of the *Titanic* and read the box. This model was made by Revell-Monogram and featured the company's Internet address (www.revellmonogram.com). Drew put the model back on the shelf and looked at Ian. "Let's go home and look at what Revell has on its Web site. If we don't find anything there, we'll buy one of the models we've seen today, probably that aircraft carrier at Toys 'R' Us." Ian brightened at the thought of doing something sooner rather than later.

Once at home, Drew logged on to America Online, started to type in the Revell-Monogram Web address, and then stopped. "I can't remember how they wrote the name. Was there a hyphen in there?" he asked aloud. Ian just looked at him. "I don't know." Drew had an idea. "Go get your *Titanic* box. Revell made that one so the address should be on there somewhere." Ian returned with the box and Drew found the web site address.

Drew and Ian Franklin visited the Revell-Monogram site and found current models and new releases. They also learned that Revell was a subsidiary of Hallmark Cards. Nowhere on the site was any information about ordering models. Instead, the Revell site had a search engine so the visitor could find dealers nearest their own location. Drew was frustrated and Ian was confused. "Why won't they sell them to us, Dad?" Drew shook his head. "Probably because they're not set up to take small orders, only orders from stores. Or . . ." "Can we go buy that one at the last store we went to today?" Ian interrupted. "Maybe," Drew answered. "First, though, let's try searching for other stores that might sell online." He clicked on the Favorites icon and selected Yahoo! to begin searching, not really knowing what to look for. He, too, was getting confused.

Ian sat and fidgeted while Drew typed several different queries. He typed in "models" and more than 5,000 sites were found. He changed that to "model ships" and Yahoo found about 80 sites. Looking these over, Drew saw that they were nearly all museum-related. Next, he used "hobby shops" and more than 200 sites came up. "Let's look at a few of these," Drew said wearily, "and if we don't see anything, we'll go buy one today."

Several Web sites were run by model building enthusiasts, offering articles, tips, and pictures of their collections. Two sites stood out, however: Model Expo and Internet Hobbies. Drew and Ian looked through the online catalogs, which were exhaustive. At Model Expo, many types of model planes, trains, ships, trucks, and cars were featured. Prices ranged from a few dollars to more that $200 for remote-controlled, large-scale vehicles. One wooden steamboat model featured an optional miniature steam engine and remote control for $250! Drew clicked on "plastic ships" back at the catalog's opening page, because that type of model was what he had assembled thirty years before. He and Ian then saw pictures, descriptions, and prices for dozens of ships available from several manufacturers. Prices were one-half to one-quarter of the prices they had seen in the stores earlier that day.

The story was the same at Internet Hobbies. This online store featured similar prices but more manufacturers than Model Expo. "Still," Drew thought, "the basic types of models I'd like to start with are the same at both places." The *Arizona* and *Missouri* battleships were $7.49 at Model Expo and $6.99 at Internet Hobbies, while the *Nimitz* aircraft carrier was available for $9.99 at Model Expo and $8.99 at Internet Hobbies. "I wonder about shipping costs," Drew thought. He checked and found very similar charges. Interestingly, Internet Hobbies charged a flat rate of $7.50 for orders up to $75; then the percentage stayed at 10 percent of the order. Model Expo had a flat $5 per order charge that rose to 10 percent of the order after $50.

Drew called Ian, who had become bored and had gone to his room to play, back to the computer. After describing more than the six-year-old wanted to hear, he asked Ian for his top choices from what they had viewed. They settled on two models, the *Arizona* and the *Queen Mary* luxury liner. Ian went back to his room. Because of the small order, Drew felt the Model Expo store had offered a better value. He clicked on the icons to place the models in his shopping cart. After quickly checking that Ian was still not around, he also placed the *Missouri* and *Massachusetts* battleships and the *Nimitz* into the cart. These, he thought as he checked out, would be good for Christmas and for Ian's next birthday. The total, with shipping charges, came to $42.38. As he entered the required credit card information, Drew smiled. Although it had taken all day, he was getting five model ships for only $10 more than the cost of the single model he had held in his hands earlier. And no sales tax!

Questions:

1. What actions could bricks-and-mortar retailers take to maintain their sales of such models? Is there a threat to their business? How important is this part of their business?

2. What could Model Expo and Internet Hobbies do to protect their business if Revell-Monogram and other model kit makers decided to sell directly from their Web sites? Why haven't these manufacturers done so?

3. Construct a multi-attitude model for this purchase. Use two bricks-and-mortar stores and the two featured online retailers and at least four appropriate attributes. How could such a model be used by shoppers like Drew and Ian Franklin? How could bricks-and-mortar retailers use the results? Online retailers?

4. How would the collection of sales taxes on electronic commerce transactions change the model-buying scenario in the case?

CASE 33

The Negotiation Ratio

This case was prepared and written by Professor Roger Dickinson, University of Texas at Arlington; and Professor William W. Keep, Quinnipac College. Reprinted by permission.

Negotiation is the process used to resolve the terms under which retail buyers and suppliers conduct business. Although some may think suppliers offer products to retailers on a "take it or leave it" basis, the latter regularly negotiate with their suppliers on product prices, special discounts and incentives, buyback guarantees on unsold merchandise, and so on. This give and take especially occurs with larger retailers, with retailers that sell private brands, and in cases where retailers have high channel power relative to the suppliers.

Much negotiation in retailing is based on the power of the retailer relative to the supplier. In some cases, suppliers have increased their power by tightly controlling distribution in a given geographic area. Thus, Stearns and Foster commonly restricts the sale of its bedding products to the leading department stores in an area and Bulova generally limits the sale of its watches to "better quality" jewelry stores. In such cases, retail buyers are likely to work hard to keep these suppliers content. On the other hand, retailers have increased their power due to the popularity of private brands and the increased importance of large retail chains.

A useful tool in analyzing buyer-seller relationships is the "negotiation ratio." The numerator of this ratio is the quantitative value (expressed in dollars) of the sum of benefits the buyer receives.

The denominator is the cost of those benefits to the supplier. For example, a retailer may be offered a $1,000 cooperative advertising allowance as an alternative to a $1,000 price discount. In computing the negotiation ratio, in this instance, it is important to bear in mind that a retailer may view cooperative advertising as being worth less than $1,000 (due to restrictions placed by the manufacturer on an ad's use) and that a manufacturer may view the additional cost to be less than $1,000 (since the cooperative advertising allowance would be used to replace $1,000 in the manufacturer's current national advertising budget). Under most circumstances, a retailer would seek concessions and a manufacturer would be wise to offer a deal with the highest negotiation ratio (offering the greatest benefit to the retailer per dollar of cost to the supplier).

Let's see how the negotiation ratio could be used to evaluate a group of concessions or a supplier's marketing program. Suppose, for example, a supplier offers to reduce its prices by an additional 5 percent on all purchases during an 18-month period, guarantee to buy back unused merchandise equal to 10 percent of sales, and offer an extended warranty to the final consumer (a two-year versus the standard one-year warranty). In computing the value of these concessions, the buyer would need to make assumptions about the amount of purchases, the percent of unsold stock, and the value of the extended warranty to the final consumer. And to complete the negotiation ratio, the supplier needs to determine the total costs of these concessions.

A supplier may also use the negotiation ratio as a way of fine-tuning its offer. It may find that a three-year warranty has less costs to the supplier but has higher perceived value to a retail buyer than the buyback offer. The costs and benefits of other combinations can also be computed.

The negotiation ratio shares some of the weaknesses of other planning tools and processes. Its value depends on the accuracy of the buyer's and seller's assumptions regarding future outcomes (such as total sales within an 18-month period) and the value of alternative concessions (such as the value of a buyback guarantee versus an extended warranty). In addition, the ratio does not analyze the impact of a concession on future buyer-supplier relationships or on competitive conditions (competitors may demand the extended warranty if this is successfully marketed to final consumers). Furthermore, including additional variables and outcomes in multiple time periods increases the complexity of the negotiation ratio concept.

Questions:

1. Discuss the pros and cons of the use of the negotiation ratio.

2. Describe how the negotiation ratio may be affected by a situation of high channel power by a supplier.

3. Compute a negotiation ratio for the $1,000 cooperative advertising allowance and the $1,000 price reduction example cited in this case. List your assumptions. (Note: There is more than one correct answer.)

4. Compute the negotiation ratio for the second example cited in this case with the additional 5 percent on all purchases during an 18-month period, the buyback guarantee, and the extended warranty. (Note: There is more than one correct answer.)

CASE 34

Old Navy: A New Tune for an Old Sailor

This case was prepared and written by Professor Richard C. Leventhal, Metropolitan State College. Reprinted by permission.

Despite the success of The Gap, Inc.'s traditional stores (which include The Gap, GapKids, babyGap, and Banana Republic stores), the firm's top executives recently determined that the firm still did not serve a large proportion of its potential customers. For example, The Gap, Inc.'s research showed that middle-market shoppers (with an annual income of $20,000 to $50,000) rarely buy in regional shopping malls, where Gap has most of its stores. As a result, The Gap, Inc. was unsuccessful in attracting the middle-market apparel market, one that spends about $75 billion a year on clothing and accessories.

Thus, in 1994, The Gap, Inc. (whose Web site is http://www.gap.com) opened its first Old Navy Clothing stores. The stores were positioned to combine the style and quality of the chain's The Gap stores, with the low prices and large selection of an apparel-based discounter. Old Navy aimed at consumers who traditionally shopped at either department stores (such as Sears and J.C. Penney), or at discounters (such as Wal-Mart, Target, and Marshall's). The Gap, Inc. initially converted 48 underperforming Gap stores around the country to Old Navy stores, as a market test of this concept. The test not only convinced the firm that its initial belief about a large untapped market was correct, but also taught it some valuable lessons about the middle-market shopper. For example, the popularity of multiple-item purchases of basic commodities (such as socks and underwear in bulk) led to Old Navy's bundling these items in packages of three or more and to providing shopping carts.

At first glance, a typical Old Navy Clothing store resembles many other apparel-based discounters with its concrete flooring, exposed duct work and insulation, shopping carts, and central checkout counters. However, upon a closer look, several key differences are apparent. Old Navy's clothing is displayed in a manner more similar to The Gap and Banana Republic stores or Ralph Lauren/Polo and Tommy Hilfiger sections in department stores. Old Navy's layout includes high-school lockers that are stripped to bare metal. The lockers, with several doors missing, serve as attractive display cases. Old Navy conceals its overhead storage space with canvas flaps that lend a somewhat nautical quality to the store. The checkout counters are made from polished press board and galvanized metal, instead of Formica plastic-laminated surfaces that are so popular at discounters. Unlike much apparel that is usually sold in this price range, Old Navy clothing is more distinctively styled. It also uses many more sales promotions than The Gap, Inc.'s other chain units. Thus, Old Navy might offer customers a gift with each purchase, such as a baseball hat or dog tags with the Old Navy logo.

Old Navy uses less costly fabrics, wider production allowances, and lower rental costs to enable it to reduce its costs and its prices. Although acrylic and wool blends are popular for sweaters at Old Navy, The Gap and Banana Republic stores sell mostly wool sweaters. The seam allowances at Old Navy are less consistent, so a shopper may have to try on several pairs of jeans in the same style and size to find one that fits best. Store rental costs are also reduced by situating in shopping strips or "power" centers, built around a Wal-Mart or a Home Depot, rather than in more expensive regional shopping center locations. As a result, Old Navy's price points can be as much as 40 percent lower than at The Gap.

A potential threat to The Gap, Inc. is that Old Navy may cannibalize (take away) sales from The Gap, Inc.'s other retail units. To protect against such cannibalism, The Gap, Inc. has worked hard to reposition The Gap and Banana Republic. As of 2000, there were more than 520 Old Navy stores; in that year, Old Navy accounted for 35 percent of The Gap Inc.'s overall retail sales. Some retail analysts estimate that sales at Old Navy sales will soon exceed those at the Gap.

Questions:

1. What are Old Navy's competitive advantages and disadvantages versus full-line discount stores such as Wal-Mart, Kmart, and Target?

2. Should Old Navy participate in scrambled merchandising? If yes, how? If no, why?

3. Has Old Navy defined its target market adequately? Explain your answer.

4. How can The Gap, Inc. prevent Old Navy from cannibalizing sales from its other store units?

CASE 35

Patagonia: An Environmentally-Focused Specialty Retailer

This case was prepared and written by Professor Gail H. Kirby, Santa Clara University. Reprinted by permission.

Patagonia was founded by Yvon Chouinard in 1957 in Ventura, California, as an outlet for the sale of his hand-made mountain climbing equipment. In 1972, Chouinard began to manufacture, distribute, and sell apparel items aimed at consumers who had a passion for mountaineering,

143

skiing, snowboarding, and other outdoor sports. From the firm's beginning, Chouinard insisted that his clothing be as technically sound as his climbing gear. The firm prides itself on field testing its products under extreme conditions. Today, Patagonia has a large mail-order operation, with 15 company-owned U.S. stores, 3 in Europe, and 5 in Asia/Oceania. Its Web site is (http://www.patagonia.com).

Chouinard believes Patagonia exists to serve as a model for corporate responsibility. His long-standing philosophy has been to run the firm along "self-sustaining" principles. In 1984, Patagonia began tithing -- distributing 10 percent of pre-tax profits (now about 1 percent of sales) to preserving and restoring the natural environment via a program it calls an "earth tax." Grants are distributed twice a year, generally to small grassroots groups that seek to protect a part of a forest, a stretch of river, or a specific species. Chouinard adds that "no one can wait for government to impose a levy, because by then the planet will be beyond repair." Chouinard foresees an era when people "will consume less but consume better."

Patagonia is a classic ecologically aware, socially progressive, entrepreneurial firm. Its unique mission can be seen from the job description for a new chief executive officer (CEO) that appeared in the *Wall Street Journal*. The ad said the firm required a CEO who could surf and kayak, was committed to open communication and high product quality, who agreed that Patagonia should continue to pledge 1 percent of sales to controversial environmental and social causes, wanted slow growth, and was committed to reducing environmental pollution. Ultimately, Patagonia decided to divide the responsibilities among a four-member team with each member responsible for his or her area, but with major decisions made collectively.

Beginning in spring 1996, Patagonia made a commitment to use only organically grown cotton in their cotton garments. The company switched to organic cotton because it believed the pesticides, herbicides, and other chemicals used in growing traditional cotton are detrimental to our soil, air, and ground water. This affects not only humans, but also birds and wildlife. In contrast, its certified organic cotton is grown using such natural methods as the introduction of beneficial bugs that eat harmful insects, the use of cover crops to control weeds, and the use of compost and other natural fertilizers. These methods are rarely used in place of traditional chemicals.

The change to organic cotton has its costs. Organic farming is not only more labor-intensive, but also additional costs are incurred in the ginning, spinning, and knitting or weaving of organically-grown cotton due to the small runs. These higher costs forced Patagonia to raise the prices of its cotton apparel items by $2 to $10. Patagonia devoted several pages of its Spring 1996 catalog explaining its switch from traditional to organic cotton.

Besides the switch to organic cotton, Patagonia has an Internal Environmental program, where two-thirds of its waste is reused (through reusing boxes, recycling paper, and having composts at its main offices). Patagonia has even created a fabric recycling program, including the development of a post-consumer recycled cloth.

A quick flip through a Patagonia catalog reveals differences between it and most other apparel catalogs. For example, the Patagonia catalog contains broad product descriptions of the fabrics, the construction of inner and outer layers, the applicability for given activities (such as mountaineering, skiing, and snowboarding), and weight of each good. The environmental influence is immediately apparent. Organic cotton goods and post-consumer recycled fabrics are clearly labeled. And a two-page spread on the inside front cover of a recent catalog, for example, was devoted to describing toxic chemicals that were released from a hazardous waste dump and their affect on local residents' quality of life.

Questions:

1. What factors in our physical environment have been important in shaping Patagonia's marketing strategies? Comment on Patagonia's approach.

2. Assess Patagonia's decision to utilize company-owned specialty stores as its major store-based retailing channel.

3. Discuss the pros and cons of Patagonia's selling selected lines of merchandise through department stores.

4. Describe the pros and cons of Patagonia's establishing factory outlets for excess stock and off-season merchandise.

CASE 36

Planning a Pool & Wellness Facility

This case was prepared and written by Professor Patricia M. Anderson, Quinnipiac College, based on input from the trustees and staff of the Shoreline Foundation in Guilford, Connecticut; and MBA students Eric Blumenthal, Dyan Grant Enright, Tim Elliott, Cathy Laydon, Dale Norton, and Brenna McVety. Reprinted by permission.

The Shoreline Foundation is a group with 1,100 members, in Guilford, Connecticut, that has used borrowed facilities (such as a neighboring school, camp, or retirement community pool) for swimming, exercise, day camp, and after-school enrichment programs. Virtually all members live in one of four suburban communities: Branford, North Branford, Guilford, and Madison. Members come from one of two demographic groupings: older adults or families with children.

After raising the necessary funds, Shoreline's directors have decided to build their own facility. Although they have identified a site, they need to decide what type of facility best meets the needs of their members and the residents of the surrounding communities. A professor teaching a marketing research class at a nearby college agreed to do Shoreline's research as a class project. About 1,300 questionnaires were sent to foundation members and other relevant groups in the target area. Responses were coded by town, and 174 usable responses were received within two weeks of the mailing (the deadline for incorporating responses into the data base).

Table 1 summarizes the survey results. The first two questions allowed multiple responses. Question 1 obtained data on selected pool and other activities by household member. Question 2 dealt with the planned frequency of use for the pool and the other facilities. Questions 3-6 asked when facilities would be used, maximum commuting time, maximum yearly membership dues, and likelihood of joining. Questions 7-9 provided data on place of residence, gender of respondent, and the respondent's current membership category.

An analysis of the questionnaires by the class revealed that respondents who would use the facility for multiple seasons were willing to pay more than those who planned to use the facility for a single season. In general, the greatest differences in responses were between individual and family member segments; those willing to pay a higher annual fee were family members who planned to use the facility multiple times per week. Family members also differed from individual members by age (family-member respondents had an average age of 48 years; the average age of individual-member respondents was 68); annual fee they were willing to pay (family members would pay $400 versus $250 for individual members), and maximum commuting time (individuals would commute up to 18 minutes; families would commute a maximum of 16 minutes).

There were several significant differences among respondents by place of residence. Guilford/Madison respondents would pay up to $400; the maximum fee for other respondents was $300. Guilford/Madison residents were also less likely to use the facility in the summer (55 percent versus 63 percent for other residents). Lastly, Guilford/Madison residents were on average "very likely" to join, whereas other respondents were "likely" to join.

Questions:

1. Evaluate the data in Table 1.

2. Define the target market for the Pool & Wellness facility based on the data in Table 1.

3. Develop a fee schedule for the Pool & Wellness facility. Your schedule should reflect individual and family memberships and summer only memberships.

4. What additional data does Shoreline need to plan its facility better? Where can it be obtained?

Table 1
Responses to Questions About a Shoreline Pool & Wellness Facility

1. In what pool activities would you and/or household participate in the planned facility? Please answer for yourself and household. If you will not use pool, skip to question 2.

	Men	Women	Children/Young Adults				
			Preschool	Elem.	Jr. High	High School	Total
Swim Lessons	5	19	28	76	12	4	144
Swim Teams	2	4	5	46	16	16	89
Swim Laps	64	66	2	13	8	8	161
Recrectional Swim	87	101	19	81	36	23	347
Aquatic Therapy	18	38	0	0	0	0	56
Mild Exercise	20	46	1	2	1	1	71
Vigorous. Exercise	87	0	0	1	3	3	94
Water Sports	10	7	2	18	16	10	63

2. How often would you and/or your household members participate in these activities at the planned facility?

	Monday-Friday		Sat.-Sun.	1-2 days	1-2 days	
	1-2days	3-5 days	(weekends)	a month	a year	Total
Pool Activities	103	78	93	22	1	297
Land Aerobics	24	24	16	5	2	71
Open Gym (basketball)	36	21	36	11	1	105
Equipment Room--Nautilus	44	46	42	12	4	148
Wellness Programs	35	13	15	12	2	77
Multipurpose room for:						
Adult Meetings	9	2	4	12	6	33
After School--ages 4-12	44	0	14	8	1	67
Teens--ages 13-18	13	11	23	8	3	58

3. When would you or household members use the facility you described in questions 1 and 2?

(97) Summer; (149) Fall; (149) Winter; (142) Spring; Weekdays (M-F): (37) 6-9 A.M.; (60) 9:00 A.M.-Noon; (33) Noon-4 P.M.; (87) 4-7 P.M.; (44) 7-10 P.M.; Weekends (S-S): (31) 6-9 A.M.; (57) 9 A.M.-Noon; (68) Noon-4 P.M.; (48) 4-7 P.M.; (19) 7-10 P.M. *NOTE*: 48 would go 3 seasons; 87, 4 seasons; 43 chose one time slot; 87 chose two.

4. The most time you would commute to facility is:

(16) 10 minutes; (89) 15 minutes; (51) 20 minutes; (9) > 20 minutes.

5. The most you would pay per year to use this "Pool & Wellness" facility is.

(16) under $250; (74) $250-$300; (58) $301-400; (15) $401-500; (136) family membership; (36) individual membership. (Respondent chose one.)

6. How apt are you and/or your household members to join this facility?

(95) Very; (51) Likely; (19) Somewhat; (1) Not very; (2) Not at all.

7. You live in: (25) Branford; (16) North Branford; (79) Guilford; (32) Madison; (20) Other.

8. Gender: (21) Male; (98) Female; (24) Both (Some answered for household).
Age: 16 to 40: 26%; up to 47: 51%; up to 64: 75%; up to 96: 100%.

9. Membership category?
(86) Day Camp; (35) Aquatic Fitness; (4) Swim Lessons; (7) Enrichment Programs; (4) Walking Club; (12) Other.

CASE 37

The Prince of Cruises: Choosing a Store Location

This case was prepared and written by Professor Allan R. Miller, Towson State University. Reprinted by permission.

Michael Charlotte has been a travel agent for over 15 years. For the last seven, he has worked as an outside agent specializing in cruise travel and tours, primarily for groups (such as members of senior citizen groups, fraternal organizations, and religious-based organizations). As an outside agent, Charlotte operates as an independent contractor for the travel agency, Go Somewhere Vacations. Charlotte and his agency divide the commissions on bookings he generates, generally about 10 percent of the vacation price. In contrast, an inside agent is an employee of the agency and is usually paid on the basis of a salary.

Go Somewhere Vacations is the largest travel agency in Bel Air, Maryland, which is a residential town located about 30 miles north of Baltimore. The agency is on the main street in Bel Air's central business district.

Recently, Charlotte decided he wanted to fulfill his lifelong dream of operating his own agency. He has a moderate base of clients who he feels would continue to book their vacations through him. In addition, Charlotte feels he can expand his client base. As in the past, he plans to continue specializing in cruise travel and tours. He wants to call his agency The Prince of Cruises.

Charlotte is considering three alternative types of locations for his new agency: a home/office arrangement (in which the agency would be operated out of a converted garage space in his home), leasing a store site in a local Bel Air shopping center (about one-quarter mile from Go Somewhere Vacations' current location), or renting space in an office building in downtown Bel Air. Regardless of the location chosen, each alternative would require approximately a $17,500 investment for office furniture and furnishings, computer equipment and modem hookups, and telephone systems and wiring. However, each alternative has totally different characteristics in terms of its trading area and customer traffic.

By operating the agency out of his house, Charlotte would save rental expenses. The home/office arrangement would also enable him to conduct business on weekends and in the evenings, when most agencies are closed. However, the ability to attract walk-in clients would be severely limited due to the absence of signs, the lack of pedestrian traffic, and the need to comply with Bel Air's strict residential zoning regulations. The home/office setup would also require an additional $7,000 expense to properly wire, panel, and insulate Charlotte's former two-car garage. Lastly, Charlotte would have to develop an arrangement with an authorized travel agency to be able to sell airline tickets from a home office.

Although the home/office alternative would take him a longer time to develop a new client base, Charlotte's expenses would be lowest under this alternative. Charlotte projects commissions of

$40,000 for the first year if he operates out of his home, half of which would be derived from his existing client base. Once the minimum required client base is developed, he could then move to another location.

Secondly, Charlotte could rent retail space in a local Bel Air shopping center at an amount of approximately $4,000 a month. The agency would have to be open seven days a week and evenings (under shopping center rules). This facility would require at least two agents and a receptionist-office manager. Charlotte forecasts that this location could generate 100 walk-ins per day, of which five could be converted to bookings. He also feels that bookings will be higher at this location than at any other due to the ability to attract street traffic, closeness to other stores, and the trading areas of adjacent stores.

The third option is to rent an office in the downtown business district. This office would be open during the week, Monday to Friday. An additional staff of at least two would be necessary, an agent and a receptionist-office assistant, with resulting salary and benefit expenses of $50,000 a year. Rent and other office expenses would run approximately $2,500 a month. It is projected that 50 visitors a week would walk into the office. Mike feels he can convert three of these walk-ins. This type of location would be ideal in attracting business travelers, but the average commission on domestic air travel is significantly less than on cruises.

Questions:

1.   Develop a methodology for estimating the trading area of each of these locations.

2.   Which location could be considered a parasite store? Explain your answer.

3.   Describe how Charlotte could assess the level of saturation of Bel Air in terms of travel agents.

4.   Which location do you recommend? Explain your answer.

CASE 38

The Racquet Club

This case was prepared and written by Professor Joe K. Ballenger, Stephen F. Austin State University. Reprinted by permission.

Well, at least, the sauna still works!

Introduction -- The Community

The Racquet Club is a full-service workout facility in a small town in the Southwest. The town has a population of about 40,000, with around 60,000 in the county. A regional university with a population of approximately 12,000 is also in the town and serves as its largest employer. There are several medium-sized manufacturing facilities in the area, as well as a medium-sized medical community. The town is about 20 miles from another similar-sized town, and one and one-half hour's drive from a couple of larger cities.

Positioned at the Top

The Racquet Club has several competitors, but none of them would be considered as direct (head-on) competition. The smaller competitors are positioned toward niche markets based on specific athletic activities. For example, there is the Muscle Gym for more serious male and female body builders. On the university campus is the Wellness Activity Club, which is mainly set up for the university-sanctioned student athletes and faculty members. The university itself, with its kinesiology classes and activities, serves as a competitor also. These last two are less expensive for the users than the private Racquet Club and the Muscle Club because they are subsidized by the state, and student fees cover most of the other costs to join and use.

On the other side of town (about 6 miles away) is the Living Branch, a higher-end "wellness" facility that specializes more in massage and life-style therapy products. Within the last two months, another private competitor, Dancing for Life (one which was just down the street from the Racquet Club and that mostly appealed to women who preferred aerobic dancing), went out of business. Several of these customers joined the Racquet Club after the closing.

The Racquet Club -- Merchandise Mix

Opened in 1982, the Racquet Club is a full-service health and fitness facility. It is the largest club of its kind in the county with annual revenues of $480,000, and a total membership of 1,250. Since it opened, there have been only two successive owners (the founder and one other) before the current ownership team took over in May 1999. Sales have grown about 50 percent since May with a 40 percent increase in the number of members. The Racquet Club offers a merchandise mix that is both wide and deep. Some of the equipment and the complementary services offered are as follows:

- Modern weight rooms with free weights and machines.
- A modern cardio/aerobics machine room with several types of equipment.
- Personal trainers for an extra fee.
- Four racquetball courts, in need of some repair and maintenance.
- An Olympic-sized swimming pool.
- A hair salon.
- Two large rooms for yoga, ballet, aerobic dancing, and other classes.

- Separate locker rooms for men and women with wet areas (hot tubs, wet saunas, and a coed dry sauna).

The prices per month range from $45 for a single membership to $70 for a family. All of this sounds pretty good, doesn't it? But, there is another side to the Racquet Club.

Healthful Health Club?

There may be some clouds on this sunny horizon, however.

Following are several comments that have been overheard in the men's locker room and around the club since the new owners took over the business:

- "Do we have to pay extra to get some soap in here?"
- "Of course, the hot tub is cold; they didn't pay the electric bill."
- "I wonder if the women's locker room smells this bad."
- "Yeah, they replace a shower nozzle with a cheap one, and they think that fixes the problem."
- "The ladies' aerobics class must be over. We have no cold water in the shower now."
- "Have they ever heard of maintenance in this place?"
- "I told them there were ants near the hot tub, but they don't listen to me." (This comment was from an employee.)

One customer did a little research on his own. He placed a used bandage in the shower stall to see how long it would stay there. The bandage was not removed from the shower for three weeks!

Questions:

1. Which services offered at a health club would be considered expected services and which would be considered augmented services? Explain your reasoning for each service you list.

2. In the context of the case, explain the difference between cleanliness and perceived cleanliness.

3. List and explain five reasons why customers would patronize a health club.

4. What types of marketing research tools could be used to determine what customers think about their experience at the Racquet Club?

CASE 39

Sanchez Property Management

This case was prepared and written by Professor Michael R. Luthy, Bellarmine University. Reprinted by permission.

Sanchez & Sons Contractors recently completed construction of its newest property, the Desert Cactus Shopping Mall in Southwest Arizona. This is a fully enclosed, three-level structure with a food court composed of six eateries and five anchor stores: Dillards, J.C. Penney, Best Buy, Famous Barr, and Toys "R" Us. Of the remaining 124 spaces for smaller individual stores, 95 are currently leased, and mall management is negotiating with several parties for the remaining ones. The physical layout of the facility is such that there is a large central open area on the ground floor (called the central galleria) that currently is envisioned as a rest area for mall patrons and will not be developed into stores.

Although the Desert Cactus facility will not have its official grand opening until the September 23-24, 2000 weekend, the property management firm operating the mall has received letters and telephone requests from the following groups to use Desert Cactus facilities:

- The Tucson chapter of the American Red Cross has asked to use the center court area for a three-day blood drive just prior to the Thanksgiving holiday in preparation for the additional blood needs the community will have during the Thanksgiving through New Year's period.
- The Salvation Army has requested permission to set up donation kettles with bell ringers at the major entrances to the mall during operating hours for 24 days starting December 1, 2000.
- A representative from Taos Junior High School has asked that foreign language classes from the school (French, Spanish, German, and Japanese) be allowed to sing holiday carols two evenings during the month of December in the mall's galleria as part of their class assignment.
- Several of the area's Boy Scouts of America troops are seeking permission to set up a staffed display booth during Scouting Week in October to attract new members and explain what Scouting is all about.
- The local Girl Scouts troop has asked permission to set up a booth to sell cookies to the public during its cookie/fundraising drive early next year.
- A local religious group has requested access to the mall to distribute literature and possibly solicit donations.
- Several local and regional fire departments would like to set up several displays during Fire Safety Week in September in the mall and want permission to use a portion of the parking lot for the Firefighters Olympics, which is a demonstration-oriented activity designed to educate the public as to what firefighters do.

Although the above requests are the only formal ones received to date it is likely that other groups and organizations will approach mall management with similar requests.

Questions:

1.   Should Sanchez management allow any non-tenant groups or organizations to use mall facilities? Explain your answer.

2.   If it does, what kinds of activities should or should not be permitted?

3.   What will be the costs to, and the responsibilities of, any groups or organizations allowed to use the facilities?

4.   Should there be a maximum amount of time any one group or organization may use the facility in a given period (calendar year) or a limit to the number of groups using the facility at one time? Explain your answer.

5.   How will you explain your new policy to tenants who may object?

CASE 40

Service Orientation (or Service Differentiation) in China

This case was written and prepared by Professor Kenny K. Chan, California State University, Chico. Reprinted by permission.

Over the past 20 years, the People's Republic of China (PRC) has experienced tremendous economic growth. In just two decades, for example, per capital gross domestic product quadrupled. There were thought to be 60 million Chinese consumers earning at least $975 (U.S.) a year in 1993; some in the more affluent areas of China are at least as affluent as the average consumer in Malaysia, Thailand, or Indonesia. Some analysts predict that the number of affluent consumers in China could soon rise more than threefold to 200 million. Due to increases in consumption, the market for consumer durables in China (as measured in terms of both purchasing power and consumption) will be larger than most of the present East and Southeast Asian markets today.

Only a few years ago, Chinese shoppers had no choice but to shop at crowded state-run department stores or local Chinese-owned shops. Typically, Chinese shoppers were denied such expected customer services as being permitted to try on or return merchandise. Chinese salespeople were typically unmotivated and inattentive. Pre-purchase sales assistance was minimal, at best; and post-purchase service was nonexistent.

Since until recently, China was a seller's market, there was little incentive for firms to have a service orientation. Simply put, retailers were able to sell their goods and services despite the lack of a market orientation on the part of Chinese retailers. Of equal importance is the prevailing management philosophy that places a greater strong focus on short-term profit over long-term strategic competitiveness. This mentality is certainly not conducive to the adoption of a service orientation in retailing.

Lastly, many Chinese consumers do not expect to receive a service orientation from retailers. A 1999 survey of 900 residents from Guangzhou, Shanghai and Beijing confirmed that many consumers in the PRC associate "marketing" with the physical aspects of it and might not appreciate the sudden emphasis of a service orientation. See Table 1. In summary, respondents placed low importance on value-added services, did not view service intangibles as important elements of the product, and were relatively unimpressed with such "western" niceties as return policies, formal complaint procedures, or attentive service. The two most important service attributes to PRC consumers are quality guarantees and value pricing.

There are some signs that PRC consumers' buying behaviors are changing. For example, shoppers with "bulging wallets" are beginning to demand a better shopping environment. They avoid department stores that do not have such amenities as escalators and central air-conditioning. This has forced some shopping districts to renovate their facilities and to rethink their service orientation.

The new emphasis on service delivery quality has surprised many multinational retailers that have aggressively targeted the China market with retail facilities. These retailers hope to gain a competitive edge on the established state-run and other local Chinese-owned stores through providing service. These retailers are conducting research to examine what services Chinese consumers now view as expected versus augmented and how they can most effectively use a service orientation to build a sustainable competitive advantage in China.

Questions:

1. How does improving customer service help build a sustainable competitive advantage?

2. What differences in Chinese culture and tradition may have inhibited PRC customers from welcoming a service orientation with open arms?

3. Aside from the consumers, what other controllable and uncontrollable variables must marketers bear in mind when incorporating services in their retail strategy in China?

4. Borrowing from the traditional product life cycle model, design a plan to introduce service excellence as part of your retail mix in China.

Table 1
Most Important Criterion When Selecting Retail Stores

Service Attribute	Frequency	Percent
Quality guarantees (assurance)	461	51.2
Value pricing	142	15.8
Product quality	68	7.6
Convenient location	52	5.8
Attentive and friendly service	35	3.9
Assortment	30	3.3
Store reputation	29	3.2
Comfortable atmosphere	25	2.8
Service-centered	22	2.4
Salespeople attitude	9	1.0
Discounts	7	0.8
Thank you call/note after substantial purchase	7	0.8
Formal complaint procedures	5	0.6
Referrals from friends and relatives	4	0.4
Customer assistance	4	0.4
Total	900	100.0

CASE 41

SpaceJams: The Jam of Retailing

This case was written and prepared by Professor Connie Ulasewicz, San Francisco State University. Reprinted by permission.

SpaceJams is the name of a start-up company designing and manufacturing a line of outerwear modeled after the actual space suits worn by NASA astronauts. The owners, Ted and Sam, are new to the garment industry. Their background is in the field of law where they both currently practice. Ted has always been a space buff. As his kids grew older, they were sent off to space camp in the summer and really got excited about the possibilities of space exploration. Their interest in space led to the purchasing of all products that were space related: books, videos, T-shirts, sheets, and towels. However, Ted found there was a real void in the market for garments that replicated the actual space suits worn by astronauts. He sincerely felt that most kids would love the idea of playing and keeping warm in a specialty space snowsuit. Ted started researching the NASA space suits and the idea of manufacturing children's snowsuits based on their design. At the same time, his partner Sam explored the market potential for this product.

Knowing little about the traditional channels of retail selling, Sam contacted some friends who owned a children's toy store, as well as a children's buyer from a department store in his area. Both of these contacts thought the idea for snowsuits, based on space suits, was good but they wanted to actually see the products before they would give more feedback. The potential buyers explained that if they were to purchase, initial buys would be small until there was customer response and they further explained that payment terms were 30 to 60 days after receipt of the merchandise. Sam also explored the idea of Internet sales. He felt strongest about this sales method for he knew all of the national sites for space buffs and figured he could link the SpaceJams site up to theirs.

Meanwhile, Ted located a coat manufacturer that could replicate what he wanted. His biggest challenge was finding a manufacturer that could model the plastic circular hose openings on the front of the suit. Ted was also very clear that he wanted to include all the seaming, zippers, and patches that were on the real space suits. The sampling process began; after three attempts over a six-month period, a prototype was developed that met his specifications. In order to negotiate what he felt was a reasonable cost of $55 per snowsuit, Ted was required by the sewing contractor to place an initial order for 600 pieces. Although it felt risky with no firm retail orders to back up the production, Ted felt sure the suits would sell and placed the order.

With Sam's sales and marketing research in hand, along with the SpaceJams prototype, the two owners decided to design a Web site to generate product interest and eventually, sales. Their product photographed well and their Web site looked quite sharp. Because their product was only available in the one color of white, it was easy to photograph and display on the Web. They decided to set the retail price for their product at $110. With a $55 first cost from the contractor for the initial 600 pieces, this gave them a 100 percent markup. They felt the product looked like it was worth $110.

To their enjoyment, customers agreed with the price and the product and started to place orders. Within one month, they had sold 100 pieces. Excitement continued as retail stores began to show an interest in carrying the SpaceJams product. The stores inquired as to what the wholesale costs would be, their expectation being that they would purchase the snow suits at $55 and retail them at $110. This is when Sam and Ted started to panic. If they sold stores the SpaceJams suits at $55, they would just be covering their expenses. If they wholesaled their product at $75, the storeowners said they would be retailed at $150. This was $40 over what they sold for on the company Web site and the stores were not pleased with being undersold. They clearly needed to develop a strategy to further the sales growth of their product. Could they keep everyone happy?

Questions:

1.   Should Sam and Ted continue to wholesale and retail their SpaceJam suits from their Web site? Explain your answer.

2. Are Sam and Ted required to have the same retail price on their Web site as in the retail stores that carry their product? Explain your answer.

3. What special sales strategies might Sam and Ted have for working with retail customers?

4. Should there be different considerations relative to expanding their business to the television retailer or the catalog retailer? Explain your answer.

CASE 42

Thomson's Computer Books

This case was prepared and written by Dean Raymond A. Marquardt, Arizona State University-East; and Lynn Samsel, doctoral candidate, University of Nebraska-Lincoln. Reprinted by permission.

Thomson's Computer Books has a reputation for stocking a wide selection of computer books and manuals, including hard-to-find books and technical material. Its customers generally are computer "nerds" who seek specialized texts that are not available elsewhere and consumers seeking computer manuals for current or older versions of major software packages. Many of the latter desire manuals that go beyond the documentation provided by software producers.

Thomson's two stores are about three miles apart in Plainview, a Midwestern city of 200,000 residents. Thomson's North location, consisting of 2,300 square feet, opened October 1, 1997. It is at the center of town in a high-traffic strip center. Four employees work there, three full-time and one part-time. The store has a toll-free number for out-of-town customers, and makes 36 percent of sales to people who live out-of-town (even out-of-state). By appealing to people in a four-state area, Mae and Bill Thomson have been able to lift the sales of this store. Thomson's North has a good following among purchasing agents in the Plainview business community as "the" source for hard-to-find items. Although 35 percent of sales are to institutions, Thomson's North is steadily building its retail traffic as people learn of it and discover its low prices.

Thomson's South store has 1,000 square feet and opened November 1, 1999. It is across the street from a community college with a small bookstore of its own. The neighborhood surrounding the community college is old and stable -- a lower-middle-class residential area. One full-time employee works at the South store. Unlike Thomson's other shop, the South store has no real institutional business. The South store is located in a small strip center with four stores and eight parking spots. Although the South store did some fairly effective radio advertising when it opened, its recent advertising via flyers sent to previous customers and new radio spots has had little effect on store traffic or sales. Table 1 contains selected financial data for the two stores for 1998 through May 2000. Table 2 shows a profit-and-loss statement for each store for 1999.

Bytes 'N Books (BNB) is Thomson's main competitor. It is in a strip shopping center in the central part of the city and has gross sales exceeding $1 million. BNB charges slightly higher prices and occupies 5,000 square feet. Like Thomson's North, BNB has a toll-free phone number for out-of-town customers. BNB also has a separate section for parents to leave their children to entertain themselves with educational software and video games while the parents shop elsewhere in the store. BNB's sales are 20 percent institutional and 80 percent retail. Unlike both Thomson's stores, BNB carries a full line of greeting cards, some stationery items, and some magazines.

Because 40 percent of Plainview's population owns computers or uses them on the job, Mae Thomson believes the sales potential for Thomson's Computer Books has not been fully reached.

Table 1
Selected Financial Information for Thomson's Computer Books -- North and South Stores
(January 1, 1998 to May 31, 2000)

North Store	1998	1999	Five Months Ending 5-31-00
Net sales	$309,876	$371,864	$137,594
Cost of goods sold	213,008	235,762	87,372
Gross profit	98,868	136,102	50,222
Operating expenses	124,555	127,376	54,804
Net profit (net loss)	(25,687)	8,726	(4,582)

South Store	1998	1999	Five Months Ending 5-31-00
Net sales	----	$3,827	$ 8,998
Cost of goods sold	----	2,635	5,831
Gross profit	----	1,192	3,167
Operating expenses	----	7,568	9,250
Net profit (net loss)	----	(6,376)	(6,083)

Note: The North location opened on October 1, 1997 the South store opened on November 1, 1999.

Table 2
Profit-and-Loss Statements for Thomson's Computer Books -- North and South Stores
(Fiscal Year 1999)

	North Store	South Store
Sales		
Software manuals/learning aids	$157,920	$ 526
Programming books	53,106	520
General computer books	50,214	1,225
Technical manuals	44,969	934
Wiring diagrams	19,448	264
Computer disks	12,859	217
Computer accessories	5,926	64
Miscellaneous	27,422	77
Total sales	$371,864	$3,827
Total cost of goods sold	235,762	2,635
Total gross profit	$136,102	$1,192
Operating Expenses		
Wages	$ 39,310	$ 1,954
Rent	31,880	1,045
Advertising and promotion	9,958	256
Freight and postage	6,340	45
Interest expense	5,242	----
Insurance	3,759	----
Taxes and permits	3,541	11
Telephone	3,425	186
Legal and accounting	3,180	332
Utilities	2,999	116
Operating supplies	1,760	165
Office expense	----	3,117
Miscellaneous	15,982	341
Total operating expenses	$127,376	$ 7,568
Total profit (loss)	$ 8,726	($6,376)

Questions:

1.   Analyze the financial data in Tables 1 and 2.

2.   What are the difficulties in evaluating the data in Tables 1 and 2?

3.   What should Mae and Bill Thomson do next with the North and South stores? Give separate recommendations for the two stores.

4.   Offer short-run and long-run financial goals for each of the two Thomson's stores. Explain your answer.

CASE 43

Trawick Hotels

This case was prepared and written by Professor Michael R. Luthy, Bellarmine College. Reprinted by permission.

Trawick Hotels and Resorts is a national chain of hotel properties based in Denver, Colorado. The company owns and operates three brands of properties, each of which caters to a different market segment. Trawick Resorts represents the high end of service, location, and price. Trawick Traveler is the organization's budget, no-frills offering, and Trawick Hotels is the firm's mid-price chain that mainly appeals to business travelers.

The Peoria Trawick is a new facility that has recently opened. This hotel features 254 deluxe rooms, each with voice mail, data ports, iron/ironing boards, coffee makers, hair dryers, and cable television. A free breakfast is included for all guests. The hotel's onsite facilities include an indoor pool and whirlpool, a business center (with fax, photocopy, and computer teleconferencing capabilities), a gift shop, free parking, and a concierge service. Corporate meeting rooms are also available.

The general manager has presented you with the forms designed to measure guest satisfaction with its overall hotel and room service experience. See Exhibits 1 and 2, respectively.

Exhibit 1
Guest Satisfaction Property Survey

We are committed to making your stay a 10! So we need your honest comments to let us know what we are doing right, and where we must improve. Please give us just a moment of your time to share your comments with us. Thank you.

Please be sure to fill the response oval completely with an X.

	EXCELLENT									POOR
Check-In Experience	(10)	(9)	(8)	(7)	(6)	(5)	(4)	(3)	(2)	(1)
Cleanliness upon Entering the Room	(10)	(9)	(8)	(7)	(6)	(5)	(4)	(3)	(2)	(1)
Maintenance and Upkeep	(10)	(9)	(8)	(7)	(6)	(5)	(4)	(3)	(2)	(1)
Overall Breakfast Experience	(10)	(9)	(8)	(7)	(6)	(5)	(4)	(3)	(2)	(1)
Friendliness of Personnel	(10)	(9)	(8)	(7)	(6)	(5)	(4)	(3)	(2)	(1)
Overall Satisfaction	(10)	(9)	(8)	(7)	(6)	(5)	(4)	(3)	(2)	(1)

If you marked any of these categories less than a 10, please let us know what we need to do to earn a 10. Thank you.

_____
_____
_____
_____

Were there any employees you would like to recognize?

_____
_____
_____

Room Number_____   Departure Date _____
Name _____
Address
_____
City _____   State _____   Zip _____
Phone Number   (   ) ____--_____

Exhibit 2
Room Service Survey

Room Service
Your comments are especially valued as they help us continuously improve our room service. Please take a moment to complete the enclosed survey. We would appreciate if you would leave the completed form either on your food tray or at the front desk. Thank you.

Date _____ / _____ / _____   Time _____ AM / PM
Room # _____   Server _____

Optional:
     Name _____
     Address_____
     City _____   State _____   Zip _____
     Phone Number (   ) _____

Please rate your room service experience today from 5 to 1; circle one choice in each category:

	Excellent	Good	Average	Fair	Poor
Operator Promptness	5	4	3	2	1
Operator Courtesy	5	4	3	2	1
Prompt Delivery	5	4	3	2	1
Courteous Delivery	5	4	3	2	1
Quality of Food	5	4	3	2	1
Order Correct	5	4	3	2	1
Value for Price Paid	5	4	3	2	1
Overall Room Service	5	4	3	2	1
Dining Experience	5	4	3	2	1

Additional comments:

_____
_____
_____

Thank you for ordering Room Service. Our goal is your complete satisfaction. If we can be of any further assistance, please call us at extension 7523.

If you have any additional comments or suggestions as to how your experience today could have been improved, please write:

Peoria Trawick Hotel
Attention: Director of Food & Beverage
1313 Main Boulevard
Peoria, IL 60022

For your dining comfort and convenience, our service includes tray pickup. Please call Room Service when finished with your meal so we may pick up your tray.

Questions:

1. Why are these surveys designed the way they are? What is the rationale for these specific questions?

2. With time before the hotel opens, if you were asked to redesign these two surveys, what would you add? What would you eliminate or change?

3. Design a response card/survey for use at the hotel's restaurant.

CASE 44

Venice Island: A New Retail Development Opportunity

This case was prepared and written by Professor Lisa A. Henderson, Drexel University. Reprinted by permission.

Manayunk, located just seven miles north of Center City Philadelphia, is one of the city's chicest shopping and entertainment districts. Once a center for textile production situated along the landmark Manayunk Canal, it is also recognized as a national historic district. On most weekends, Main Street, the primary avenue of retail trade, is filled with visitors from the surrounding areas of Pennsylvania and New Jersey. Because of its unique blend of shops and restaurants, Manayunk has become a destination shopping location. During their stroll along Main Street, shoppers may browse for antiques, shop at the Nicole Miller boutique, enjoy lunch at a sidewalk café, or even see a movie.

With a village atmosphere reminiscent of Soho in Manhattan, Main Street offers a shopping experience paramount to any shopping mall. A unique variety of both merchandise and service retailers share this fashionable address. In total, there are over 65 one-of-a-kind boutiques, galleries, and home furnishings retailers. In excess of 30 restaurants and eateries provide a unique dining experience to visitors and local residents. With United Artists at one end and the Arroyo Grille at the other, this neighborhood business district stretches for over one mile. The wide variety of service retailers found in Manayunk includes beauty salons, interior design studios, fitness centers, and a movie theatre. Fashion apparel, accessories, athletic gear, antiques, fine art, and home furnishings comprise the broad assortment offered by merchandise retailers. The mix of apparel retailers range from independent designer boutiques, such as Nicole Miller, to corporate chain stores, such as Banana Republic. Manayunk also offers a diverse selection of home furnishings retailers. Home Grown, which features hand-made crafts, and Pottery Barn, which offers branded home furnishings, are just a few examples. In addition, there are a wide variety of restaurants to suit any taste. In addition to Japanese, Italian, Mexican, Southwestern, and French restaurants, a cozy selection of pastry and coffee shops can all be found along Main Street.

In contrast to many neighborhood business districts, the activity in Manayunk extends beyond the close of the shopping day. As many shoppers are selecting their final purchases, crowds are just beginning to arrive at Main Street's entertainment venues. With its extensive array of restaurants, bars, and nightclubs, Manayunk enjoys the reputation of Philadelphia's hottest nightspots.

Manayunk's unique architecture and picturesque landscape is rooted in a rich historical background. The Lenni Lenape Indians, the first to inhabit the area, called the now Schuylkill river "Ganshewchanna" or "noisy stream." They referred to the valley it passed through as "manaiung," meaning "our place of drinking." When English settlers arrived 1824, they adopted the name of Flat Rock. The name was later changed to Manayunk, meaning, "where we go to drink." In this newly established town, settlers built textile mills and used the water from the Schuylkill River to supply power to the factories. By the end of the century, Manayunk factories were used to produce cotton, wool, carpet yarns, silks, hosiery, dress goods, cashmere, jeans, and other articles. They were even used for the production of Civil War uniforms. In 1912, the Manayunk canal was linked to a major waterway transportation system. This provided businesses with increased trade and further established Manayunk as a center for textile production. This early mode of transportation utilized mules to pull the barges of textile production down the Manayunk canal. These canal towpaths are now used as pedestrian trails, which provide recreation and enjoyment to Manayunk residents.

Venice Island, separated from Manayunk by the historic canal, runs parallel to Main Street. The distance of the island spans twice the length of the shopping district area. Venice Island, despite the extensive commercial development on Main Street, has primarily existed as industrial property. Based on the overwhelming success of Manayunk, the city has now decided to develop Venice Island as a residential and commercial property. Plans for the two-mile-long island include 36,000 square feet of retail space, 1,278,000 square feet of residential space, two recreational parks on either side of the island, and a connecting riverside pedestrian trail. In addition, there are plans for six bridges at various places on the island, which will provide access to and from Main Street. See Exhibit 1.

Exhibit 1
Plans for Venice Island

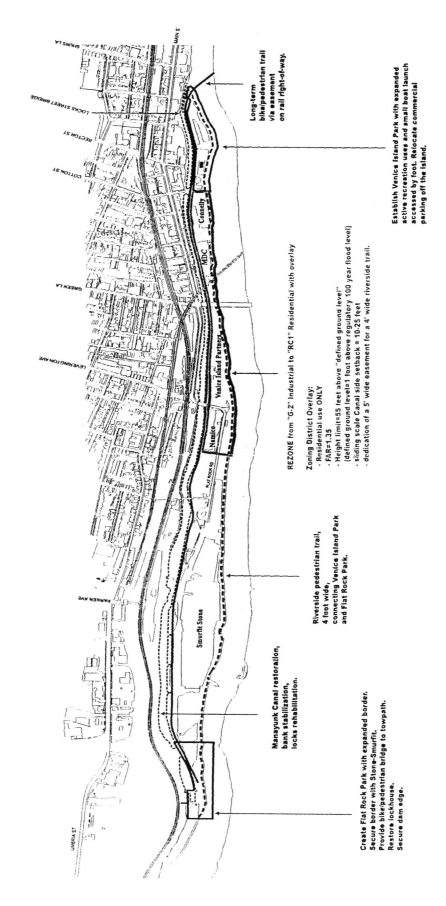

Create Flat Rock Park with expanded border.
Secure border with Stone-Smurfit.
Provide bike/pedestrian bridge to towpath.
Restore lockhouse.
Secure dam edge.

Manayunk Canal restoration,
bank stabilization,
locks rehabilitation.

Riverside pedestrian trail,
4 foot wide,
connecting Venice Island Park
and Flat Rock Park.

REZONE from "G-2" Industrial to "RC1" Residential with overlay

Zoning District Overlay:
- Residential use ONLY
- FAR=1.35
- Height limit=55 feet above "defined ground level"
  (defined ground level=1 foot above regulatory 100 year flood level)
- sliding scale Canal side setback = 10-25 feet
- dedication of a 5' wide easement for a 4' wide riverside trail.

Long-term
bike/pedestrian trail
via easement
on rail right-of-way.

Establish Venice Island Park with expanded
active recreation uses and small boat launch
accessed by foot. Relocate commercial
parking off the island.

165

Questions:

1. Analyze the direct competition located in Manayunk and identify strategic opportunities.

    Key merchandise store competitors include:

Apparel	Shoes/Accessories	Home Furnishings
Women's	*Men's/Women's*	Cosmopolitan Home
Abbe's Place	Benjamin Lovell	Home Grown
Allure	Mainly Shoes	Palais Royal Linens
Banana Republic		Platypus
Best Friends		Pottery Barn
Ma Jolie Atelier		Restoration Hardware
Next Boutique		
Nicole Miller		
Paul Hian Designs		
Public Image		
Worn Yesterday		

    Women's and Men's
    Smith Bros
    Something's Different
    SportsWorks
    Neo Deco
    Men's
    Pyramid

    Children's
    Turtledove

    In addition, there are 12 galleries and craft stores, 3 gift and stationary stores, 4 jewelry stores and 1 florist on Main Street.

2. Based on your analysis, what location format should be used for the new Venice Island development?

3. The 36,000 square feet of retail space on Venice Island will accommodate approximately 36 retail outlets at an average of 1,000 square feet. What mix of retail ownership would you recommend? What assortment of service and merchandise retailers would you recommend?

4. Develop a promotional mix for the new Venice Island retail development.

CASE 45

Walgreens: Where Does it Locate?

This case was prepared and written by Professor Susan C. Strickler, South Dakota State University. Reprinted by permission.

Sioux Falls, South Dakota's largest city, is located in the southeast corner of the state. While Sioux Falls' population is currently 124,000, the city has an estimated consumer market of 350,000 people (this includes consumers from nearby Iowa and Minnesota). These shoppers come from a distance of 80 miles to the west and north and 40 miles to the east and south. Sioux Falls' economy has experienced tremendous growth over the past 15 years as can be seen from the development of regional medical centers, credit-card service centers, and retail store establishments

While there are several prime retail areas within the city, the most important retail location in South Dakota is the intersection of 41st Street and Louise Avenue. Over 50,000 cars travel on 41st Street on a daily basis. Residential growth is located to the south of 57st Street. Light industrial and business developments are occurring in the northern area of the city. Several low-income housing developments have been scheduled to begin in the northeast. Two elderly housing developments have also been recently completed at 49th and Louise and at 66th and Louise.

Many mass merchandisers and discount retailers have retail outlets within the city limits of Sioux Falls. These include Target (1 store), Wal-Mart (1 store), ShopKo (2 stores), Kmart (3 stores), Lewis Drug (5 stores), and HyVee Food and Drug (5 stores). With the exception of Target, each of these retailers has a pharmacy operation within each store.

Walgreens' customer service philosophy focuses on customer convenience and accessibility. Walgreens seeks to have a pleasurable shopping environment and to run each store in an efficient manner. Unlike some of its competitors, Walgreens targets consumers who use a drug store more than five times a month. Walgreens attracts the higher frequency shopper by better understanding his or her wants and needs. For example, market research by Walgreens found that more frequent drug store shoppers view shopping convenience as more important than price. Walgreens' research also found that its pharmacy is the number one generator of consumer loyalty. A third important research finding is that households headed by 55- to 64-year-olds spend 34 percent more on medicine and medical supplies than the average U.S. household; households headed by 75-year-olds and older members spend 86 percent more than the average household.

Currently, Walgreens operates 2,894 stores in 40 states and Puerto Rico. It plans to open its 3,000th store during spring 2000, and to have a total of 6,000 stores by 2010. In addition to bricks-and-mortar locations, Walgreens fills prescriptions through its Web site.

Recently, Walgreens has expressed an interest in opening additional stores in the Sioux Falls area. Walgreens' strategy is to saturate the Sioux Falls market by opening as many locations as is economically feasible. Walgreens feels that a market saturation strategy is especially appropriate for an older population that may not be very mobile. Walgreens has currently found three locations in Sioux Falls to implement its market saturation strategy. It is also reviewing two to three additional locations based on such factors as pedestrian and vehicular traffic, concentration of the elderly shoppers, and closeness to key competitors. With the exception of a location at 10th and Cliff, where Walgreens was rejected by the property owner, Walgreens has successfully negotiated for the other properties.

Exhibit 1 depicts all the major retailer locations within Sioux Falls. The map uses the following letters to represent each major retailer: WG = Walgreens, T = Target, W = Wal-Mart, S = ShopKo, K = Kmart, L = Lewis, and H = HyVee.

Given Walgreens' market penetration, where would you locate two more sites in Sioux Falls?

Questions:

1. Is the Sioux Falls market appropriate for Walgreens' expansion plans? Explain your answer.

2. Why is the Sioux Falls market so interesting to Walgreens?

3. What is the optimal location for Walgreens in Sioux Falls? Why?

Exhibit 1

Locations of Major Chain Pharmacies in Sioux Falls

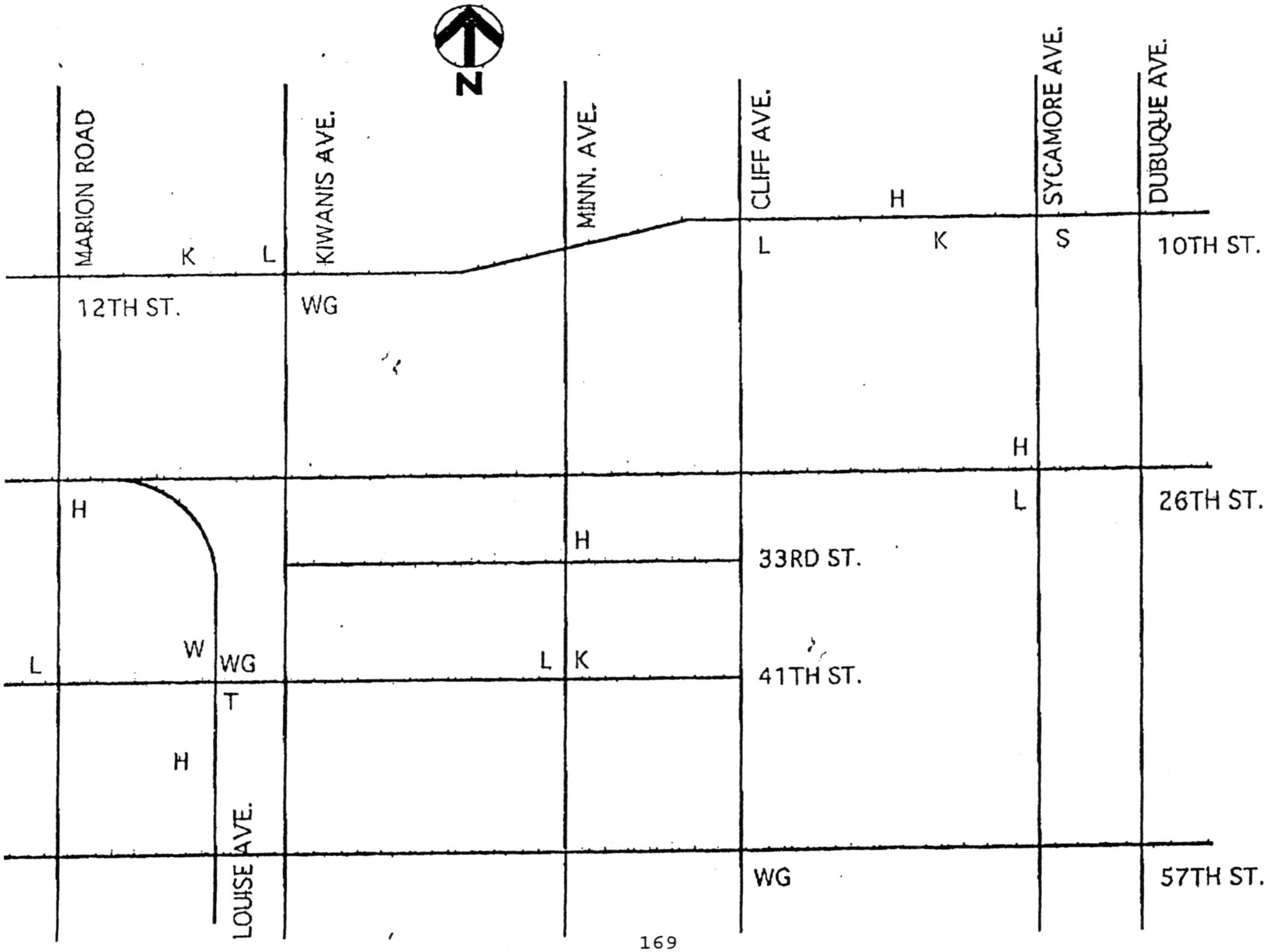

169

CASE 46

Williamson-Dickie: Using Dual Channels in the Apparel Industry

The material in this case was prepared and written by Stan Rapp, Cross Rapp Consulting Group; and Professor Jack Eure, Southwest Texas State University. Reprinted by permission.

For years, there seemed a belief existed that a manufacturer distributing through traditional retail stores could not also market products via direct marketing. More recently, however, manufacturers' use of dual channels (traditional retailers and direct marketing) has became a standard practice in the sale of such diverse goods and services as computer hardware and software, financial services, hotels, and airline travel. IBM and Compaq, for example, sell their computers through direct channels at the same prices as their traditional retailers. A dual distribution strategy lets a manufacturer directly target key customers, stimulate repeat purchasing activity through special offers to loyal customers, and builds long-term relationships.

Williamson-Dickie (W-D), the maker of Dickies brand of work clothes, has effectively made the transition from just using indirect distribution through retailers to a dual channel strategy (that includes direct marketing). Steve Lefler, W-D's president, reasoned that besides boosting domestic sales, a good catalog would stimulate international sales. The catalog would also reduce reliance on W-D's superstore-based customers, many of whom only stock W-D's best-selling lines. Athough W-D's smaller stores still stock a full product line, their importance has dropped.

In the early 1990s, W-D faced a series of problems in developing its mail-order operation. When W-D initially planned its mail-order catalog operation, this strategy was seen by its small independent retailers as a form of unfair competition. Furthermore, W-D needed to generate and maintain a final customer data base to successfully pursue its direct marketing strategy.

The first W-D catalog, mailed in 1991, was an unattractive piece sent to consumers who had requested additional product information. Soon thereafter, W-D realized the need to reorganize its phone call center, add additional operators, and totally redesign the catalog. Lefler soon noticed that the number of customer inquiries it typically received was insufficient to support the expense of an attractive four-color catalog. And W-D had to devise and maintain a customer data base.

Lefler and his colleagues decided to use W-D's carton labels, packing slips, and inspection forms to communicate the existence of the firm's mail order catalog. Although the inside pocket of each W-D garment always contained an inspection slip, in the past nothing else was ever communicated on the reverse side of the slip. So, W-D added the statement: "Ask your dealer about other Dickies products or call (toll-free number) for a free catalog." This simple tactic resulted in W-D's compiling a data base of nearly 400,000 names. W-D even runs an annual sweepstakes (in which winners are drawn from 3 million entry blanks that are inserted in garments and from entry blanks available at 6,000 displays in retail locations) to build and update its data base. W-D currently mails out 270,000 catalogs at a time, with a 6 percent response rate.

Of the retailers that resented W-D's move to a dual distribution strategy, many were small firms that were already hard-pressed by giant superstore competitors. Thus, W-D took special care in dealing with these retailers. For example, Lefler sent each complaining retailer a letter explaining how the company was not taking sales from its small dealers. The letter explained that W-D's mail-order prices were slightly higher than at traditional retailers. In addition, W-D explained that its mail-order customers are first referred to a local retailer if W-D's inventory management system verifies that this retailer has recently ordered the purchaser's preferred style and color in the buyer's size. According to Lefler, 98 percent of the callers do not order from the catalog, but are inspired to go to their local store to try on a new item.

According to a retail consultant, even though W-D's dual distribution strategy can be easily adapted to other firms, few companies are now taking advantage of this opportunity.

Questions:

1. Comment on W-D's decision to use a dual distribution strategy. What should its goals be? Why?

2. Describe the steps W-D should have gone through in planning and implementing its direct marketing strategy.

3. Did W-D do an adequate job of reassuring retailers that dual distribution could benefit them? Explain your answer.

4. What other steps should W-D take to deal with disgruntled retailers?

CHAPTER-BASED EXERCISES

Student's Name _____
Class/Section _____
Instructor _____

CHAPTER 1 EXERCISE

Distribution Decisions for a New Stereo Store

The owner of a new stereo store is uncertain with regard to several distribution decisions, including these:

- Should merchandise be purchased directly from manufacturers or should a leading wholesaler be sought out?
- What assortment of brand names and models should be carried?
- What kind of promotion should be used?
- Who should be responsible for storing, shipping, and price-marking merchandise?
- What kind of support (e.g., advertising, displays, etc.) should be expected from suppliers?
- Should exclusive, intensive, or selective relationships with suppliers be sought?
- How should store fixture suppliers be selected?

The store owner has hired you to help with these decisions.

Questions:

1. What information must you obtain from the store owner before making any suggestions?

2. What criteria would you consider for each of the decision areas noted in this exercise before making recommendations?

Student's Name _____
Class/Section _____
Instructor _____

CHAPTER 2 EXERCISE

Brian Laine Insurance: Planning a Service Business

Brian Laine worked for Prudential Insurance as a salesman for eight years after graduating from college and enjoyed all of them. However, he reached the point where opening an independent insurance company became important. So in 1995, Laine opened his own company. Because of the firm's small size and unknown name, Brian Laine realized he would have trouble selling commercial insurance and decided to concentrate on homeowners' insurance.

In the beginning, Laine selected names from a local telephone directory to solicit business. Although progress was slow, this endeavor proved profitable by 1997, especially with renewals and referrals. During all of this time, Laine concentrated on advertising in the Yellow Pages and newspapers and appeared before local civic and consumer groups. Several group life-insurance plans developed out of these appearances.

Laine encouraged homeowners to buy all their insurance from him, and several did. He has also taken pride in promptly answering all phone calls, in following up with his insurance companies, and in suggesting additional coverage based on life cycle changes that affect each client (e.g., the birth of a child or a client's need to consider retirement planning).

During late 1998, premiums reached the point where Brian was able to match his previous income with Prudential. In fact, Laine is now facing these lucrative alternatives: (1) To open a large office and hire a full-time staff. (2) To merge with a slightly larger company. (3) To bring his accounts with him and return to work as a salesman at Prudential.

Questions:

1.   Has Brian Laine done a good job of planning his service strategy? Explain your answer.

2.   How can Laine better utilize the principles of relationship retailing?

3.   Develop a customer service strategy for Brian Lane.

4.   What are the pros and cons of each of the alternatives now confronting Brian Laine?

Student's Name _____
Class/Section _____
Instructor _____

CHAPTER 3 EXERCISE

Bill Janis: Evaluating a Retailing Opportunity

Bill Janis, a recent college graduate, is seeking to purchase a business with the financial assistance of his father. Bill has always been an entrepreneurial type, is fascinated by retailing, and has a high energy level. He is keeping in mind these criteria in the search for an appropriate opportunity.

- Bill does not want to become a franchisee. He does not want to pay franchising fees, contribute to a national advertising program, or have his ability to manage a business restricted.

- Bill wants to purchase an established business that has not met its full potential. In this way, the risks of failing will be reduced. He will consider a moderately successful firm that has absentee management or a complacent owner; this will allow him to apply his talents.

- Bill wants a service-based business, as service retailers are growing at a faster rate than goods-based retailers. A service firm also requires less inventory investment.

- Bill wants a business with some barriers to entry. He does not want to look at upholstery and carpet-cleaning firms or sixty-minute film processing studios, as they require low capital investments and relatively little training. He wants to avoid oversaturation and price competition.

- Bill wants to own the real estate on which his firm is located. This will allow him to use depreciation as an expense, to control maintenance, and to be free from concerns about lease renewal.

Questions:

1. Comment on Bill's criteria for selecting a retail opportunity.

2. What goods/service category would you recommend to Bill?

3. Do you think that Bill is ready for his own business? Why or why not?

4. What kinds of information should Bill acquire before making a decision?

Student's Name _____
Class/Section _____
Instructor _____

CHAPTER 4 EXERCISE

Aerobics Unlimited: Evaluating Two Franchisees

Aerobics Unlimited is a franchisor with 45 outlets in the eastern United States. Its franchises have been considered an attractive investment by franchisees for a variety of reasons: its good reputation and proven track record, availability of company assistance, and low initial investment ($5,000-$15,000) vs. several hundred thousand dollars or more for a hamburger franchise. In one large state, the average Aerobic Unlimited franchise recently reported profits of about $40,000 (excluding the owner's salary).

Despite the overall success of Aerobics Unlimited, the firm has had some failures among its franchisees. Common problems leading to franchise failures are: the franchisee giving up on a store location too quickly, uncleanliness, lack of good instructors, low dedication to the store, not complying with company requirements, etc. In contrast, successful franchisees have hard-working owners, who are persistent and strictly adhere to company policies.

Exhibit 1 shows the characteristics of a successful and unsuccessful franchise operation.

Exhibit 1
A Successful Versus an Unsuccessful Aerobics Unlimited Franchise
(during a recent year)

	Successful Outlet	Unsuccessful Outlet
Income:	$ 455,000	$ 257,000
Expenses:		
Owner's salary	30,000	30,000
Payroll	144,500	90,000
Rent, property tax	38,750	38,000
Royalty (rent override)	15,300	8,600
Franchise fees (advertising)	63,000	28,200
Utilities and sanitation	28,800	18,250
Taxes and insurance	19,650	14,300
Maintenance and repair	20,800	12,500
Interest	17,600	5,000
Depreciation	23,000	12,000
Miscellaneous	15,400	7,500
Total expenses	$ 416,800	$ 264,350
Profit (loss)	$ 38,200	$ (7,350)

Questions:

1.	What are the advantages of an Aerobics Unlimited franchise in comparison with operating an independent aerobics business?

2.	Evaluate Exhibit 1.

3.	What suggestions can you make to Aerobics Unlimited (as the franchisor) based on Exhibit 1?

4.	What are the risks of becoming an Aerobics Unlimited franchisee?

Student's Name _____
Class/Section _____
Instructor _____

CHAPTER 5 EXERCISE

A Traditional Department Store Decides to Confront Off-Price Chain Competition

Dennison's is a traditional department store chain located in suburban Chicago that is confronting heavy competition from off-price chains. In recent years, a number of developments have occurred which have caused the store's apparel division merchandise manager to be especially concerned:

- The number of off-price chains within 4 miles of Dennison's main store has recently increased to 5. In addition, the move to better locations by some off-price chains is threatening several of its branches' apparel business.

- The off-price chains are becoming more aggressive in buying. In some instances, they are contracting with manufacturers for current season merchandise instead of concentrating on irregulars, end-of-season goods, and odd lots.

- Dennison's customers frequently complain that Dennison's merchandise is available at 30-40 per cent savings elsewhere. Dennison's will match any store's price for identical merchandise.

The division merchandise manager has been asked to draw up a plan to respond to the increased competition from off-price chains. Among the options to be considered are to:

- Refuse to buy from merchants who also sell to off-price chains.
- Focus on high fashion and on Dennison's fashion leadership niche.
- Increase service levels and store atmosphere appeals.
- Compete head-on through special sales, clearance centers, shopping center cooperative sales, and early markdowns.

Questions:

1. What advantages does Dennison's have in comparison to off- price chains?

2. Should Dennison's continue to match off-price chain pricing on identical merchandise when a customer complains?

3. Evaluate each alternative strategy.

4. Which strategy should Dennison's pursue? Why?

Student's Name _____
Class/Section _____
Instructor _____

CHAPTER 6 EXERCISE

Tops Luggage: Planning and Implementing Web Site

Tops is a luggage manufacturer that has sold much of its luggage on a private-label basis to large chain-based luggage retailers and major department stores. While Tops' luggage features high-quality construction and materials (such as fabric, zippers, and wheels), the Tops brand has no recognition since its retailer customers use their own brand designation on Tops' products.

Tops is now planning a Web site to sell luggage under its own brand. Tops assumes that the site sill give Tops access to additional geographic markets, will help develop its brand name, and will reduce dependency on several key accounts.

Tops' site will feature two of Tops' most popular models: a valet pack which enables a user to store two jackets and slacks on a hanger, and carryon luggage model featuring wheels made from in-line skate components and multiple compartments. Tops plans to promote is Web site through one page ads in magazines with major travel–related magazines. The ads will feature testimonials from airline crews as to the durability of Tops luggage.

Tops plans to include the following on its Web site:

- The history of the company
- A description of the materials used and construction details for its models
- A color chart
- An order form with an easy-to-use shopping cart
- A listing of important travel-related sites such as airline listings, weather reporting, and so on.

Questions:

1.   What are the pros and cons of Tops' proposed retail strategy?

2.   Develop suggestions for improving Tops' proposed site using the following criteria: cross merchandising, customer service, free shipping, one-click ordering, and selection.

3.   How can Tops avoid channel conflict with its current retailer customers due to its proposed dual channel of distribution strategy.

Student's Name _____
Class/Section _____
Instructor _____

CHAPTER 7 EXERCISE

Peter's Antiques: Regaining Lost Customers

Warren Peters has owned and operated an antique business in southern Florida for twelve years. Until recently, Warren was quite successful. However, annual sales have fallen despite increases in inventory costs. As a result, no profits are currently being earned.

When Peters opened, he carried only antique clocks and furniture. As business improved, he added rifles, china, silverware, millinery, and art. His shop is located on a shopping strip neat a major highway. Tourists and local residents alike patronize the store, which is noted for its low prices.

Originally, 70 per cent of Peters' sales were to local people. Only 30 per cent were to tourists and 20 per cent to local customers. This change has not occurred for the other antique dealers. A profile of local patrons and tourists is shown in Exhibit 1.

Exhibit 1
Description of Antique Customers

Characteristic	Local Patron	Tourist
Age	52 years old	42 years old
Education	12.7 years	14.6 years
Family size	3	4
Family income	$22,000 yearly	$33,000 yearly
Occupation collar worker	Retired or white-	White-collar worker
Possessions apartment, t.v., washer, dryer	Average owns home, fine camera, stereo	Average owns a
Item purchased silverware	Rifle, furniture	Pot-bellied stove,
Average purchase	$125	$200

Questions:

1. Comment on the demographic profile of the antique customers shown in Exhibit 1. What other information is useful to Peters?

2. How can Peters reduce his customers' perceived risk? Be sure to comment on each type of perceived risk in your answer.

3. How does the consumer behavior process operate for antiques?

4. Make several consumer-behavior based suggestions for Peters to improve his business.

Student's Name _____
Class/Section _____
Instructor _____

CHAPTER 8 EXERCISE

A Jewelry Store Turns to Research

Walter Kravat worked as a manager for a major jewelry store chain until two years ago when he started his own store. Situated in a high-traffic neighborhood shopping center, the store has a new storefront, display cases, fixtures, and carpeting. Walter has positioned the store as a full-service, full-markup retailer. Besides Walter and two salespersons, the store has a full-time jeweler who is responsible for repairs, jewelry redesigning, and insurance appraisals. The store is an authorized dealer for a wide selection of watch brands such as Seiko, Pulsar, Movado, and so on.

After being in business for two years, the store has not met sales expectations. Walter, after talking in-depth with several friends, feels that several factors may be jointly responsible for the lack of success.

First, consumers are likely to judge a jeweler's pricing policy based on discounts offered on watches. Walter discounts Seiko and Pulsar brands by 10 per cent. Department stores typically offer these brands at 20-30 per cent off list during special sales. Furthermore, many discount houses feature "gray market" items (watches not imported or guaranteed by the U.S. authorized importer of these brands) at 30-50 per cent off list. Walter will not stock these "gray market" watches, since they were not designed for the U.S. market.

Second, department and discount stores in Walter's area are very aggressive in their jewelry advertising. In many cases, however, their standard prices are no lower than Walter's regular selling prices. Nevertheless, these stores are significant competitors due to their credibility, and offering of money- back privileges (Walter allows exchanges but no cash refunds).

Third, operating one store does not allow Walter to use media available to department stores, discount stores, and retail catalog showrooms.

Walter wants to research the feasibility of three strategies which he feels may help increase sales. These strategies are: (1) To create store traffic through the use of special promotions. One week per month, the store would feature special purchases, markdowns on slow-moving merchandise, and so on. (2) To develop a "designer selection." This will consist of antique, estate, and one-of-a-kind jewelry and watches. (3) To become more price aggressive by quoting prices on the phone, allowing bargaining, and matching department store sale prices.

The strategy selected will be based on marketing research findings. Walter is willing to pay a consultant $500 per day for up to 7 days plus up to $5,000 for expenses in conjunction with the study.

Questions:

1. Develop a marketing research proposal to present to Walter.

2. Outline project costs and time requirements for your research proposal.

3. Develop a questionnaire to define the problem area and evaluate alternative strategies.

4. Describe how you plan to analyze the data from the questionnaire responses.

Student's Name _____
Class/Section _____
Instructor _____

CHAPTER 9 EXERCISE

Trading-Area Analysis for a Home Improvement Chain

Made-to-Last Paint is a 25-store home improvement chain featuring paint, hardware, lumber, do-it-yourself supplies, and seasonal goods.

The chain's stores span four counties in two states; the distance between the furthest stores is about 80 miles. All stores are located in affluent suburban areas. Generally, stores are in freestanding locations with ample parking.

Made-to-Last Paint is in the process of re-examining its trading-area strategy as a result of a preliminary analysis by a retail consultant. Parts of the consultant's report follow:

There appears to have been no rational strategy on which store locations have been based. Among my preliminary findings are:

a. High waste in advertising. About 40 per cent of the readers of the firm's major newspaper for advertising, *The Daily Sun*, live further than 5 miles from a current Made-to-Last Paint store.
b. That many poorly performing stores could have been identified prior to their opening. Three of 7 poorly performing stores are located in areas with apartment houses and cooperatives. Dwellers in these units are not inclined to purchase paint, hardware, lawn supplies, and snow removal tools. Another store is the sole unit in its state. Two other units are located in extremely affluent areas served by landscape gardeners, carpenters, and general contractors instead of do-it yourselfers.
c. That executives in the firm are unfamiliar with census tract data.

The firm is now convinced that it needs to regularly use trading-area analysis. It also realizes that an overall evaluation may involve store elimination in some markets, and store expansion in others.

Questions:

1. How would trading-area analysis differ for a chain than for an independent retailer?
2. What are the steps that Made-to-Last Paint should pursue in evaluating its trading areas?
3. What characteristics of trading areas would you assume would be associated with success for Made-to-Last Paint? Explain your answer.
4. Is the *Census of Population* a more appropriate source of trading area data than the *Survey of Buying Power* for Made-to-Last Paint? Explain your answer.

Student's Name _____
Class/Section _____
Instructor _____

CHAPTER 10 EXERCISE

Nancy's Flowers: Site Selection Within A Regional Shopping Center

While Nancy Adams is considering regional shopping center locations for a proposed florist shop, she is not sure they are optimal. Advantages of such locations are an excellent pedestrian traffic base, good affinities with clothing and gift shops, and the benefits of shopping center promotions at such times as Mother's Day, St. Valentine's Day. On the other hand, Nancy recognizes that many of the benefits of a regional shopping center location would not directly affect her store:

- The Christmas/New Year's seasonality has less of an effect on a florist than a general merchandise retailer.
- The high rent may be wasteful in light of anticipated mail/phone business.
- Traffic congestion, parking difficulties, and not being able to own a location are other disadvantages.

Nancy is evaluating two locations in the same regional center. The first is in a "boutique mall" in a separate wing of the center. Other "boutique mall" tenants include a wine shop, a gourmet cheese store, an antique clock store, and a ladies' high-fashion clothing store. The boutique mall is adjacent to the main mall and has direct access to the mall via a series of doors. Advantages of this location are slightly more convenient parking, and a rent 30 per cent below that of a main mall location. The proposed site would be about 1,500 feet from a major department store. The second site is within 300 feet from the major department store in the main wing, adjacent to a women's shoe shop and a camera store.

Each site requires about the same renovation expense, has similar lease restrictions and terms (except for the rent differential), is of similar size, and will be available within 8-10 months.

Questions:

1. Do you recommend that Nancy locate in a regional shopping center? Why or why not?
2. Develop a checklist of factors for Nancy to consider in assessing each location.
3. How would your checklist in question 2 differ if it were for a central business district location?
4. Of the two specific sites in a regional center being investigated by Nancy, which would be better for her? Why?

Student's Name _____
Class/Section _____
Instructor _____

CHAPTER 11 EXERCISE

Mystery Shoppers Visit the Microwave Oven Department at Kelly Stores

Kelly Stores, a large chain of appliance stores, regularly employs mystery shoppers to evaluate sales force product knowledge, enthusiasm, and selling skills. The mystery shoppers are part-time personnel who pose as sales prospects and evaluate sales personnel without the salesperson's knowledge of their true role.

Recently, Kelly Stores decided to utilize mystery shoppers for microwave oven purchases, because of the product's industry sales growth and Kelly's declining market share. A report based on the data compiled by two mystery shoppers who evaluated 30 different salespeople at a total of 20 chain locations was writ- ten by Kelly Stores' vice-president of operations. Portions of the report follow:

- Few salespeople understand the safety features incorporated into microwave ovens and are able to adequately explain radiation emission levels, safety interlock features on doors, etc.
- 40 per cent of the salespersons did not explain the ideal uses of microwave ovens.
- Few salespersons tried to ascertain consumer needs. Almost all tried to sell the top-of-the-line, largest capacity model, even to singles.
- Most salespeople exerted undue pressure for customers to purchase an extended guarantee. This tended to undermine confidence in the newly-purchased product. On the other hand, accessories for microwave ovens were not pushed by any salesperson. These accessories are stocked by Kelly Stores. A trade magazine reported that the average microwave oven customer buys $75-$100 in accessories shortly after the oven purchase.

Questions:

1. Develop an evaluation form for mystery shoppers to rate the sales force.

2. Evaluate two presentations by microwave oven salespersons in stores close to your house using the form. (The form is to be completed after the sales presentation).

3. What problems does the mystery shopper program identify for Kelly Stores?

4. Develop a plan to correct these problems.

Student's Name _____
Class/Section _____
Instructor _____

CHAPTER 12 EXERCISE

Operating Noble's House

Ed and Virginia Noble own and operate a small gardening supplies store called Noble's House in a middle-class suburban area. The Nobles have been in business for seven years and have made a moderate profit, in addition to their combined annual salaries of $75,000, each year.

As of this date, Noble's House has these balance sheet data:
- Current liabilities of $75,000
- Current assets of $37,000
- Fixed assets of $191,000
- Fixed liabilities of $50,000

The net sales for this year are expected to be $200,000. After deducting for the cost of goods sold and various operating expenses, net profit should be 8 per cent of sales. Of particular concern to the Nobles is their store's erratic cash flow. During peak seasons, cash flow is very good; but in January and February (when sales are low and they must make advance purchases for the spring), it is quite unsatisfactory.

Questions:

1. What is the net worth of Noble's House? Comment on this.

2. Calculate asset turnover, profit margin, and financial leverage for Noble's House. Explain your findings.

3. Compute the return on net worth and the return on assets for Noble's House. Explain your findings.

4. How can Noble's House reduce its cash flow problems?

Student's Name _____
Class/Section _____
Instructor _____

CHAPTER 13 EXERCISE

Developing a Crisis Management Plans

As director of operations for a major department store chain, you have been asked to develop a crisis management plan for a number of contingencies. The store's management has directed you to develop plans for the following contingencies: loss of power due to a hurricane or other natural disaster, the sudden resignation of a key employee, and a key supplier going bankrupt.

Each plan needs to:
- Communicate the situation to all affected parties. This should include vendors, current customers, future customers, the general public, government agencies, and so on.
- Identify the chain of command for each crisis. For example, the retailer's information technology should be in charge of problems relating to the firm's Web site, while the retailer's director of security needs to direct operations involving store theft.
- Develop a strategy to minimize the potential loss.

Questions:

1. Develop a crisis management plan for loss of power due to a hurricane.

2. Develop a crisis management plan for the sudden death, disability or resignation of a key employee.

3. Develop a crisis management plan for a key supplier going bankrupt.

Student's Name _____
Class/Section _____
Instructor _____

CHAPTER 14 EXERCISE

Private Branding at a Major Computer Retailer

A major computer retailer is considering developing a private brand for its desktop computers, modems, monitors, and disks and related supplies. To increase credibility for these products, the retailer will provide long warranties on these products. The retailer will also work with its vendors to ensure that specifications for these products will be of high quality. All disks, for example, will have a lifetime warranty. All private label products will be subjected to rigorous testing in both laboratory and field-based environments.

The retailer feels that there are a number of major benefits to this strategy:
- Many of the retailer's smaller vendors have no brand image. The private label brand of the retailer would establish greater credibility to these products.
- If the private brand strategy would be successful, the retailer could encourage brand loyal consumers to become store loyal.
- Many small vendors would be happy to private label their output subject to the retailer's specifications.
- Private label products could be easily identified as to place of purchase. This would facilitate returns and credits for customers who did not have a receipt.
- Due to large quantity purchases, savings in promotional costs, and so on, these private label products would represent excellent value to the customer.
- The private label strategy would reduce price competition among these products.

Questions:

1. What are the pros and cons of the retailer's private brand strategy.

2. What additional tactics does the retailer have to plan and implement to better ensure success? Explain your answer.

3. What strategies could a manufacturer brand implement to counter the private brand's success?

Student's Name _____
Class/Section _____
Instructor _____

CHAPTER 15 EXERCISE

Buying at Off-Price Stores Versus Traditional Retailers

A buyer's position in most off-price stores differs significantly from the same position at a department or specialty store chain.

- Off-price buyers are able to make decisions on their own. Department store buyers, in contrast, may need approval from as many as five levels of merchandising executives.

- Department store buyers seek to buy goods and replenish then at the item level; off-price buyers seek goods based on the appropriate classification mix (they are not as concerned about individual items).

- Off-price buyers, in many cases, will try to place orders with vendors with which they can maintain good relationships.

- Off-price buyers prefer vendors who sell to department stores. They need to prove to customers that they are saving money.

- Off-price buyers will purchase irregulars, end-of- season merchandise, cancellations, etc. They are less concerned than department stores with their effect on store image or on the sale of full gross margin merchandise.

- Off-price buyers are more concerned about maintaining high stock turnover. Merchandise is evaluated weekly; slow-moving merchandise quickly receives markdowns.

Questions:

1. Compare the position of buyer for an off-price chain with that of buyer for a department store.
2. How would the negotiation process differ between department store and off-price chain buyers and their suppliers?
3. Are cancellations, end-of-season merchandise, and irregular merchandise appropriate for traditional department and specialty stores? See Table 11-1 in the text.
4. What are the implications of a manufacturer selling identical merchandise to off-price chains and to traditional department and specialty stores at different price levels?

Student's Name _____
Class/Section _____
Instructor _____

CHAPTER 16 EXERCISE

Men's Discount Clothing (MDC): Planning Monthly Purchases

Ben Jason owns Men's Discount Clothing (MDC), a store based in downtown Milwaukee, Wisconsin. The retailer buys imported suits, sport jackets, raincoats, and slacks. All garments have the MDC label; and all alterations are included in each garment's price. MDC's retail price lines are low to moderate, the firm advertises weekly in Milwaukee's major newspaper, and has a convenient location with ample parking.

In reviewing MDC's financial records, the firm's accountant has raised some concerns. The accountant feels that Ben is overly optimistic in forecasting sales. Ben defends this practice as due to uncertainty with delivery dates. To Ben, over ordering reduces the effects of slow delivery. The accountant would also like Ben to develop a yearly plan relating to sales, reductions, and inventory levels. Ben likes to plan only 1-2 months ahead due to inaccuracy with plans beyond this time period.

Men's Discount Clothing's sales, reductions, and inventory levels for the most recent fiscal year are shown in Exhibit 1.

Exhibit 1
Men's Discount Clothing : Sales, Reductions, and Inventory Levels
(Most Recent Fiscal Year)

Actual Month	Actual Retail Sales	Reductions	Beginning of Month Inv. Level (at Retail)	End of Month Inventory Level (at Retail)
January	$210,000	$ 20,000	$100,000	$ 80,000
February	190,000	30,000	80,000	150,000
March	350,000	10,000	150,000	100,000
April	250,000	10,000	100,000	100,000
May	260,000	10,000	100,000	25,000
June	470,000	15,000	25,000	150,000
July	220,000	40,000	150,000	90,000
August	140,000	20,000	90,000	150,000
September	290,000	10,000	150,000	120,000
October	220,000	12,000	120,000	250,000
November	420,000	30,000	250,000	300,000
December	510,000	30,000	300,000	150,000
Total Year	$3,530,000	$ 237,000		

Questions:

1. Based upon Exhibit 1, what should MDC's planned purchases at retail have been each month?

2. If the firm has a 40 per cent markup at retail, compute its open-to-buy at cost for each month.

3. Compute MDC's monthly inventory turnover.

4. Evaluate the accountant's arguments.

Student's Name _____
Class/Section _____
Instructor _____

CHAPTER 17 EXERCISE

Smith Appliances: Dealing with Intensive Price Competition

Smith Appliances is a major regional chain specializing in refrigerators, televisions, washing machines, stereos, and dish- washers. It has been established for over 30 years and is respected in the community. Its pricing strategy is to take normal markups, and to permit some bargaining by customers. In general, the store would not sell merchandise unless its markup at retail would exceed 15 per cent. It now finds that it must re-examine its pricing strategy in light of several developments.

Smith Appliances recently has had significant competition from retailers who give price quotes on the phone. Typically, these retailers place ads in local papers stating they will beat any price. They have no retail store, no displays, and prefer to stock only high turnover items. Generally, they will ship merchandise if a customer calls in his/her order with a credit card deposit; goods are usually delivered within 2-3 days. All merchandise carries the manufacturers' full guarantees. Discounters' prices are 10-15 per cent below Smith's.

In addition, the firm finds that the average customer has become more price conscious. This may be due to an extension of the influence of off-price chains on apparel and footwear, and to increased price advertising by Smith's traditional competitors. One major competitor actively promotes that it will beat all advertised and quoted prices.

Smith Appliances is concerned about what pricing strategy to undertake in response to changed competitive developments. Some alternatives it is considering are:

- Do nothing. The firm is currently successful and should not erode profit margins.
- Focus on full service. Include such services as microwave cooking classes, washing machine and dryer hookup, and reduced installation charges for dishwashers and wall ovens.
- Match all prices, providing the firm can verify price levels through phone calls or advertisement copy.

Questions:

1. Evaluate each alternative.
2. Which alternative strategy should Smith Appliances pursue?
3. How can Smith prevent shoppers from visiting its store, examining its product samples, getting product feature and warranty information, and then saving 10-15 per cent by going to a discounter?
4. How should an appliance manufacturer react to increased retail price discounting? Distinguish between short- and long-term implications in your answer.

Student's Name _____
Class/Section _____
Instructor _____

CHAPTER 18 EXERCISE

Betty's Dress Shop: Planning A Retail Image

Betty's Dress Shop has been at its present location for 5 years. The firm specializes in "off the rack" and custom-made dresses. Most of its customers have purchased garments in asso- ciation with weddings and formal functions. Betty's Dress Shop is located in a strip location on a major thoroughfare. Neigh- boring stores are a 7-Eleven and a discount candy/chocolate store.
Betty's Dress Shop's retail strategy is comprised of

- A product mix of custom-made dresses (70 per cent) and off-the-rack dresses (30 per cent).
- All garments are sold with alterations included. A skilled fitter/tailor is on the premises.
- All off-the-rack dresses stocked have limited distribution. This limits price competition with department stores and other specialty stores in the area.
- The price line is between $200-$750; the average dress purchase is $350.
- The firm has a low-key approach to selling. Sales personnel are paid on a salary; and are encouraged to be honest about the fit and appearance of each garment.

Nevertheless, Betty is concerned about the store's overall image. Her feelings are based on extended discussions with the store's customers and with local residents. Betty feels that many people are unaware of the store's existence. The store is set back from the thoroughfare due to zoning requirements; this gives the store poor visibility. The store also has poor affin- ities with neighboring stores.

The store has a cluttered appearance. This is due to several factors. One, no double-tiered racks are used. Two, when it is busy, store personnel have little time to put tried-on garments back on the racks. Three, the sewing machine and clothes' steaming machine are visible. Four, the store also sells sweaters, shorts, and costume jewelry.

The store has been put together piecemeal as Betty could afford to make improvements. Thus, the store fixtures, carpeting color, clothes racks, and storefront are not coordinated.

Questions:

1.   What should Betty do as a result of her preliminary feelings?
2.   How could these problems be avoided?
3.   Explain how Betty can determine her optimal space needs using the model-stock and sales-productivity ratio approaches.
4.   What factors should Betty consider in reassessing her customer service strategy?

Student's Name _____
Class/Section _____
Instructor_____

CHAPTER 19 EXERCISE

Ellie's Leather Goods: Modifying a Promotion Strategy

Ellie Farmer owns a two-year-old leather goods store that features luggage, women's bags, attache cases, and wallets. The store is situated in a community shopping center anchored by a junior department store in an affluent neighborhood. Its fixtures are chrome and glass, and it utilizes plush carpeting and silver/black stripes on the walls. This outlet's customers are more knowledgeable, less susceptible to sales presentations, value conscious, style (fashion) conscious, more likely to comparison shop, and less likely to buy an item as a gift than those shopping at older, more traditional leather goods stores. Many unique, high-priced goods are carried in the store.

Until now, Ellie has relied on personal selling, in-store displays, special mailings to loyal customers, and word-of-mouth communication in her promotion strategy. But, Ellie believes the time is right to begin advertising. She is currently devising a strategy that takes these factors into account:

- The store is based on a full-service, fair-profit-margin concept -- personal service, a generous return policy, and repair services are provided.
- First-quality, popular brands are carried. All products are genuine leather. No synthetics are sold.
- Ads should not be dominated by price. A "classy" look is necessary.
- While flyers and penny-saver newspapers have excellent geographic fit for the store, garage sales, used furniture vendors, car washes, and others are advertising in these media.
- Customer demand is seasonal, and it varies by product category. For example, attaché cases are good gift items and have high holiday sales. Luggage is popular during May and June, as consumers prepare for vacations.
- Between $10,000 and $15,000 is available for yearly advertising.

Questions

1. Develop an overall promotion plan for Ellie's Leather Goods.
2. Develop a yearly media plan for Ellie Farmer. Explain your answer.
3. Which types of sales promotion should Ellie use at her store? Explain your answer.
4. How could Ellie determine the effectiveness of her new promotion plan?

Chapter-Based Exercises

Student's Name _____
Class/Section _____
Instructor _____

CHAPTER 20 EXERCISE

Michael's Market: Studying Key Industry Data

Michael Manning owns and operates Michael's Market, a three- year-old fruit and vegetable store. Michael's Market is a mid-sized store in Pittsburgh that emphasizes product quality and freshness. Recently, Manning decided to compare his store's performance with other fruit and vegetable stores.

Accordingly, he collected the appropriate data from his own records and from a number of sources including Dun & Bradstreet's *Industry Norm Report.*

	Annual Results for Michael's Market	Annual Results for a Typical Fruit and Vegetable Store
Net sales	$ 1,250,000	$ 1,500,000
Gross profit	$ 275,000	$ 415,500
Net after-tax profit	$ 45,000	$ 34,500
Quick ratio (times)	1.0	0.9
Current ratio (times)	2.1	1.8
Collection period (days)	5.5	8.1
Sales to inventory (times)	24.8	40.3
Assets to net sales (%)	21.1	17.8
Return on net sales (%)	3.6	1.5
Return on assets (%)	17.1	7.0
Return on net worth (%)	38.5	16.5

Questions:

1. Comment on the annual performance of a typical fruit and vegetable store.

2. Compare Michael's Market's performance with that of the typical fruit and vegetable store.

3. How do you recommend that Michael's Market respond to these findings?

4. What are the limitations of Michael's Market's using data from such sources as *Industry Norm Report* as a means of benchmarking?

RETAIL MATHEMATICS PROBLEMS

STORE LOCATION PROBLEMS
(Chapter 9)

__ 1. Cities A and B are 50 miles apart. City A has a population of 400,000 and City B has a population of 100,000. According to Reilly's law, what is the point of indifference for City B?
    a. 5.0 miles   c. 25.0 miles
    b. 16.7 miles   d. 33.3 miles

__ 2. If City B, from the prior problem, has a population increase of 20 per cent over the next three years while City A has an increase of 10 per cent, what will the point of indifference be for City B?
    a. 5.0 miles   c. 25.0 miles
    b. 17.5 miles   d. 32.5 miles

__ 3. Respectively, Cities A, B, and C have 5,000; 10,000; and 12,500 square feet of retail selling space allocated to gift items. Potential customers live 10 minutes from City A, 15 minutes from City B, and 20 minutes from City C. The effect of travel time is 1. According to Huff's law, what percentage of customers will shop in City A for gift items?
    a. 9.3   c. 34.4
    b. 27.9   d. 37.2

__ 4. If the effect of travel time in the prior problem is really 2, what percentage of customers will shop in City A for gift items?
    a. 18.0   c. 34
    b. 28.7   d. 40

__ 5. A community has 40,000 residents; 30,000 of them regularly shop in that community. These shoppers spend an average of $200 per week in the community. What are the expected annual sales in the community?
    a. $ 6,000,000   c. $312,000,000
    . $60,500,000   d. $416,000,000

__ 6. If the percentage of residents in problem 5 who shop in their community goes to 80 per cent and the average expenditures stay constant at $200 per week, by what percentage will expected annual sales in that community increase?
    a. 1.1   c. 3.3
    b. 2.2   d. 6.7

  _ 7. An area has a population equal to 0.4 percent of total U.S. population. Residents make 0.6 per cent of total U.S. retail purchases. The area's effective buying income is 0.3 per cent of total U.S. effective buying income. What is the area's buying power index?
    a. 0.35 per cent   c. 0.44 per cent
    b. 0.41 per cent   d. 0.48 per cent

  _ 8. Based on the following data, which area has the highest buying power index?
County

	A	B	C	D
% of U.S. retail sales	0.5	0.4	0.3	0.2
% of U.S. population	0.3	0.2	0.5	0.3
% of U.S. EBI	0.2	0.3	0.2	0.5

    a. A   c. C
    b. B   d. D

  _9. A town has 9,000 residents who buy appliances in that town. Annually, they spend $5.2 million on appliances. In the town, 14,000 square feet of selling space are allocated to appliances. What is the index of retail saturation for appliances in the town?
    a. $171   c. $371
    b. $271   d. $571

  _ 10. A new 4,000-square-foot appliance retailer is expected to open in the town noted in problem 9 in a few months. When it opens, what will the index of retail saturation be?
    a. $191   c. $371
    b. $289   d. $578

OPERATIONS MANAGEMENT PROBLEMS
(Chapter 12)

  _ 1. A retailer's current assets are $200,000. Its fixed assets are $250,000. Current liabilities are $75,000 and fixed liabilities are $125,000. What is the firm's net worth?
    a. $ 75,000   c. $250,000
    b. $125,000   d. $275,000

  _ 2. A retailer's fixed assets are $300,000. Current liabilities are $135,000 and fixed liabilities are $250,000. It has a net worth of $78,000. What is the value of the firm's current assets?
    a. $15,000   c. $163,000
    b. $50,000   d. $463,000

— 3. A retailer has net sales of $500,000, total assets of $1,000,000, and a net profit of $60,000. What is its asset turnover?
    a. 50%   c. 100%
    b. 56%   d. 200%

— 4. What is the profit margin for the retailer in problem 3?
    a. 4%   c. 10%
    b. 6%   d. 12%

— 5. What is the return on assets for the retailer in problem 3?
    a. 4%   c. 10%
    b. 6%   d. 12%

— 6. A retailer has these financial results: current assets, $400,000; fixed assets, $1,000,000; current liabilities, $420,000; fixed liabilities, $920,000; net sales, $8,000,000; and net profit, $120,000. What is its net worth?
    a. $ 60,000   c. $500,000
    b. $160,000   d. $580,000

— 7. What is the asset turnover for the retailer in problem 6?
    a. 3.4 x   c. 20.0 x
    b. 5.7 x   d. 66.6 x%

— 8. What is the profit margin for the retailer in problem 6?
    a. 1.5 %   c. 15.0%
    b. 1.8%   d. 17.5%

— 9. What is the return on assets for the retailer in problem 6?
    a. 1.5%   c. 8.6%
    b. 5.0%   d. 11.5%

— 10. What is the financial leverage ratio for the retailer in problem 6?
    a. 8.8   c. 12.0
    b. 10.3   d. 23.3

— 11. What is the return on net worth for the retailer in problem 6?
    a. 50%   c. 125%
    b. 75%   d. 200%

— 12. A retailer has net sales of $500,000, a gross profit of $220,000, operating costs of $100,000, and other costs of $10,000. What is its cost of goods sold?
    a. $ 70,000   c. $180,000
    b. $170,000   d. $280,000

__ 13. What is the net profit before tax for the retailer in problem 12?
    a. $ 70,000   c. $180,000
    b. $170,000   d. $300,000

__ 14. During January, a retailer has net sales of $30,000. Fifty per cent of these sales are on credit and payment will not be received until March. Payments in January for customer credit purchases made in prior months equal $5,000. The retailer's cost of goods sold and operating expenses for January total $28,000. What is the retailer's cash flow in January?
    a. -$8,000   c. $3,000
    b. -$3,000   d. $8,000

__ 15. During October, a retailer has net sales of $25,000. All of its sales are in cash. The firm buys merchandise costing $30,000 in October, but has deferred billing privileges. It only pays for half of the merchandise in October. Its October operating expenses are $5,000. There are no other costs in October. What is the retailer's October cash flow?
    a. -$13,000   c. $ 5,000
    b. $ 2,000   d. $10,000

FINANCIAL MERCHANDISE MANAGEMENT PROBLEMS
(Chapter 16)

__ 1. Compute the cost of goods sold, if sales = $1,000,000; beginning inventory (at cost) = $600,000; ending inventory (at cost) = $150,000; purchases (at cost) = $200,000.
    a. $ 50,000   c. $650,000
    b. $250,000   d. $950,000

__ 2. What is the gross profit of the retailer in problem 1?
    a. -$150,000   c. $100,000
    b. $ 50,000   d. $350,000

__ 3. If the operating expenses of the firm in problem 1 are $50,000, what is its net profit or loss before taxes?
    a. 0   c. $125,000
    b. $50,000   d. $300,000

__ 4. A retailer uses a perpetual inventory system. Compute the firm's end-of-month inventory at cost, if monthly sales (at cost) = $500,000; monthly sales (at retail) = $750,000; monthly purchases (at cost) = $250,000; and beginning inventory (at cost) = $600,000.
    a. $ 75,000   c. $350,000
    b. $150,000   d. $400,000

— 5. What is the cost complement for Adams Stationery?

Adams Stationery
Calculation of Merchandise Available for Sale
July 1, 2000 - December 31, 2000

	Cost Method	Retail Method
Beginning inventory	$75,000	$200,000
Net purchases	50,000	55,000
Additional markups	-	10,000
Freight-in	1,500	-
Total merchandise available for sale	$126,500	$265,000

a. 0.375   c. 0.477
b. 0.471   d. 0.490

— 6. If Adams Stationery has sales, markdowns, and employee discounts that total $100,000 during the time period noted in problem 5, what is the ending retail book value of inventory?
a. $153,500   c. $165,000
b. $155,000   d. $265,000

— 7. A physical inventory of the merchandise of Adams Stationery as of December 31, 2000 showed a valuation of $160,000 (at retail). Compute the stock shortages that occurred during the period from July 1, 2000 to December 31, 2000.
a. $5,000   c. $100,000
b. $6,500   d. $105,000

— 8. Calculate the closing inventory at cost for Adams Stationery as of December 31, 2000.
a. $45,600   c. $76,800
b. $60,800   d. $83,200

— 9. A toy store has average monthly sales of $80,000. Its sales for December were $100,000. What is the monthly sales index for December?
a. 33   c. 125
b. 80   d. 400

___ 10. If the October monthly sales index is 200 for the company mentioned in problem 9, what are October's sales?
a. $120,000
b. $160,000
c. $200,000
d. $300,000

___ 11. A firm plans its average monthly stock at retail to be $34,000 and its average monthly sales to be $20,000. What is its basic stock?
a. $4,000
b. $7,000
c. $14,000
d. $34,000

___ 12. For the firm noted in problem 11, its August sales are planned to be 50 per cent greater than average monthly sales. If the store uses the per cent variation method of inventory level planning, what should the August inventory level be?
a. $30,000
b. $37,500
c. $42,500
d. $51,000

___ 13. A camera retailer uses the weeks' supply method of inventory planning. If average weekly sales are $4,000, and a three-week supply of merchandise is desired, what is the planned inventory level?
a. $4,000
b. $8,000
c. $12,000
d. $24,000

___ 14. A small appliance dealer estimates May sales to be $300,000 and plans reductions to be 20 per cent of sales and ending inventory to be $65,000. Beginning inventory is $85,000. What should be the planned purchases for May?
a. $240,000
b. $320,000
c. $340,000
d. $380,000

___ 15. If the appliance dealer in problem 14 receives $60,000 in merchandise by May 10, what is the open-to-buy for the balance of the month?
a. $180,000
b. $260,000
c. $280,000
d. $320,000

___ 16. The small appliance dealer noted in problems 14 and 15 plans merchandise costs to be 80 per cent of selling price. What is the open-to-buy at cost as of May 10?
a. $144,000
b. $208,000
c. $224,000
d. $256,000

___ 17. A health food retailer has $100,000 in monthly operating expenses and planned monthly sales of $400,000. Reductions are planned to be $8,000. A profit goal of $40,000 is established. What is the required initial markup?
a. 24.5%
b. 36.3%
c. 37.0%
d. 40.0%

___ 18. A mail-order retailer has an average inventory at retail of $300,000 and net annual sales of $4,000,000. What is the annual stock turnover rate at retail?
a. 7.5 x
b. 13.3 x
c. 16 x
d. 17 x

___ 19. A clothing store has a gross margin of $25,000 and net sales of $100,000. What is the gross margin percentage?
a. 15%
b. 25%
c. 40%
d. 80%

___ 20. A computer retailer has net sales of $150,000 and average inventory at cost is $20,000. What is the sales-to-stock ratio?
a. 5.0 x
b. 6.0 x
c. 7.5 x
d. 8.0 x

___ 21. If the retailer in problem 20 has a gross margin percentage of 15, what is the gross margin return on investment (GMROI)?
a. 105.0
b. 112.5
c. 210.0
d. 240.0

___ 22. A plant shop sells 20 plants a day and needs 5 days to order, receive, and display merchandise. What is the reorder point?
a. 7
b. 20
c. 70
d. 100

___ 23. If the plant shop in problem 22 desires a 7-plant safety stock, what should the reorder point be?
a. 7
b. 27
c. 77
d. 107

___ 24. A luggage retailer finds the Poisson probability distribution useful in estimating safety stock. If the estimated reorder point is 80 and the retailer desires a 95 per cent probability of not running out of stock, what should the safety stock be?
a. 88
b. 89
c. 94
d. 101

___ 25. A retailer estimates annual sales to be 1,000 units. The average item costs $50; insurance and other carrying expenses equal 10 per cent of the cost of each unit; and order costs are $20 per order. What is the economic order quantity?
a. 89
b. 101
c. 122
d. 145

PRICING IN RETAILING PROBLEMS
(Chapter 17)

— 1. A retailer can sell 75 typewriters per month at a price of $200 each or 250 typewriters per month at a price of $175 each. What is the elasticity of demand (expressed as a positive number)?
   a. 0.40
   b. 1.00
   c. 1.65
   d. 8.08

— 2. If the retailer in problem 1 can sell 200 typewriters at $155, what is the elasticity of demand (expressed as a positive number) between the prices of $175 and $155?
   a. 0.48
   b. 1.83
   c. 2.44
   d. 2.56

— 3. A men's specialty shop uses a markup of 45 per cent at retail for branded shirts. What is the markup equivalent at cost?
   a. 45%
   b. 55%
   c. 82%
   d. 122%

— 4. A ladies' specialty shop buys merchandise for $15 and sells it for $25. What is the markup at retail?
   a. 40%
   b. 60%
   c. 100%
   d. 150%

— 5. A bookstore buys books for $8 and sells them for $10. What is the markup at retail?
   a. 20%
   b. 80%
   c. 120%
   d. 180%

— 6. A retailer purchases appliances for $10 and desires a 40 per cent markup at retail. What should the retail price be?
   a. $11.70
   b. $13.00
   c. $14.28
   d. $16.67

— 7. A retailer purchases milk for $1.00 per half gallon and seeks a 30 per cent markup at retail. What should the retail price be?
   a. $1.30
   b. $1.43
   c. $1.65
   d. $2.86

— 8. A belt shop requires a minimum markup of 40 per cent at retail on leather belts. If the store owner feels that a line of leather belts should retail for $25.00 each, what is the maximum price he or she will pay per belt?
   a. $10.00
   b. $15.00
   c. $16.00
   d. $17.42

Retail Mathematics Problems

_ 9. The belt retailer noted in problem 8 sells plastic belts for $10 and seeks a 25 per cent markup at retail. What is the maximum price he or she will pay per belt?
a. $5.00   c. $7.50
b. $6.00   d. $9.00

_ 10. A retailer has purchased a line of sports jackets for $85 each. The selling price is $125 per jacket. What is the markup at retail?
a. 32.0%   c. 53.0%
b. 42.0%   d. 63.0%

_ 11. A retailer has purchased a line of suits for $100 each. The selling price is $175 per suit. What is the markup at retail?
a. 42.9%   c. 75.0%
b. 57.1%   d. 175.0%

_ 12. A retailer has net annual sales of $125,000. Retail expenses are $75,000. Net profit is $25,000. Compute the maintained markup at retail.
a. 20%   c. 60%
b. 33%   d. 80%

_ 13. A retailer has net annual sales of $2,000,000. Retail expenses are $260,000. Net profit is $400,000. Calculate the maintained markup at retail.
a. 13.0%   c. 20.0%
b. 16.5%   d. 33.0%

_ 14. For the retailer in problem 13, the retail selling price is $10.00. What are merchandise costs?
a. $3.33   c. $12.00
b. $6.67   d. $14.92

_ 15. The retailer in problem 13 has planned retail reductions of $100,000. What is the initial markup?
a. 33.0%   c. 41.0%
b. 36.2%   d. 43.4%

_ 16. If the retailer in problem 13 has planned retail reductions of $600,000, what is the initial markup?
a. 36.2%   c. 48.5%
b. 41.0%   d. 63.0%

_ 17. A retailer buys merchandise for $20.00 a piece. Half is sold for $25.00 and half for $35.00. What is the maintained markup?
a. 25.0%   c. 37.1%
b. 31.4%   d. 42.8%

206

18. A retailer buys items for $6 each. Two thirds are sold for $12 and one third for $9. What is the maintained markup?
    a. 37.0%   c. 44.4%
    b. 41.5%   d. 48.2%

19. Reclining chairs are reduced from $250 to $140 each. Calculate the off-retail markdown percentage.
    a. 20%   c. 44%
    b. 25%   d. 60%

20. A home furnishings retailer has additional markups totaling $850 on a line of table lamps. Net sales of the lamps equal $8,000. Compute the additional markup percentage.
    a. 7.5%   c. 10.6%
    b. 8.1%   d. 16.1%

KEY BUSINESS RATIOS PROBLEMS
(Chapter 20)

1. A retailer has accounts receivable of $60,000, total current liabilities of $40,000, and $55,000 in cash. What is the quick ratio?
   a. 1.4   c. 2.0
   b. 1.5   d. 2.9

2. Assume that the retailer in problem 1 has total inventory on hand of $120,000. What is the current ratio?
   a. 0.65   c. 4.6
   b. 3.00   d. 5.9

3. A clothing store has accounts receivable totaling $50,000, accounts payable totaling $45,000, and net sales of $50,000. What is the collection period?
   a. 50   c. 227
   b. 183   d. 365

4. Assume that the retailer in problem 3 has accounts receivable of $15,000 and net sales of $30,000. What is the new collection period?
   a. 91   c. 274
   b. 183   d. 335

5. A firm has total assets of $400,000, total liabilities of $250,000, and annual net sales of $1,000,000. What is the assets-to-net-sales ratio?
   a. 5%   c. 30%
   b. 7%   d. 40%

_ 6. Assuming that the firm in problem 5 has accounts payable totaling $175,000, what is the accounts- payable-to-net-sales ratio?

a. 9.5%   c. 15.0%

b. 12.5%   d. 17.5%

_ 7. A retailer's net dollar profit after taxes is $50,000. Annual net sales are $200,000 and total current assets are $300,000. What is the return on net sales (profit margin)?

a. 20%   c. 113%

b. 25%   d. 170%

_ 8. If the retailer in problem 7 had annual net sales of $240,000, what would be the return on net sales?

a. 20.8%   c. 94.2%

b. 66.7%   d. 141.7%

_ 9. A toy store has a net worth of $500,000 and net dollar profit after taxes of $45,000. What is the return on net worth?

a. 7.0%   c. 9.0%

b. 7.5%   d. 17.5%

_ 10. If the toy store in problem 9 had a net worth of $470,000, what would be the return on net worth?

a. 6.1%   c. 9.6%

b. 7.4%   d. 27.4%